Japan Dreams

Japan Dreams

Notes from an Unreal Country

Mark Peters

Li te ra

Japan Dreams: Notes from an Unreal Country, by Mark Peters.

Second edition 2016.

First edition published 2011.

Cover design by Mark Peters, layout by Litera.

www.litera.com.au

ISBN-13: 978-0-9 941 934-1-4

10 9 8 7 6 5 4 3

Contents

Preface

SOMETHING CURIOUS IS HAPPENING in Japan, and it has been going on for a long time. It is the replacement of things with virtual substitutes of themselves. The phenomenon is not peculiar to Japan, but Japan is where it is strongest. It is one of the characteristics that we find most fascinating about the place, even though we sometimes cannot quite put our finger on it.

Ancient Japanese gardeners constructed views to remind visitors of famous wood-block print landscapes, which themselves were representations of real scenery. Many theme parks scattered around Japan are idealised replicas of towns in other parts of the world. Instead of golf courses and baseball grounds, we find driving and hitting ranges. Mechanical horses with giant video screens give us the feeling of riding a horse down a forest lane without the threat of being thrown. Virtual pets (Tamagotchi) vie with mechanical pets (Aibo). Some women have an operation to reconstruct their hymen, making them virtual virgins. Wherever we go in Japan, machines have electronic façades – user interfaces – which are virtual substitutes for the machines themselves, which already insulate us from the physical world. There are artificial ski slopes, artificial beaches. In all these cases there is something good that we want to recreate, such as the beauty of a view of Mount Fuji, but there is something bad about it, such as the fact that Mount Fuji cannot be seen from where we live, so we make a new version, which has the positive characteristics of the original, but not its drawbacks.

This is not to be confused with the plain distinction between *inside*, how things really are, and *outside*, their appearance. That is much less interesting, because it is already ubiquitous. No, virtuality is a three-part phenomenon: it has an ideal original (which doesn't really exist), a real original (which has disadvantages), and the virtual substitute (which has only the ideal qualities). One of the most intriguing aspects of Japanese virtuality is that it is both old and new. It links the ancient Japan with the technological Japan in ways that are often surprising.

Like some early Japanese travel writing and the modern genre of shi-shosetsu, *Japan Dreams* is documentary, autobiography, meditation, fiction. The subjects of the tale unfold in a blend of recounting, remembering, pondering, and imagining. There are times when my thoughts are straight and true; there are times when they err.

This book is more than just a personal account of a journey into Japan, a sketch of a country and a culture; it is a discourse of virtuality and, in the sense that some of it is truer than fact, fictitious. This is a real story, but many of its events virtually happened.

So, I may have glimpsed the future – it is not real and it is in Japan. Of course, the future can never be real, it is at best virtually there. But in Japan the same can be said of the present and the past too. In Japan, nothing really exists; it is a floating world, a fluid world of appearance, of image and illusion, icon and artifice.

Notes

I PREFER TO USE THE ORIGINAL order of Japanese names: family name followed by personal name. Common Japanese names, in my experience, only ever have these two parts.

The Japanese know, better than anyone, that the content of a conversation is often less important than its mood, or the simple fact of it. This may be why I have translated only some conversations.

Sometimes a word born in one language takes up residence in another. *Karate*, *tsunami* and *origami* are examples that have made themselves at home in English and are no longer treated as strangers. *Soroban*, *genkan* and *ko-gyaru*, however are still exclusively Japanese, although *ko-gyaru* has something of a past life in English. For reasons of personal taste, I have italicised all Japanese terms, except for Japanese proper names.

Two types of diacritic marks used in Japanese have been omitted for easier reading: the macron, which indicates a long vowel sound, and the apostrophe that indicates a terminal *n* in the middle of a compound word.

Much as I am captivated by the *kanji* writing system, I have adhered to a policy of rendering all Japanese in the *romaji* script for reasons of technical simplicity and general readability.

The Counterfeiter

Point of departure

THE HOUSE BEHIND ME is silent and closed, slumped already in a deep summer slumber. The old green letterbox wobbles on a single screw. I must fix that on my return.

With the afternoon sun in my eyes, I peer down the road for the first sight of the taxi. My fingers shuffle my impedimenta: guidebook and dictionary, passport and Japanese banknotes, itinerary and vouchers. I check every item once more. Across the road, Centennial Park is hot and deserted.

A suitcase and a backpack sit on the footpath beside me. To any passer-by, it is obvious I am setting off on a journey. Tomorrow morning I will arrive in Tokyo – a travel-dazed anonymous stranger in a city I seem unable to imagine.

The taxi should be here by now. Another glance at my watch; more paces along the kerb.

In the last couple of days I put my tiny affairs in good order, hoping the accumulated disarray of their neglect wouldn't overwhelm me when I return. I thought clearing my affairs would also clear my mind to concentrate wholly and continuously upon Japan.

One letter lies at the bottom of the letterbox. It is for me, from England, and in a hand I don't recognise. Hearing a car draw to a stop behind me, I push the letter into a pocket and reach for my luggage. I climb into the taxi, and by that act, become part of a migratory pattern.

Real Japan

We, the non-Japanese, the gaijin, the hypnotised and the cauterised, the Japan-crazy and the Japan-sick, the avid and the jaded, flock to a mythologised land. Drawn from our European traditions, we are travellers in a procession that has run for five hundred years. We hope, despite constant failure, that one day we might attain repose in something that is the real Japan. We just never seem to get there.

Why is the journey so difficult and apparently endless? Is there something amiss with the Japan we find or something awry with the Japan we seek?

Today it seems that almost everyone who travels to Japan is stricken with the urge to write about it. Poor Japan; it gets remade every time a visitor puts pen to paper. Leafing back through the literature of encounters with the country it is possible to see that the intensity of the struggle to become acquainted has hardly varied at all.

In relatively early days, travellers were already going to great lengths to find the 'real' Japan. Isabella Bird recounts in *Unbeaten Tracks in Japan* how, the day after arriving in Yokohama in 1878, she already longed 'to get away into real Japan.' She worked hard at it, travelling north over terrible roads as far as Hokkaido. Ever since then, *gaijin* pilgrims have been repeating the pattern. There has been a persistent need to put sole to soil and pace the place. Oliver Statler more than once made the pilgrimage to the eighty-eight sacred places of Shikoku. He circled the island, endlessly sifting through the mythology and hearsay for the true reality of Kobo Daishi, the great figure of Japanese Buddhist history. Through his search for the truth Statler sets himself apart from the Japanese people he meets, who all seem remarkably indifferent to it or, at best, of the opinion that when it comes to Kobo Daishi the truth is what we want it to be. In *Japanese Pilgrimage* Statler also recounts the great walks undertaken by the abstemious American scholar Frederick Starr in the first quarter of the 20th century. We might assume Starr found the reality of Japan, because he ultimately proclaimed Japanese life more 'real.'

Alan Booth walked the full length of Hokkaido, Honshu, and Kyushu in 1977 and wrote an engaging book about it: *The Roads to Sata.* Reversing the journey sixteen years later Craig McLachlan walked the 3,200 kilometres from Cape Sata to Cape Soya, he says, to find, like so many others, the real Japan. The first 3,199 kilometres of his odyssey apparently consisted of something else entirely. His book, *Four Pairs of Boots*, closely modelled on Booth's, does not match it for originality.

While reading it one senses a copy of another text, a representation of a representation, rather than a first-hand report. And the 'real Japan' he seeks? Still 'out there' he informs the gathered pressmen at the final step. Alan Booth finishes on a similar note, though in his case the irony is intentional. Booth recalls that an old man in Hokkaido told him that one cannot understand Japan by living in Tokyo. No, agrees Booth, that's the reason for looking at other parts. Looking's no good, retorts the old man. Not just looking as a tourist would, but actually walking through it, offers Booth. The old man is still not satisfied, so Booth explains that he will be talking to all the people he meets along the way. You can't understand Japan just by talking to people, the old man says. 'How then?' asks Booth. You can't understand Japan is the answer.

But not all visitors to Japan are long-distance walkers. Peregrine Hodson writes in *A Circle Round the Sun*:

> Some people think the old Japan is the real Japan. I also used to
> think it was the real Japan and I thought if I was patient, like
> Daruma, I might one day find enlightenment and understand it
> all.

Ah, yes, old Japan. Nostalgia. Look at a few of the book titles; they make a veritable industry of lament. Alex Kerr's first book on Japan is called *Lost Japan*. His follow-up book is on the same line. Elizabeth Kiritani's book is called *Vanishing Japan*. In the title of his last book on Japan, the same Alan Booth managed to use both adjectives: *Looking for the Lost: Journeys Through a Vanishing Japan*. All worthy books, but helping to suggest that what the visitor will encounter in Japan these days will not be the real Japan, but a noisy clanging automaton, a mega-machine, or some soulless, tawdry wraith, stripped and beaten by globalisation. Fiction promulgates this notion just as often. In *number9dream* by David Mitchell, a soup of fantasy, dream, memory, ghosts, cyberselves, mistaken identity and misapprehension:

> All Japan has been concreted over. The last sacred forests have
> been cut down for chopsticks, the inland sea has been paved
> over and declared a national carpark, and where mountains
> once stood apartment buildings vanish into the clouds. When
> people reach the age of twenty their legs are amputated and
> their torsos are fitted with interfaces that plug directly into

sophisticated skateboards – for use in the home or office – or
into grander vehicles, for longer journeys.

Matthew, in *The Lady and the Monk* by Pico Iyer, believes something similar. He is perpetually unfulfilled by what he encounters in Japan, constantly hoping a more valid experience is just around the corner.

Much travel writing implies that one's sense of individuality can only be reaffirmed through the seeking out of different places and events, not, apparently, by seeing the commonplace and feeling something new; not by being just like everyone else yet sensing something unfamiliar and bigger than oneself. It is as if the truth is always *out there*. Yet the familiar, re-represented, can sometimes cause us the greatest shock. I've often thought that the prosaic leads most directly to knowledge; perhaps only by living and paying tax in a country can one ever know it. But maybe even this is unattainable; even our own countries can remain mysteries to us. Though I have lived in Australia for over twenty years I more than ever feel like a stranger abroad. So how do we ever hope to penetrate to the inner truth of another place?

The quest for the real Japan implicitly dismisses first impressions, outward appearances, and superficiality. The difficulty of penetrating these surfaces is compounded by the fact that a surface can only be perceived as such once one has been behind it. By definition, when you get to the real core, you can go no further. So, ironically, any 'real' Japan is inherently conditional on the impossibility of deeper penetration. But how can we ever be certain we have finally arrived? Might not our 'real' Japan be just another mask?

The idea of an ultimate, remote, *real* Japan necessarily conjures up some other shallower Japan, much easier to find. But judging by the extremes visitors go to in their search, this illusory or decoy Japan must present a *substantial* obstacle on their path to the real thing. This might well be significant. Anything as large and resistant as this surface Japan is surely worth a visit in its own right, I suspect, if only to experience its power to distract or confound. And perhaps surfaces have a depth of their own. Come to think of it, why is the Japan of surfaces ever thought to be unreal in the first place? Might it be because our yardstick of reality is the Japan we have mythologised: that inscrutable land of oft-cited paradox and contradiction, refinement and savagery, arrogance and deference? Is our reality just a matter of attitude, a question of which of our preconceptions get pandered to? Have we *defined* Japan as something that cannot be understood, cannot be attained?

What we feel sure of is more than what we know, it is the extent to which we are happy with our answers. And what is real is only what we know, not what we are content with.

Prosaic beginnings

My Japan was a fiction from the start. As a teenager I read *Shogun* by James Clavell. The alien logic concerning death, sex, wealth, defecation – all the taboos of my culture perceived from the other side of the earth – was deeply intriguing. I was charmed by the femininity, stirred by the masculinity, inspired by the aesthetics and awed by the political power of the characters in the book. Seen through the comfortably familiar perspective of the English character Blackthorn, Japan was a difficult but soluble puzzle – at once a challenge and a source of satisfaction. Sadly, I can't see the book in the same light now. I reread it recently, and was disappointed by its implausibility and inaccuracies. That is because *my* Japan has changed. Yet in that first encounter *Shogun* triggered something of a reading frenzy in me.

I was meant to be studying painting at Liverpool's School of Art, but I developed a hunger for information on Japan. One of my first steps was to call the Japanese embassy in London's Grosvenor Street. Enthralled almost to the point of speechlessness by the beautiful voice of the woman who answered the phone, I managed to request 'information on Japan,' which was duly sent and consumed. I scoured my college library and the second-hand bookshops of Liverpool for more. James Kirkup's *Tokyo*, a picture of Japan seen through the eyes of the 1960s, was particularly evocative. My reading expanded to include Shinto and Zen Buddhism, but learning about Japanese philosophy through the filter of the English language felt like trying to explore a country by looking at its maps. Japanese thought, I quaintly decided, could only be truly understood by understanding the Japanese language. It was surprising to discover that at the time only three places in

England offered courses in Japanese. No courses were available in Liverpool, so I bought *Teach Yourself Japanese* instead, and laboriously plodded through its lessons in commendable scholastic solitude. Learning a language in solitary confinement is a gloomy pastime. I even applied for jobs in Japan. I was becoming what the Japanese call *nihon kichigai*, Japan-crazy.

But like many a youthful infatuation, nothing came of it. Other, more immediate interests held sway. When my degree was finished, I formed a rock band. When that split up, I returned to Australia and started my first proper job. Later, I travelled extensively but never to Japan. Over time I entered various partnerships, some personal and some commercial, moved from one house to another, and eventually went back to university. For two decades Japan faded into the background.

Then something changed. A mid-life reassessment found me asking what kind of person I wanted to be. A multi-lingual one, as it happened. And to my surprise, Japanese emerged as the first language of choice. I enrolled in evening classes at my university and dredged up twenty-year-old memories of '*kore wa pen desu*,' '*watashi wa...*' and '*ichi, ni, san...*' Soon I was avidly reading about Japan all over again; the madness had returned like a childhood sweetheart coming back in a dream. Having greater wherewithal now to turn dreams into reality (how appropriate) I prepared for my first visit to Japan.

Images unreflected

The taxi surges away from the kerb, then brakes hard for the roundabout. We turn towards the airport.

Mid-week flights, my preference, usually mean empty aircraft and unharried flight attendants with plenty of time to chat. The flight attendant who serves my lunch appears impressed when I observe that her surname, Nishida, translates directly to the English name Westfield. She tells me that her personal name, Miho, means beautiful rice-plant, and coyly challenges me to find an English girl's name that matches that. We chat about my travel plans, and, as we talk, I find her increasingly attractive. Her humour is of the gentlest, most playful sort, and her soft brown eyes express much more than she says. Her voice, echoing that of the embassy receptionist so many years ago, is quite exquisite; it has a soft and loving feel that flows over her carefully enunciated English consonants. She walks tall, with a grace and balance that must be useful aboard an aeroplane.

The plane is almost empty and Miho, with so few passengers to attend to, appears to be at a loose end. She repeatedly comes to my seat to ask if there is anything I need. She jokingly pleads for something to do – so I keep ordering drinks. Soon, I am unable to take my eyes off her, completely enchanted by her prettiness, wit, and an appealing *sangfroid* edged with a *frisson* of nervousness at potential *faux pas*. Indeed, the word 'Parisienne' keeps coming to mind. Before I know it I am asking to meet her socially in Tokyo. I am excited and surprised when she agrees.

Having plenty of time to myself I check all my things once again, even going through all my pockets. I pull out the unopened letter.

dear leo,

my ability to get in touch with people is in inverse proportion to the length of time for which i haven't. this is a personal flaw which every now and then i think about trying to do something about. fortunately there is a kind of quantum tunnelling effect which occasionally puts a random spin on the logical consequences of

$P(\text{write}) \sim e^{-\alpha t}$

as it happens, you've been in my thoughts rather more than usual recently. some of this was caused by a climbing holiday, and some by a moderately perplexing dream. by my calculations it's been a year and a bit since we last spoke. um, sorry. it's not the most appallingly wantonly neglectful i've ever been – far from it, as it goes – but please consider me appropriately contrite and abject.

there was a time lapse in the last block of text. it is now many days since i started this letter and today's burst of verbal outpourings was catalysed by dreaming about you again last night. i dreamt i was talking to you on the 'phone. i was using the cordless 'phone, it was late evening and i was standing in my front door looking out onto the darkening garden. i kept lapsing into german, but otherwise we were communicating very well for two people who've never <u>spoken</u> to each other.

what am i to make of your significant increase in participation in my neural activity?

i'm sure i could come up with a wonderful materialist explanation if i put my mind to it. additionally, i am anxious to avoid getting caught up in 'the meaning of dreams.' all this notwithstanding, my life has not been without its share of dream related weirdnesses, and there are more things in heaven and earth et cetera. it's true, i become more unnerved by coincidence than someone with a basic grasp of statistics should, but whatever the reason, i am feeling a distinct pressure to get this letter to you as soon as possible... i hope it doesn't take a year and a bit to write back!

i could fire off a load of questions at this point about how you are and what you're doing. i rely on you to tell me what's interesting – you require no prompt from me.

what i will do is send you an extra-light (airmail weight restrictions) imaginary hug, remind you how much i've always lionised you, even when i appeared to have vanished off the face of the earth, and sign off.

i hope to hear from you soon, and i'll be thinking about you (whether i want to or not, apparently).

lots of love, as ever,

tyger

tyger lives in England and, as she says in the letter, we have never spoken to each other. We met, that being the best available word, in an Internet talker known as Underworld, hence the *noms de plume*. From our first typed conversation I was amused by her word play, her surprising trains of thought, her arch literary style, and a remarkable intellect that sometimes left me gasping with admiration. Her reading had been serious and broad, and she was able to discuss a wide range of subjects with clarity, intelligence and a maturity not usually found in people of twenty years. Whenever we talked I felt that I was being kept on my toes intellectually, yet she seemed to revel in our conversations as much

as I, and it was not long before an intimate and deeply satisfying attach-
ment grew between us, despite the fact that we existed for each other
only as ephemeral illuminated text on the phosphor screen.

Our relationship had flared, then lapsed into occasional short exchanges, and finally faded away. I'd often hoped for renewal of our correspondence, which at its height could last for ten or twelve hours at a
stretch, but as each month slipped by I became increasingly resigned to
not hearing from tyger again.

And now there is this slightly odd letter, the first hard evidence of
tyger incarnate.

As I Crossed a Bridge of Dreams

And then there is Japan

THERE IS JAPAN and then there is Japan. Whatever they are, they are not the same. We expect one but always meet the other. We find the first, but seek the second.

I look for Mount Fuji in the semi-darkness as the plane approaches Narita airport. I don't really expect to see it, but I look anyway, and suddenly there it is. So much bigger than I had expected, bursting up through the mists below, centred in its own perfect isolation, dark and symmetrical. An island in a sea of cloud.

The plane descends towards Narita in the metallic minutes just after dawn. Tiny valley farms, neatly inscribed between woods, flicker by below the wings. Miho comes to my row to say goodbye. I offer her my business card. She reads it thoroughly and questions me about everything, even though she already knows most of the answers. She presents her own, and pencils her mobile number on the back. I pretend the same degree of interest in her card, but not as convincingly. As the wheels touch down the rain lightly stripes my window. I watch Miho by the doorway, wondering if I will see her again. On my way out of the fuselage I promise to call her, but her response is professionally neutral.

The airport sounds are muted. Few people are active. With other tired passengers I pass through counter formalities and step out into a cold morning. Determined to make an immediate start with the language, I carefully compose Japanese words to buy a bus ticket to the Hilton in Shinjuku. My words are understood, and I feel a small elation at that, though the clerk answers me in perfect English.

I hand over my luggage and find my seat. An employee steps up into the bus to thank us all for travelling with his company, and bows deeply. As the bus draws away from the airport, we pass buildings of a cold, uniform grey. At this hour of the morning, in the weak sunlight, it is not a welcoming first impression. The bus rushes along the highway towards Tokyo and I absorb the detail. My decoding of *katakana* and *hiragana* script is ponderously slow at this stage. Love hotels, scraps of thick forest, tiny buildings that must be houses, and several wide rivers flash by until finally the buildings of Tokyo proper loom out of the haze. The city looks vast, treeless, unplanned, and quite unlovely. At one stage the highway is enclosed by high walls incurving on both sides. Then, massive fly-overs writhe above a drowning river, sealing it into a tunnel-tomb, trapped by office towers on both banks.

My reward for arriving so early at the hotel is to be upgraded to a better room, mine apparently still occupied. The receptionist passes me a letter. It is from Satomi, an animated Japanese girl I met a few weeks before in Australia, and who lives here in Tokyo. Up in my room, I scrabble together the things I want for the day, and I'm back out on the streets within ten minutes.

Office workers are beginning to fan out in large numbers from the nearby railway station, heading for their workplaces around Shinjuku. The disciplined march of thousands of people walking in one direction is martial and impressive, like an ant colony on the move.

I first explore Nishi-Shinjuku. A lift rockets me to the top of the towering Tokyo Metropolitan Centre, where I attempt to get my bearings. This turns out to be difficult, because Tokyo is truly huge and no clearly identifiable centre exists. The massive urbanisation extends from horizon to horizon, unbroken except for a few isolated and densely wooded parks. Apart from these dark arboreal oases the view is all unremitting solid white concrete. The city is so vast it is almost an artwork, the epitome of something: uniformity, artificiality, or environmental insensitivity. From my vantage point I count forty-three construction cranes – so much for the Asian economic downturn, though from this distance it is difficult to tell whether the cranes are working or silently mourning, offering up prayers over open graves.

In many places across the city large frames hold green netting up to the sky. They turn out to be golf driving ranges. They call up memories of the old gasometer frames of England. In the south-west the now delicate outline of Mount Fuji is dimly visible. I read once that it is lucky to see Mount Fuji on one's first day in Japan, so I should feel doubly favoured.

Back at ground level I wander Shinjuku streets at random. I have no real objective at this stage; I just want to attune to everyday things first. It's a kind of calibration. Already I feel that I am making up a story I will later recount, acting out my own part in it, kneading the ingredients; dreams, flawed memories, lies and unintended inaccuracies, but no guns, no murders, no car chases, no explosions and certainly no self-discovery.

I find myself outside the electronics shops near Shinjuku station. Multitudes of tiny mobile phones are racked on counters at the kerbside, all colours, all models, all priced and with specifications neatly noted too; so unlike the semi-secretive methods of Australian phone shops, I think. At a bank of vending machines I discover, with some wonder, that hot coffee is available for 120 yen. I buy a can. The coffee is warm and sweet, but drinkable. Later in the trip I learn that coffee can be a little expensive in cafés, and is usually served in a cup of genteel proportions, so the machine variety is a useful option, particularly when I want to be rid of small change.

After the novelty refreshment I venture inside the electronic shops. The wealth of choice is truly staggering. Within each market sector – minidisc players for example – there are dozens of models and colour variants available for prodding and caressing. The shops fill several storeys and carry all forms of equipment, from the professional to the novelty. The Japanese fondness for miniaturisation reveals itself everywhere. The controls on gadgets are now so tiny that one has to use fingernails rather than fingers to operate them, and there are signs that the miniaturisation process has not yet finished.

Finding all the little novelties is engrossing work, and decoding what the signs say is rather satisfying, like solving a puzzle. At times during the trip I will play it like an adventure game in real life, treating problems as challenges to my ingenuity, and the language as a secret code that must be deciphered before I move to the next stage. I feel like Alice in Wonderland, unsure of the reality of things, everything suggestive of hidden layers and secondary meanings, a juxtaposition of the inhumane and the animal, the animate and the inanimate, the refined and the earthy, deep philosophical challenges embedded in the most innocent of questions, and serious consideration paid to the utmost nonsense.

I stroll around to the front of Shinjuku station and enter the first of many music shops. I'm keen to find pre-recorded minidiscs, and expect to see them in large numbers, but I don't. The CD is king here, just like everywhere else, and the minidisc is a distaff cousin, not in line for the throne. Some shops don't even bother to stock the pre-recorded format. The only pre-recorded minidisc I feel half inclined to buy is *Tapestry* by Carole King. Outside the shop I plug it into my machine and pop in the earphones. My noise now competes with Tokyo's noise.

And loses. Tokyo *is* cacophony. Everything that has electricity also has a voice. Lifts and escalators speak to me, phones say *arigato gozai-mashita* when I put down the receiver. Trains tell me what they are doing (so do their drivers, just for good measure), and the same goes for buses, and for cruise ships and cable cars. Announcements are being made everywhere. Music is pumped out of shops. The traffic is as busy at 3 AM as it is at 10 AM. The ringing, chiming, beeping mobile phone is ubiquitous. A descending octave tone constantly chimes around the railway stations. It reminds me of the distant soundtrack that plays in some computer games. Against this background noise the people are subdued, even silent.

The shops will continue to intrigue me. In Singapore I'd loved to just wander around the Japanese department stores, Takashimaya, Seibu, and Isetan. It's the strangeness of so many things and the density of clever, weird, tricky and downright cute variations on familiar themes. A toothbrush that generates a stream of ions to enhance cleaning (I buy one), a ballpoint pen filled with both green and purple ink, so that it changes colour as one writes (I buy one). Then there are the food departments, where I will daily buy things I don't recognise, eat them and try to decide what they are. Sometimes I identify flavours, often I don't.

In a search for somewhere to have lunch, I head towards Takashi-maya Times Square. The cafés are upstairs and so is an I-Max theatre with a 3-D feature coming up in about an hour. After ordering in Japanese (and understanding the price given to me in Japanese – another small success), I eat, then walk into the theatre and take my seat. A button on the headset toggles the soundtrack between English and Japanese. The movie begins and gives me a headache right away. The reason for this is that the makers of 3-D films seem compelled to over-use the third dimension: objects rush in towards my face, then recede into the distance, focus shifts violently from near to far, and so on. This creates the need for constant change of eye-focus and vergence, which is soon tiring. Despite this, I enjoy the film. Feeling a little tired, I walk back towards the hotel, planning to have a short nap before evening. A girl on the street hands me a piece of advertising for a nearby shop. It is a small packet of tissues, a more thoughtful idea than a plain A5 flyer. I already know that being given this is a bit unusual. I've noticed that such things are often not handed to foreigners, in the presumption, I presume, that we couldn't read them anyway. Later I discover that some Japanese are even loath to sit next to *gaijin* on public transport. It may just be that they fear our tendency to strike up incomprehensible conversations, but I sense a gentle racial discrimination.

My plan to nap inevitably backfires, and I stay asleep until early morning.

I've been led to believe that the Tokyo subway system is horribly difficult to use. My first experience is quite the opposite. I have no problem with the ticket machines, the signs, the automatic barriers, or finding out where I am once on the train. Actually the only problem I have on the train is my own height (1.9 metres). Several times over the next few days I will bump my head as I get off, and when standing inside the train I'm unable to see the station names as I pass through.

After leaving the train at Tokyo station I walk around parts of the Imperial Palace gardens. There is little of interest here; the palace itself merely peeks above the trees and is only just visible from one spot. Getting inside is difficult, to say the least. In a small museum in the grounds I marvel at a pair of strikingly beautiful carved wooden birds – a foretaste of other aesthetic pleasures.

On the other side of the station lies the fabled Ginza district. It is hard to imagine why it is so famous. It is a modern shopping district with a few quaint back streets. The Sony showrooms dazzle me with engineering and technical inventiveness. Under the indulgent eye of the staff I play with assorted pieces of electronics. A little microphone that is not available in Australia attracts my attention; if I can find one on sale I will buy it.

If I want to call Satomi and Miho today, I had better buy a phone card, but this is not as easy as I expected. After some searching, success comes in the convenience shop of a western-style hotel.

'*Irasshaimase*,' says the clerk, with a little bow.

'*Konnichiwa. Denwa kaado wa arimasu ka?*'

'*Hai.*' She nods and bends down to open a drawer.

'*Ikura desu ka?*'

'*Sen en desu.*'

'*Arigato.*'

'*Arigato gozaimashita.*'

Fantastic! A complete transaction in Japanese, and I have what I wanted. I'm pleased with myself, and walk out of the hotel full of confidence and eager for more conversation. First I phone Miho, who is meeting friends and shopping, and terribly curious to know how I am enjoying Tokyo so far. She sounds keen to see me again, and we talk about meeting tomorrow, but instead of arranging a definite time and place here and now she seems to want to defer arrangements until some later time. I don't quite know what this signifies.

Satomi reunion

I also call Satomi on her mobile. Her voice is sleepy.

'*Moshi moshi?*'

'Kawamoto-san?'

She giggles at my feigned formality.

'Yes! Maaku, good day! Where are you?'

We discuss where and when to meet. I outline my plan to first see an hour of *kabuki* at the nearby Kabuki-za theatre then meet Satomi afterwards. Satomi suggests this is a bad idea for some undisclosed reason – she is given to vagueness at times – so we arrange to meet as soon as possible at Shibuya, outside the Shu Uemura shop.

I arrive first and kill time by pacing along the line of shops. Satomi rushes up behind me and grabs me by the arm – worried I am walking away.

'Maaku! Don't walk off!' she cries.

I spin around and collide with her kiss. She is laughing. Satomi is tall and slim, and has a small child's face. Her hair is always cropped short and softly spiky. She is carefully dressed in a long grey wool dress under a darker grey winter coat. We adjourn to a coffee shop and chat.

First impressions can be deceptive. When I met Satomi in Australia she scuffed about in loose jeans and an old ski jacket. Here in Tokyo she is as chic as all the other young women who throng the streets in dark, elegant clothes, black more often than not, a tone that suits their skin and hair colour perfectly. The explanation for the difference in Satomi's style is that the Japanese see Australia as a dress-down place where appearances are not important, and visitors can be more re-laxed about how they look. They may be right, but they sometimes overdo it by persisting in casualness on occasions when even Australi-ans dress up. Anyway, I've brought my best clothes to Japan, because I correctly expected that standard Australian casualness might be wrong here.

Shibuya is a busy place at any time, even more so than Shinjuku. The pedestrians surge in waves as the traffic lights change. Their uni-formity of height and colouring somehow emphasise their numbers. The girls look so good. And I've never seen so many miniskirts in November. All over, women are wearing sexy black Lycra boots with high heels and chisel toes. Others stalk around on huge platform boots. Many of the guys have a retro beatnik look I like too: spiky hair and rectangular glasses, but a few of them also wear dopey floppy hats that give them the air of assistant gardeners. Dyed hair is in abundance, straw blonde at times but streaky brown usually. At first it looks odd to me, but I soon accommodate to it. Some of the younger girls have deep tans, pink lipstick and wear Da-Glo vinyl clothes. The look has a certain rebellious sexiness to it, though it would probably look infantile in Australia. Some guys stride around in sharp double-breasted or single-breasted three-piece suits, having come straight from the office. Later in the evening I expect to see a few staggering along blind drunk, but harmless.

After a strong coffee Satomi and I move to another coffee shop. It turns out Satomi has arranged to meet a friend of hers, Asako, at eight o'clock, in time for a dinner booking for the three of us at 8:30 PM. I still don't know why it was important to meet so early, but it doesn't really matter too much. Asako arrives, and we catch a taxi to the restaurant. She is another cosmopolitan Japanese woman, living in both Paris and Yokohama and running her own jewellery buying business. Her face is oval with a strong nose and cheekbones resembling an Indian squaw. Like Satomi, she speaks French and English, and has the objectivity to see her own country as something of an outsider. The girls are great company, the food is *oishii*, delicious. Satomi introduces me to a drink that is to become one of my favourites: *umeshu*, a syrupy plum liqueur with a tart edge, great on ice.

Soon the girls are keen to go – they have a *karaoke* night planned for me. We take another taxi to a small lane near Roppongi, and are shown upstairs to a sound-proofed door. Inside, a long curved couch, a small drinks table, and a sophisticated electronic *karaoke* system fill the room. This is a *karaoke* box, not a *karaoke* bar. The advantage, for me, is that no other people will be able to hear me sing. This is also the big benefit for other people. Asako immediately punches a number into the machine and starts singing into the microphone. *Ah, good,* I think, *the music has a voice track on it, we don't have to sing alone.* I'm very wrong. Asako's singing is so good I mistake it for the real thing, and I think there is more than one voice simply because of heavy reverb on the vocal track. Satomi picks up a mic and sings her selection. She is a great singer too. At the end of her song she hands me the mic and my moment has come. I forget which song I'd selected, but I know I'd selected it purely for ease of singing. It makes no difference. I am disastrous. I know it, they know it, and I know they know it. At times we do things so badly that we embarrass ourselves. And at other times we do so much worse that even witnesses are embarrassed too, on our behalf. This is one of those moments. Satomi and Asako cannot bear to look at each other for fear of bursting into laughter. I can see them avoiding each other's eyes but I have nowhere to hide, I have to hold out to the last bar. When I finally finish Satomi puts it very delicately, 'Maaku, you have no melody at all! None at all!' She screams with laughter. A few minutes later I have another go, this time coaxed into singing an ABBA duet with Asako. My singing feels a little better, but it may be because I am a little drunker; the drinks have been coming into the room fairly regularly. Then Satomi reappears in a pink cat costume, swinging her tail. Asako and I think this is such a good idea we troop out to the corridor to select our costumes. There are animals and clowns and Elvis suits to choose from. They are all ridiculously small on me, but it is not as if they don't look ridiculous on the girls too, and embarrassment has ceased to be an impediment tonight.

By about 3:30 AM I truly feel like Frank Sinatra, and punch song numbers into the machine as if there is no tomorrow. I finish the night with a three-song marathon, feeling more harmonious and melodic than ever before. After paying our bill we go in search of fast food, exploring little alleys lit by the last quarter of the moon. The place we find is full of sleeping people slumped like serial killer victims in front of their chips and chicken. This gives the place a surreal atmosphere.

After eating I wonder where we can go next. Satomi leaves me in no doubt. An instant after Asako steps away from the table, Satomi's hand cups my genitals and she pushes her face into mine. Through tiredness and impending hangover my desire flares up. I reach for her legs.

'Time to go,' she says.

We farewell an unsurprised Asako in the lane outside. From Roppongi to Satomi's tiny room is an expensive taxi ride made unendurable by the need for propriety.

Satomi's body, which I see for the first time in the bluish light of her bedroom, is hot and velvety to the touch and, apart from a dense black pubic tuft, completely hairless. We make love like desperate animals. It's rough and breathless and exhausting and wordless, and not enough. Within minutes Satomi is pulling at me to start again, which I do. She cruises an oceanic orgasm while I toil in the engine room, stoking the boilers, or that is how it feels. At the third attempt I have to apologise and say I'd rather sleep. Satomi's disappointment is not well concealed, but she is just as spent. We lie like fallen wreckage. I wake later, like a castaway, dehydrated and disoriented, my mouth as slack as that of a sack. The room is hellishly hot. My stumbling to and from the toilet does not wake Satomi. I kneel beside the *futon* and carefully fold it off her. The absence of even the lightest down on her glabrous skin fascinates me. I try to caress her without waking her but she stirs and reaches for me. We crash to another bruising climax, sweating and gasping, then fall asleep once more.

When I wake in the yellow light of early morning, Satomi is already dressed in black pants and a thick white sweater, and is making breakfast of coffee and muffins. She serves me in bed. I dutifully try to pull her back onto the *futon* but she twists free and kills all ardour with...

'My boyfriend is coming, you have to be quick.'

On the train back to Shinjuku, all the young men look somnolent. They mumble sleepily, their hair pillow-rubbed, their eyes puffy. The women shine like Buddhas.

Odaiba shopping

At the hotel I stumble straight into bed and sleep until lunchtime. In the late afternoon I go to meet Satomi at Shinjuku, where I find her waiting in the same black pants and a tight breast-flattening shirt. Her body momentarily captures my attention but, business-like and purposeful, she draws me back to the agenda of the day. Last night I expressed an interest in seeing Odaiba, an enormous new development across Tokyo Harbour and today Satomi has appointed herself guide. We cross Tokyo by train and catch the monorail over the Rainbow Bridge to the reclaimed land that is Odaiba. From the bridge we catch glimpses between the buildings of the pale lavender outline of Mount Fuji.

Beside the monorail station at Odaiba stands a huge metal box – purple, windowless, and several storeys high. Against the darkening sky it looks black and oppressive. Its name is Venusfort, and it is a shopping centre with romance.

Along with several young couples, with linked arms and awed expressions, we walk through the entrance and step into the dream. The interior is an idealised recreation of something Italianate, perhaps a version of old Florence. A synthetic blond masonry clads all the shops; unloaded stone pillars, unnecessary arches, and unseeing windows. The floor is a nameless compromise between authentic medieval cobbles and practical non-slip tiling. The ceiling bears faint impressions of clouds, and is now darkening in harmony with its counterpart outside. The gentle bubbling of Rococo fountains can be heard above serene synthesiser music floating overhead, and the effect is one of complete security in a foreign place, something I suppose the Japanese people yearn for.

We move around the streets in communal flow. I try to unravel the nested set of fantasies collected here. Japan is a dreamy place to start with, and Tokyo is as unreal as any place on earth can be. Odaiba is artificial in many ways; everything about Odaiba is new, even the earth beneath it. Odaiba has been designed with a purpose, to attract people. So, whatever they want, Odaiba will become. Venusfort lifts itself above these three layers of hypnosis to create yet another state of unreality. And, as if that were not enough, I notice advertisements for special 'Venusfort fantasy evenings,' which presumably add a further, fifth, level of artificial abstraction.

Detractors may say the effect is one of ersatz stylisation and superficial consumerism. Of course it is, but how irrelevant! The point is that very few people think of Venusfort that way. Single Japanese women in their mid-twenties (just to get the demographics right) tell me that Venusfort is a romantic place and good for couples. The name combines concepts of love and security, which themselves are highly compatible, but it combines them in an incongruous way. Love and war. Love and siege. Satomi tells me that the concept (I'm surprised at her use of the word) of Venusfort is aimed at women, but aren't all shopping centres aimed at women anyway?

We look around for a suitable place to eat. Having eaten pizza nearly everywhere else recently, I perversely choose French fried potatoes here. I ask the waitress for *shio*, salt. Satomi observes that I ought to say 'o-shio,' honourable salt, when I am talking about someone else's salt. Sitting across the small table from her, knees touching, I feel a physical desire again. Will we return to her place tonight, I ask, but she explains that *both* her boyfriends like sex and tonight she has promised to look after the *other* one. She finishes the explanation with a level look, curious about how I will take the news that she will have slept with three men in twenty-four hours. I simply respond that I still want to sleep with her. It is not possible, she says, with a convincingly regretful smile. There appears to be nothing more to say on the matter. No love, no siege.

After the meal we walk out of Venusfort into the brilliance of Odaiba's night-time lighting. Next door in the Toyota showrooms we are again surrounded by young couples – most of whom appear intent on leaving hundreds of incriminating fingerprints all over the cars. Satomi and I strain our ties with reality still further by driving the car simulator. This is a massive white tablet-shaped capsule suspended on six hydraulic legs that pulse and thrust in response to how the driver inside handles the controls. From the outside it resembles a monstrous bloated insect posturing for a fight, on the inside it is a mixture of perfect physical verity and disturbing spatial effects.

The controls all appear to be the real thing – a car. The two of us sit inside, legally seat-belted. I put my hand on Satomi's leg, she knocks it off again. Through the windows we watch a wrap-around projection of space. The otherwise perfect effect has two weaknesses. The resolution of the images is a little coarse, so they are difficult to interpret at times, but more off-putting, the relationships between my movement of the controls, their mechanical feedback, the motion, and changes in the scenery are dissonant. The disparities between apparent visual movement and actual physical movement have an unsettling effect on my stomach, and I am glad to get out. I crash the car four times. They are all serious incidents involving no damage. Satomi jokes that I need to take driving lessons again, the attendant hands me a slip of paper showing that I scored 30,000 points, where the best drivers have scored about 90,000. I am too queasy to care.

Meiji-Jingu

The next day I visit the Meiji shrine. Anyone who has worked with wood will be deeply impressed by the skills of the carpenters and wood-carvers who built this shrine. A large chrysanthemum design is cut right through a door 8 cm thick. Its edges are perfect, not a single splinter can be seen, and the internal surfaces are uniform and symmetrical. The railings around the shrine are upturned at their ends. The easy way to make such rails is to turn them on a lathe, then bend them in water or steam until they take on the curve. That was not how they were made; instead they were hand-carved out of solid wood, each one made singly and perfectly fitted into position. Upper surfaces are slightly raked. This is hardly noticeable, but makes the joinery many times more difficult. Joints are complex and hidden; the beams are supported using nailless techniques that can be found in Japanese wooden toy puzzles. The mastery, purity and simplicity of this building are as near to ideal as I have seen, but one needs to know what to look for. The shrine's power to impress is in the small unnoticeable things, absences, subtleties – for there is little drama or splendour here.

Meiji-jingu piques my interest in Shinto, so I look for other shrines that sound interesting. One of them is Atsuta-jingu in south Nagoya.

A couple of days later I leave Tokyo on the *shinkansen*, having still not met Miho.

Atsuta-jingu swords

Shiny bronze leaves glitter against a blue metal sky when I draw back the curtains of my room. My guest-house backs onto a small birch grove. Outside the temperatures are below zero but the bright morning sunlight mimics summer.

Atsuta-jingu is intriguing because it is one of the three places that are said to house objects once owned by the gods who created Japan. The object held here is *kusanagi no tsurugi*, a legendary sword. It was given to Amaterasu, the sun-goddess, by her rather psychotic brother Susano-o, who had found it in the tail of an eight-headed serpent he had just killed (after getting it drunk with eight buckets of *sake*). Up to this point then, the story is all perfectly plausible. However, we have only circumstantial evidence for the sword's existence. Nobody has ever seen it. Despite this, the mere idea of *kusanagi* has resulted in many other swords being left here, and the collection in the museum within the grounds of the shrine is now quite fine.

Disingenuously I ask one of the women working in the shrine if she has ever seen *kusanagi*. 'No one has seen it,' she replies, and I pretend to be thoroughly surprised. My surprise turns genuine when a truck backs up to a tree in the shrine gardens, and raises on its cherry picker arm a workman who then starts sucking up the tree's loose pine needles with a vacuum cleaner. This kind of improvement on the raw material of nature has been noted before by David Mura in *Turning Japanese* (workmen rearranging stones in a riverbed to make the river more attractive).

There is more to the story of *kusanagi*. A closer reading of its history reveals that the original was lost at sea, and that what is installed here is, and has always been, a replica. For most westerners, this revelation is disappointing. 'It's not real, then,' we might complain. But Japanese people seem quite unconcerned by this. It is as if the original sword were merely a symbol for a Platonic Ideal, and the replica is just as good a symbol.

The sword collection of Atsuta-jingu embodies another idea that engages my imagination: emptiness at the core. The collection is real, but the original reason for it gathering here is a non-entity. In western thought we perceive there to be density around the centres of things. About each absolute truth, all our various opinions cluster. Truth can only be revealed by peeling away the onionskins of deception and misunderstanding. Truth is the heart of the matter. There is a well-defined central concept, or precept, or axiom, or object, or thing of importance, about which other things, or versions, are gathered more or less loosely. Gravity collapses matter, satellites orbit. Cores and density seem to be closely related in our ontology. We do not feel comfortable with the idea that when we really get down to it there is nothing to get down to – we feel 'hollow.'

In time I try to explain this disturbing feeling to Satomi. She says it doesn't sound like a bad feeling to her.

Ise-jingu and Ago-wan

Ise-jingu and the Imperial Palace are the other two locations of godly heirlooms: a mirror at Ise-jingu, and jewels in the Imperial Palace. Ise-jingu, the shrine of Ise, is next on my agenda.

I'm told that one cannot make a day trip to Ise from where I am staying in Seto, but I am willing to give it a try.

My route requires careful planning: a bus and two subway trains to get across Nagoya itself, then two more trains and another bus. An early start is unavoidable. As I move further away from the city of Nagoya I notice manners changing. People become noisier, more carefree. Is this the Osaka boisterousness I have heard about? I am not really travelling into Osaka, but this area may come under its influence.

In *A Wild Sheep Chase* Murakami Haruki described how trips on suburban trains in Japan are often punctuated by invasions of schoolchildren, who suddenly fill the carriages with incomprehensible noise, frantic movement, and body odours, only to vanish as one at the next station. It seems things never change on the trains of Japan, because I go through the same experience several times as the train passes the local schools along the way.

It is hard to convey the effect of Ise-jingu. Under a brilliant clear sky, the nearby Isuzu River reflects blinding light through soaring cedars and cypress trees. The gravel crunches loudly underfoot, and the cold gnaws at my cheeks. I stand in front of a building both pristine and primordial. At first sight, the inner shrine replaces Meiji-jingu as my favourite building. For all the reasons I loved Meiji-jingu, I love Ise-jingu more. It is minimalistic; it has an architectural purity, an eschewal of frippery that reveals a deep unquestionable self-assurance. Beams extend well beyond the body of the building, recalling logs laid one on top of another. Some are well turned. The ends of some are coated white. Others are cased in gold, yet adornment is minimised almost to the point of invisibility, and the craftsmanship is sublime.

Ise-jingu also has an appealing abstract dimension. To reach the shrine, I endured a pilgrimage, on trains and buses, which culminated in a long slow walk through the surrounding woods. I passed though *torii*, and over a long arched bridge. It is not a hard trip to make, but not an easy trip either. I travelled for many hours and then, turning the final corner and walking up the steps to the shrine, I find that only a tiny part of it is actually visible to visitors. We are not allowed to enter, and must be content with looking in through a gate, which itself is out of reach. Finding myself here at the holiest place in Japan, a place to which all Japanese people supposedly make a pilgrimage at some stage in their lives, I experience once more that central void. One is supposed to come here, but when one does, one finds one cannot take the final step of the journey.

The shrine is sealed off from our touch. Much of what is within easy reach is permanently covered in sheets of antiseptic white plastic. I never expected to see the fabled mirror, but to see so little of what conceals it is a true disappointment – one that makes me thoughtful. I feel I have made an investment that has not returned my principal. I must examine what I really came here for, and realise it was more than just to see a building. Perhaps it was a need to be mystified, confronted, or given something new to think about. I cannot really say what my goal was, but wondering about it has somehow brought satisfaction, and my disappointment wanes.

After bearing witness to the building, which is all one can really do, I take my last look and turn to leave. My reflections continue almost of their own volition. The shrine provides a direct connection to the animist primitive I like to think lurks beneath the surface in all of us. In the presence of the shrine things seem simple and natural.

The entire shrine is built anew every twenty years or so. The rebuilding process is incremental and ritualised, taking up to eight years. Permission to proceed is sought from the *kami* spirits at several stages in the construction. The materials are taken from the surrounding forest and assembled using ancient techniques. Though ancient in design, the buildings before me certainly look new. The wood has not aged or stained, and the deep *susuki* thatch is still solid and crisply outlined. This process of cyclic renewal is significant, for only through constant replacement can we experience the shrine as it was when originally built, maybe 1,500 years ago. Had it been preserved it would now look extremely old, fragile and therefore quite unlike its original self. So which is the truer, more 'real,' more immortal shrine? One that has been left to weather and age, or one that is for ever new? Like Uchiide Beach in *As I Crossed a Bridge of Dreams* by Lady Sarashina, Ise-jingu only achieves timelessness through constant renewal.

Given the many hours it took me to get this far, it is probably rash to try to get around the Shima peninsula in time to watch the sun set-ting across Ago-wan, a bay of many small islands, but this is what I now set out to do. Though the train's progress around the coast is slow, it is made interesting by many tiny hamlets and miniature ports that don't appear on my maps. As the train leisurely trundles along its bumpy track, the sun sinks steadily towards the hills, but I am confid-ent I will arrive just in time to see it dip into the sea.

The train moves towards the descending sun, and in the opposite direction the moon rises out of the water, full, sepia-brown, and en-larged by its proximity to the horizon. Schoolboys who have been shouting and squabbling in my carriage pause to admire it. We rattle along through small tunnels and tight bends and arrive at Kashikojima at dusk. The disc of the sun is hidden in low clouds to the west, but the sky is still pink and red, and in the gloom the calm leaden sea is peppered with tiny white islands of rock, each wearing a wig of dense greenery. The sky darkens further and the islands fade away. By twisting on my heels and looking east I see that the moon, now a little higher, has made a dappled white road across the water. On one side a dying sun, and on the other a rising moon. When it is truly night-time I stroll back to the station, wondering if I should simply check into one of the luxurious hotels sitting on nearby hill-tops, rather than slog all the way back to Seto tonight. But finding that it is possible to catch an express direct to Nagoya, and that it leaves in only ninety seconds, my mind is made up and I jump aboard.

Cherry blossom transience

On the train I continue to think about the constant renewal of Ise-jingu. I do not feel any deep sense of permanence. The renewal is just as redolent of transience to me.

I let my head rest against the back of the seat and begin to drift off. My loosened thoughts slip from transience to the wonderful pathos that the Japanese call *aware*, a pity for the mortal helplessness of things.

The poignance of cherry blossom, celebrated each year in an unof-ficial flower-viewing festival called *hanami*, is its fragility and delicate transience.

Until the year 710, the capital of Japan had been moved to a new location upon the accession of each new Emperor to the throne. Shinto regards death as pollution, and a death as significant as that of an Emperor was sufficiently contaminating to render a whole city in-auspicious for a new era. Eventually the sheer logistic difficulties out-weighed the animist misgivings, and Nara was established as the permanent (from 710 to 794, at least) capital.

Transience persists even after death. The Japanese have few qualms about disturbing graves. Human remains are casually moved to make way for new developments. In *Diary of a Mad Old Man*, by Tanazaki Junichiro, the narrator laments that graves must be constantly shifted to avoid destruction. In Japan, the dead are as transient as the living.

A Kyoto woman

Having failed to interest Satomi in accompanying me to Kyoto, I travel alone. She has been here within the last twelve months and begs off, pleading pressure of work. She mollifies me with the argu-ment that if she can get some more work done now, she will be able to spend more time with me in other places.

In the first few days of my trip I run the circuit of all that is famous in Kyoto: the beautiful Kiyomizu-dera, classically framed by blazing maples; the treasures of the museums; Ginkaku-ji, the silver pavilion that is black and contains no silver; dozens of little craft shops; Nijo-jo, a single-storey palace; tiny lanes and graveyards, all washed and tended with care. There is enough to endear me to this place for a life-time. Each morning begins with the joyous anticipation of exploring another part of the city – I have never felt such affection for a place. Each day ends in exhaustion. I walk until I can walk no further, too spent to experience the other side of Kyoto: an energetic nightlife that provides the antithesis to the calm of each day.

One evening, after walking the Path of Philosophy, I return to my hotel by taxi, too tired to walk back through the city. I fall asleep in my clothes, and wake at 10:30 PM. What should I do? Try to go back to sleep, or go out? I ask the question repeatedly and eventually the win-ning argument is *if I stay here I know nothing will happen, but if I go out I don't know what I might find.* My guidebook mentions a place called 'Bar, Isn't It?', saying it 'is popular with young Japanese and foreign men desperately searching for... something.' That fits the bill perfectly.

The place is loud, crowded, hot, and smoky. In Australia I would probably avoid it. After getting my first vodka and tonic I stand by the bar and watch people dance. All the music is western and there is nothing unfamiliar about the setting: a basement bar with music memorabilia and dark murals of half-recognised musicians decorating the walls. Actually none of the staff appear to be Japanese either, I could easily be in an Australian bar catering to Japanese tourists on the Gold Coast.

Several attractive girls are out on the dance floor, but one in particular really holds my attention. She has strong eastern features, and the most cat-like eyes I've ever seen on a human being. Although chatting and dancing with her friends she has an aura of stillness and self-possession that fascinates me. I tear my eyes away briefly to order my second drink. When I look again she is moving slowly towards me through the crowd. She holds one hand out for mine, beckons with the other hand and offers the simple explanation 'I like you.' Her name, she tells me, is Takegawa Emi, and she wants to dance with me. She is surprised when I show her I know the *kanji* for her family name, though it is a relatively easy word with a literal meaning of 'bamboo river.'

Emi is tall, thin, and balances languorously on high heels. Her thick hair is tied behind her neck. She is expressionless and composed, with a quiet face dominated by huge black eyes that demand attention.

She dances with one hand on my shoulder and the other at my waist. Her head sways from side to side. When I tell her this is cute, she just smiles and says thank you. Her friends – Yoko, Kasumi, and Katsuya – are all smiling and don't seem to worry about having a giant *gaijin* suddenly pulled into their circle.

Emi holds me while we talk between dances. It touches me as extraordinarily affectionate, and I'm completely disarmed. She disappears for a few moments, and I wonder what has happened to her, but she is soon back with beers for both of us. She first opens mine and turns it to the correct angle before opening her own. Later, when I go to fetch more drinks she tags along and is happy to lean against me with her head on my chest or shoulder. We stay like this for a long time just watching people dance. This is just what I need. After days of lonely travelling, and my inability to have an easy conversation in Japanese, this articulate non-verbal contact is deeply satisfying. I ask if she is free to do something together the following day, but she and the others are going to a classical music concert some way out of town. Tomorrow will be my last full day in Kyoto, so it looks like we won't see each other again. Not for the first time it seems travel is the maker and breaker of romance. Then it occurs to me that going to the concert with Emi and her friends, enjoying their easy company, being able to sit still and have the entertainment come to me, rather than having to walk all day to see it, would be the ideal way to spend the day. I ask Emi if I can join the party and she says yes, as if there was no need to ask.

It is soon time to leave. Katsuya offers to drive me back to my hotel. We all leave the bar and squeeze into his car. I sit between Emi and Yoko, who points out the famous Minami-za theatre on the way, and later jokes that Emi's heart is *dokidoki* (aflutter) because I'm sitting next to her.

At the hotel we all get out to do proper goodbyes and again Emi holds me close. Though I didn't expect this I wonder if she wants to stay with me tonight. Everything we said about tomorrow was predicated on her calling me in the morning. Chancing my hand, I whisper the invitation into her ear; she nods and, without saying anything, waves goodbye to the others. Not a glimmer of surprise or amusement crosses their faces as they get back into the car.

In the room, Emi loosens her hair; it bursts free, a great wild black jungle. She crouches before the mini-bar and pulls out a couple of beer cans. I put my hand on her back, but she says she needs a drink first.

Later, with the lights turned down low, we undress for a shower together. Emi, I then discover, is one of Japan's shaved women. She is as hairless as Satomi, but all over her body the skin has an oddly roughened texture. Not satisfied with depilated underarms and legs, she apparently shaves everywhere, except for her head and her small, shaped, pubic flock. Her dry skin feels somehow inanimate. Even her face appears to be shaved. Where I expect soft baby hair, in front of her ears, at her temples, I touch a light and barely detectable stubble, the same on her lip and around her purple nipples.

The night is something of a fiasco. Either I drank too much, or Emi is far too tense. Whatever the explanation, we are unsuccessful in our attempts to have sex. After much painful bending I give up. Emi's reaction to this is disconcertingly hard to determine, as her face is Buddha-impassive. Within minutes she falls asleep, her body sprawled over mine like an octopus on a rock.

In the morning, Emi is refreshingly nonchalant about her nudity. She is happy to lounge naked on the bed and chat, even after I have pulled on a *yukata*. This is so unlike many western women, for whom to be plumped and plumbed is often less exposing than to be seen. I remember an American woman who slipped out of my bed and, in case I was watching her from my pillow, actually crawled across the floor to the bathroom door so I couldn't see her naked. Here, Emi bends, sits, scratches and yawns – bare and unselfconscious. I've already had a shower, but I stop by the bed and put my hands on her shoulders. Her hands move around my waist. We move our mouths over each other's body and both find a way to satisfaction, though again I am unable to enter her. She is cheerful enough, and I feel a warm affection between us that tells me we will be friends and lovers anyway.

Successful raids on Nin-jutsu Mura and a cow barn

I have long wanted to visit a remarkable Kyoto house called Nijo-jinya. It is near Nijo-jo Palace, and is unusual for the fact that it is full of secret passageways and trapdoors. I like this kind of thing. However, visits must be arranged in advance in Japanese and, as the tour is conducted in Japanese only, one needs to either understand the language or take an interpreter. Back in Kyoto, I call Emi and ask if she would make the appointment for me. She agrees, but we find our timing is bad. The house is fully booked this weekend.

'Is it a *ninja* house?' asks Emi.

'Yes, you could say that.'

'Wait a little bit, please.' She puts the phone down. A few minutes later she is back on the line, 'Maaku-san?'

She has information about a *ninja* village about ninety minutes away by car. It sounds like the perfect substitute for Nijo-jinya, and so we agree to go there tomorrow.

That evening Emi takes me on a tour of the bars around Otsu, her hometown, which lies on the shores of Lake Biwa, just east of Kyoto. Like nearly every town I visit in Japan, Otsu was once the capital of the country. In retirement it is the capital only of Shiga prefecture.

Much of what Emi tells me about her life is surprising. Her ancestors were monks by tradition, but her father broke with this to become a painter. Had he not done so, Emi, as the next generation's firstborn, would have been expected to go to the temple too. Her name, combining the characters for 'picture' and 'beauty,' refers to her father's avocation.

Emi took a degree in economics in nearby Hikone, notwithstanding the local prejudices against Otsu residents, prejudices that linger on from what she calls 'the war' – the battle of Sekigahara in 1600.

Despite her degree, and other qualifications that entitle her to teach several subjects at high school level, Emi is expected to do much of the drudgery in her office, as well as her actual job of keeping the accounts. This is because she is the only woman there. So, she arranges the office flowers, cooks for her colleagues, but eats alone when they have office occasions. She usually keeps her mobile phone switched off in the evenings because otherwise she is likely to be called by colleagues who have drunk too much to drive, and expect her to drive them home. She has five days of leave a year, and works every other Saturday. In the evenings she usually cooks for herself and her mother. She spends whatever free time remains in study to become a conveyancer, and hopes one day to set up her own practice, in partnership with a husband, since a woman on her own would stand no chance in business.

Emi recently took part in an *o-miai*, a formally arranged meeting with a prospective husband. Apparently, all the wedding plans were going well until her family, through the services of a private detective hired to investigate the boy's family, discovered that his father had a criminal record and had spent some time in gaol. Emi laughs as she relates the tale, deliberately making light of a matter that must have been something of a family bombshell at the time.

Emi has excellent qualifications in *kanji*. Though my knowledge is obviously minuscule compared to hers, this is an interest we share, and she is happy to go into extended explanations in answer to my many questions. I am surprising and delighting myself every so often, in being able to read fairly long strings of mixed *kanji* and *kana*. The meaning doesn't leap out the way it does in English; I drag it out one character at a time.

Much visual pleasure can be derived from the Japanese writing system and its multiple scripts. *Katakana* cut so much like the rapid slashes of a sword; it is appropriate that the words *katana* and *kata-kana* sound so similar. *Hiragana* curl like the eddies and ripples of a little brook, and *kanji* often look like densely woven fencing.

When we talk, Emi and I mix languages. Some days all Japanese deserts me. On others, complete sentences form on my tongue without any sense of having consciously planned them out in advance, and then I often wonder *did I say that in English or Japanese*? On a couple of occasions I am not even sure that Spanish words haven't unconsciously slipped back into my conversation.

As planned, the next day we drive away from Otsu in Emi's car and reach the turnoff to Nin-jutsu Mura, the *ninja* village, about midmorning, only to see a sign saying it is closed. Emi is ready to start discussing what to do instead but I, having come this far, and having been twice thwarted in my attempts to see Nijo-jinya, suggest we walk up the approach road, and 'just have a look at what's up there.'

The morning is cool and sunny, and it is lovely to inhale the fresh country air. At the top of the hill is a fortified gate, but both its reinforced doors are open. Emi hesitates on the threshold, but I urge her on. Beyond the gate the road descends to a strong bamboo fence. There is a small ticket office, closed, and a gate into the village itself, also closed and, I discover when I try to open it, locked too.

'Let's just walk along this fence...' I suggest. Emi is beginning to get the idea. Sure enough, only a few metres into the woods we discover an opening. We step though and soon reach a clearing on the other side. From the edge of the woods we can look down into the village, which consists of a ring of small buildings around a circular area that reminds me of a parade ground. The village is not deserted. We can hear someone sweeping, and smoke is rising from a few piles of smouldering leaves. We talk in whispers and tread quietly. We approach the nearest building and gently try one of the screens. It slides open noiselessly, and inside we can see a large *tatami*-floored room, looking a little like a *judo dojo*. We close the screen and creep towards the next building. This is a kitchen. We pause behind this building because we hear someone moving on the other side. We let them pass out of earshot, then move stealthily on.

Further around the ring of buildings we find a climbing wall made of several tree trunks standing in a row. Small notches have been cut into them. I traverse the wall, Emi mimes applause. Among the trees stand a few other walls, each of a different construction, presumably also for climbing practice.

Still undetected, we continue to creep around the edge of the village. Unaccustomed to such naughtiness, Emi is finding it rather thrilling. It sounds as if there are perhaps four people working here.

Then we almost get caught. We are tiptoeing between two buildings, and for a moment we are out in the open, when a man emerges from one of the buildings and walks across the open space. We freeze. All he has to do is move his gaze slightly to the left and he'll see us, but miraculously we go unnoticed. When he is a reasonable distance away I retreat towards cover but Emi trips and scuffs her foot noisily against the gravel. We wait, certain of having been discovered, but the man must have thought the noise was caused by one of his colleagues, because he does not come back to investigate.

We successfully work our way around the village perimeter and are returning towards the opening in the fence when Emi points to a building we haven't seen before and says, 'That is a *shuriken dojo*.'

'Oh, we must see that.'

Inside, it resembles a shooting gallery. Targets are arranged at various distances up the hillside, rising from a row of small stalls from which *ninja* would have thrown their *shuriken*, star-shaped blades about the size of the palm of one's hand. The stalls are surprisingly cramped. When I stand in one I hardly have room to lift my elbows, let alone take a full arm swing.

Then I get a mental image of *shuriken* being used in some old martial arts film I must have seen. The victim enters a room. The camera lingers on a large cupboard, its door ajar just half an inch. We see the victim moving across the room, but now we see him from *inside* the cupboard. The next moment we see him from outside the cupboard again, but something flashes, we hear a thud, and the victim stumbles. Within a second, two more thuds follow and we see him reel and fall to the floor, three *shuriken* bloodily embedded in his chest. The cupboard door eases open. The assassin's legs come into shot. They are hidden in close-fitting black trousers and soft black shoes. They pause, and then silently move out of sight.

I wander up towards the targets and just happen to look down at my feet. Half buried in the soil and camouflaged by rust is a *shuriken*. I clean the dirt off it. Each blade bears a single *kanji*, and a dragon design encircles a small square hole at the centre. The *kanji* are *te kutsu satsu utsu*, meaning 'hand strike kill win' – probably a slogan. I wonder if it is an antique, but find 'PAT. JAPAN' punched into the reverse side. Emi notices the avaricious gleam in my eye.

'Are you going to be a thief?' she asks me, seriously.

'Yes, I think I am,' I confess.

Looking down at the weapon in my hand, I know leaving it behind is out of the question. It is too appropriate a trophy of our perfectly executed incursion into the heart of the *ninja* stronghold. To take the *shuriken* is against my better conscience, but the neatness and audacity of coming away with it is just too tempting. I slip it in my pocket, and we walk back through the trees to the opening.

I tell Emi we have 'out-*ninja*-ed the *ninja*.' This verbal form takes a bit of explaining, but she understands perfectly what I mean. We have executed a stealthy *ninja*-style raid against the very proponents of the art. It is no exaggeration to say that Emi has been moved by our unauthorised escapade. Her face is aglow with excitement.

In an attempt to ease my conscience a little, but also to add a triumphant flourish to our mission, I write a note *Nin-jutsu Mura e, kimashita, mimashita... arigato*, 'To Ninja Village, We came, we saw...

Thank you.' I push the note and our 2,000 yen admission fee through a crack in the ticket office window. I then explain the *veni, vidi, vici* significance of my note. Emi tells me that Caesar's words have a standard translation in Japanese: *kita, mita, katta*. If only I'd known a moment ago.

As we walk back down the hill I suggest to Emi that we have enjoyed the village closed more than we would have had it been open. She agrees enthusiastically. Several other cars pull up at the end of the road. Their occupants see the 'closed' sign, and immediately drive away again, without even pausing to contemplate defiance. 'They are missing the fun,' says Emi. I couldn't agree more.

It is still early in the day and we must decide what to do next. Emi characteristically asks me what *I* would like to do. Here, amid silent frozen woods and dried rice paddies, with the temperature well down the scale, miles from anywhere as far as I know, this is a somewhat rhetorical question. I ask Emi what she would like to do. Cautiously, she mentions a place that is reasonably close, 'but it is not very Japanese,' she warns.

Blumen Hügel is an attempt to create the illusion of a foreign town. It sits in a lonely spot, on converted agricultural land where property prices were presumably low. Blumen Hügel is a 'German' town. This is evident as we approach in the car, because the unmistakably Teutonic buildings are visible from a distance. Closer still we hear *oom-pah-pah* beer-hall music rolling from speakers mounted on poles all over the vicinity. It is definitely the off-season, though; quiet and uncrowded.

Arm in arm we walk around the town, bemused to discover that nearly every 'house' is a shop of some kind. Some are dedicated to milk and cheese-making activities, none of which is in progress. I find that knowing hardly any German, which is true of me, and knowing no German, which is true of Emi, are two very different things. I am able to explain incomprehensible signs and names to Emi, and feel that, in her eyes at least, I might appear to be quite cosmopolitan after all.

'Vogel Strasse *wa tori-michi desu.*'

'*Ah, so desu ka.*'

Finding most of the restaurants closed we finally strike lucky and eat slightly off-theme pizza – righting or repeating the wrong I committed with Satomi in Venusfort?

Emi is on a mission. I don't know this yet. Today she has planned to do something she has never done before. What's more, the events of this morning, at Nin-jutsu Mura, have given her a new determination to make things happen, rather at odds with the more typical fatalism of the Japanese people. Emi is twenty-seven and has never seen a cow, she tells me.

'Really? I find that very hard to believe.'

'There are not so many in Kansai,' she explains.

So, Emi came here with the dream of seeing a cow. Unfortunately, the winter temperatures are keeping all the cows indoors, in a barn on the hill, and not in the fields that surround the village. But this isn't enough to stop Emi, not now. She leads me up towards the barn, saying 'I am encouraged by your vitality,' which I take to mean *I am inspired by your gaijin disregard for rules and propriety.* Emi tries to shake open the big barn doors. Even though I show her that by peering through a filthy window we can vaguely make out lumpy vaccine outlines inside, her determination is unabated and she tries a few more doors. They are all locked except one, which leads into a milk-processing room, spotlessly clean and full of stainless steel pipes. Emi strides across the floor, leaving muddy footprints, and vanishes through an inner door. I follow forlornly.

We find our way into the barn itself. The stench of methane stabs like a knife into the back of my nose, but Emi is oblivious. Close up the cows are as big as cars. We walk between their pens. A chained dog and a cat watch us warily. I find a calf and call Emi over to look at it. The calf strains its head through the bars and whips out a tongue about a foot long. The tongue wraps around our hands and leaves them smelly and sticky. I've had my fun, but Emi wants to hang around. A dairy worker sees us but carries on unconcernedly.

'My first cow experience,' announces Emi, enraptured, the calf's tongue still straining towards her.

'On this day of 1999,' I say, for posterity.

'Yes. A good day,' Emi declares.

And I agree. A good day. On the way home we pass a love hotel and I try to interest Emi in popping in with me. 'I don't want to,' she says, uncharacteristically blunt.

It is dark when we drive back into Otsu. We try, unsuccessfully, to find an Internet café so that I can catch up with my email – we have a beer instead.

The tiny old castle of Hikone

The next time I visit Kyoto, Emi offers to take me for another drive. We are to meet at 1 PM. That morning, I make a quick trip up to Kiyo-mizu-dera, one of my favourite spots.

By now I have the hang of Japanese public transport. It is possible to make travel plans that involve split-second connections, because things invariably arrive and depart on time. I know exactly how much time I have before I need to return to the bus-stop, that the bus will get me to the station with just a few minutes left to get to my plat-form, and that then the next train will put me in Otsu at 12:55, just be-fore I am due to meet Emi. That is the plan, and that is what happens.

After a couple of minutes, Emi pulls up in her tiny car. We soon settle on driving up the southern shore of Lake Biwa to visit Hikone castle.

We chat in our hybrid of English and Japanese. I enjoy speaking Ja-panese with Emi because she gives just the right amount of correc-tion, not so much that it is difficult to remember everything, nor so little that I am left floundering without the right words. And as she be-comes less preoccupied with the need to speak English and more able to think about what she really wants to say, her grammar and all the grammatical link words revert to Japanese. Only the verbs and nouns remain in English. This results in phrases like 'Saturday *ni* I have to work *da kara...*' In this way she inadvertently clarifies some of the more obscure aspects of Japanese usage for me.

The wind is blowing hard across the lake, and throwing up respect-able waves. '*Umi mitai*,' says Emi; it looks like the sea. As we near Hikone, our destination, the castle, emerges from the haze high on a hill.

The castle has a museum at the foot of the rise. It is well presented, and has a small *noh* stage at its centre. Close beside the stage is a little

Japanese tearoom. Emi wastes no time in ordering for us. While we wait for the tea I ask a thousand questions on the theme of how the old and new Japanese cultures are balanced in Emi's life. 'Do you go to *kabuki*?' 'Do you go to *noh*?' 'Do you own any *kimono*?' and so on.

'Is this a Japanese test?' she asks with a smile.

'Yes it is, and you don't appear to be very Japanese.' I laugh. Later she tells her friends about this and they are all keen to hear the questions, to see how well they do on my 'Japanese test.'

When we climb up the hill to the *donjon* of Hikone Castle I realise a clever trick has been played on us. Most Japanese castles are deliberately deceptive in that from the outside they appear to have one less floor than they really do, but Hikone plays a second deception. From afar the castle looks imposingly large because all that can be seen are the top two storeys, high above the shores of the lake. Trees, we imagine, obscure the rest. Close up however, the *donjon* is tiny, like a child's castle, and perhaps not much bigger than a large house. Inside, the framework consists of rough tree trunks, twisted and gnarled, laid across one other, under which carefully carpentered screens and frames are fitted – a pronounced contrast in techniques. This *donjon* dates from 1622 and is one of only twelve original castles left standing in Japan. Most of Japan's castles are modern concrete reconstructions. Once there were hundreds of castles in Japan. Many were destroyed during the Meiji period in a mad orgy of pacifism, condemned as unwanted reminders of an abandoned militaristic past. The bombs of World War II obliterated nearly all the rest.

We ascend the steep steps, almost ladders really, and look out from the top floor. The view over Lake Biwa and across to the mountains, thirty kilometres away on the far side, is dramatic even in these cloudy conditions. Scenes of Scottish castles and windswept lochs come to mind. On the way down, the tails of Emi's long white coat keep slipping between her feet and the steps, so she has to hold them to the side. I am similarly hampered by having to hold our shoes in their plastic bags. Castle steps are slippery and dangerous in stockinged feet.

We take a quick walk in the castle's cherry orchard and reach the car chilled and eager for warmth. We drive back towards Otsu on Route 1, following the track of the old Tokaido linking Tokyo and

Kyoto. Near Otsu, we stop at a bar and discuss what to do next. Emi in thought is the perfect picture of Japanese female pensiveness. She purses her lips, cocks her head slightly to one side, then the other, places one finger to the side of her mouth. '*Eh tooooo…*' 'Hmmm…' '*Ehhhhhh…*' '*Nan daro…*' she says. It is worth asking hard questions just to elicit this performance. We have dinner in a Chinese restaurant and then try a few more bars. Several are full and turn us away at the door, but we spend the rest of the evening and much of the following morning in dark, intimate drinking holes each of whose presence is almost undetectable from outside.

After the third or fourth margarita, Emi asks why I am vegetarian. I explain my reasons and ask her what she thinks. What she says is very interesting. While Buddhism doesn't actually advocate carnivory, its concept of reincarnation can be used to justify many things. If one accepts the premise, it can make a strong argument against vegetarianism, or in favour of eating meat. The argument goes like this: all animals are created as bodies in which souls must reside in order to solve the problems they inherited from their previous lives. Whatever those problems are, they can only be addressed by having the normal expected life of a chicken, pig, etc. This entails, for these domesticated species, being killed and eaten. In other words, the proper destiny of these animals is to be treated as food. If they were treated any differently, the whole purpose of being a chicken or a pig would be defeated, and their souls would continue to struggle with their unresolved problems.

Without actually accepting the argument – primarily because I do not take reincarnation seriously – I think hard on it. The core argument is circular: chickens are eaten, so to be born as a chicken means one's fate is to be eaten, so it is only right that one be eaten, therefore chickens are eaten…

With Emi it is easy to take an interest in each other's ideas without feeling the need to compare them with our own. Emi has voluntarily explained her thoughts, and thereby left herself open to possible contradiction. This is an indication of her trust, or that is how I read it, and I feel a grateful affection towards her. I slide my hand up under her hair and caress the back of her neck. She stops this by placing her hand under mine. Is it because someone at the bar is watching us?

At about three o'clock in the morning we finish our last cocktail. We have both had another delightful day. I suggest an early start in the morning, but Emi is looking forward to sleep, and suggests we talk at two o'clock the following afternoon. She leaves for home and I walk back to my hotel.

Mii-dera and Enryaku-ji

The morning starts with coffee and toast in a small café beside Lake Biwa. This is the first day I've had the confidence to venture out without a guidebook, dictionary, or any of the other tourist's aids I brought with me. I wander slowly around the extensive grounds of Mii-dera, one of Japan's largest Buddhist temples, situated for 1,300 years, with great foresight, just outside my hotel. It is an interesting place. Its bell is renowned for having the most beautiful sound in Japan. In one small hut a spring burps and bubbles. Water from this spring was used to bathe baby emperors. Buddhist pacifism notwithstanding, the history of Mii-dera includes many wars with Enryaku-ji, another large Buddhist temple not far away. Hard as it is to believe, these wars resulted, every now and then, in the temple's utter destruction.

At two o'clock exactly I call Emi, who says she is still waiting for Katsuya to call, and explains that we will be going in his car today. She promises to call back. Why can't we make a more definite plan? Why wait for a third party, she in her house, me just a few minutes away across town – particularly as my time here is so short. I can never really understand the reasons for what to me appear to be precariously vague or conditional plans, but I seem to run into them over and over again in Japan. All I know is that Katsuya is keen to meet me again and so the only polite thing to do is wait.

And the plan then fails completely. Emi does not call me. By three-thirty in the afternoon I've given up hope of doing very much of anything today, so I stroll back to the hotel. It's now so cold that there's little point in being outside. Then to my surprise I find Emi, Katsuya, Yoko and another of Emi's friends, Sachiko, all waiting for me outside the hotel. Emi says they have been there for half an hour. She had written my mobile number down incorrectly, couldn't call me, and so they all thought the best thing to do was wait at my hotel.

We all crowd into Katsuya's car and drive towards the summit of Mount Hiei. As Katsuya throws the car around the tight, twisting switchbacks, we all feel a little nauseous and eager to get to the top. From the summit we can see many miles up Lake Biwa to the east, and across Kyoto to the west. Kyoto tower sticks up like a little match-stick in the city's centre. The temperatures are below zero at this altitude, and the day cools rapidly as twilight nears. Near the summit, people are skiing.

We visit Enryaku-ji temple – the one that warred upon Mii-dera. It is situated north-east of Kyoto, which is significant. Evil is thought to approach from this direction; so locating the temple here serves to protect the city. We walk around the complex, but one-by-one the buildings are being shut down for the night. Some fun remains to be had; the girls run up to the big bell and swing the clapper into it, hard. The bell booms out between the giant cedars and across the great spaces beyond. From many places we have wonderful views through the trees, out over the valleys and lake far below.

The cold really bites when the sun goes down, so we drive to a new mountaintop hotel and drink coffee at 800 yen a cup. I try hard to squeeze 800 yen-worth of enjoyment out of it, but it remains just an ordinary cup of coffee. Later in the evening we descend into Kyoto and park the car in one of the huge underground car parks that lie beneath the main streets. It had been obvious to me, from the glass-walled elevators that pop up incongruously in the pavement, that something existed down there but until now I had no idea these places existed.

We dine in a restaurant on the sixth floor of a building consisting, it appears, entirely of restaurants. Our table overlooks the main street of Kawaramachi-dori, through floor-to-ceiling windows. Only I put my legs under the table, everyone else kneels on cushions in the painful, but traditional, *seiza* position. One by one, though, they all shift to a more comfortable sitting position. Katsuya orders *fugu*, the poison fish. It tastes so much like ordinary fish that I wonder why anyone risks eating it at all. Next we order *nabe*. A large bowl, in which meat and vegetables are to be boiled together, is brought to the centre of the table. Since everyone puts their own chopsticks into the bowl, Emi says, we only eat *nabe* with our family or with close friends. I see the compliment in what she says. As the meal progresses, the friends sink into each other's company quite naturally. No one feels pressure to entertain or even to take part in the talk. Sachiko, for example, just sits quietly and listens. It is this, and the fact that she looks so much smaller than Emi and Yoko, that reminds me of the dormouse at the mad hatter's tea party.

Return post

The following day I find an Internet café where 1,000 yen buys an hour on the net and a small cup of coffee. I look for tyger but she is not logged on.

Dear tyger,

This email comes with much love. I know that usually goes at the end of a letter, but I think it's important to get the main idea across early.

Absolutely delighted to get yours and discover that you are real, after all. Very lucky, too, as I left for Japan less than three hours after the letter arrived. I'm there now (syntactically correct, but semantically vague, I agree). I've found an Internet café though they are not common here. Hope this adequately excuses my execrable (but not altogether unique) lack of communication over the last few weeks.

Also hope your dreams are not as disturbing as they sounded. Try to dream of me in light snow, serenely strolling the temple gardens of Kyoto. I'll do my best, morphic resonance assisting, to make sure you do.

tyger, whenever I think of you, I always end up wishing I could touch you. Today this seems more impossible (I know, I know...) than ever. I'm so far from home and familiar things I don't think I can even touch myself. Just a second while I try...

Yes, it is possible, but the guy beside me
seemed to disapprove.

Anyway, I am on the face of the earth, so are
you, we both see the same moon, and that's
comforting to know.

Looked for you a minute ago on the talker,
forgot about time difference, etc.

Much virtual (and real) love,

Your cat,

as always,

everywhere,

Leo.

Sometimes when I take my virtual leave of tyger a funny melancholy space forms like a gasp trapped in my chest. It's not an Internet romance, but it can feel like one.

Nijo-jinya

It is not long before I succeed in visiting Nijo-jinya. At eight-thirty one morning I meet a guide outside in the street. He calls himself Kazu and starts by explaining a little of Kyoto history. I listen, as if for the first time.

When the doors open we step inside and wait in *seiza* position until this morning's tour party is assembled. A middle-aged lady leads the tour and Kazu translates what she says into English. He adds sceptical comments of his own intended, I feel, to create a conspiratorial closeness between us. The tour conductor is a member of the Ogawa family, who have owned this house since it was built, around 1600.

Jinya belong to a class of building somewhere between a home and a castle. They were intended to be defensible against attack, but to look like ordinary houses. Their owners, the lesser *daimyo*, may well have desired and been able to build themselves a castle, but the Tokugawa regulations of the day forbade the building of new ones. When these *daimyo* left their homes, as they were often required to do, they needed more than the usual degree of protection *en route*. So it was that commercial *jinya*, a kind of fortified *ryokan*, came into being. Appearance being everything, they betrayed no external signs of being anything out of the ordinary. Inside, however, they were fitted with numerous ingenious security and anti-fire devices.

Ogawa Hiraemon, a *daimyo* and the owner of Nijo-jinya, was in the habit of providing lodging to other *daimyo* visiting Kyoto. Over thirty years he refined and augmented the features of his inn, turning it into an early project home. Indeed, the very idea of Nijo-jinya has always been more important than the reality. Not one of the spectacular security gadgets, it transpires, was ever used seriously. The idea of them was sufficient to discourage attacks. On the other hand, the fireproofing was remarkably effective. The building survived the great 1788 fire of Tenmei, which razed the surrounding neighbourhood.

The casual and uninformed visitor would have difficulty finding anything unusual in Nijo-jinya, except the high quality of the construction and perhaps one or two unusually positioned beams. But the building's array of cunning devices is as extensive as it is imaginative. Dark corners hide holes in the floor, designed to trip intruders and break their legs. A staircase can be raised and concealed in the ceiling. The building appears to have only one storey, but there are two, or three if we count the cramped, tunnel-like mezzanine where guards were meant to lie in wait. A cupboard has a false back, concealing a compartment large enough for someone to hide in. The nails in the floors are angled and hold the boards slightly away from their supporting beams, so that they squeak and give notice of anyone trying to approach unheard. The beams in one corner of the corridor are arranged so they can be used as the rungs of a ladder, enabling access to an escape hole in the ceiling.

Ian Fleming is rumoured to have declined to use this house in the movie of *You Only Live Twice* on the grounds of excessive implausibility. A place stranger than fiction, where art dare not imitate life for fear of ridicule. Gouverneur Mosher writes lovingly and evocatively of it in his wonderful little book, *Kyoto: A Contemplative Guide*.

After an hour or so, during which I have had little opportunity to stand up straight, the tour is finished and I invite Kazu for a cup of coffee around the corner. We talk about *nin-jutsu* and the other martial arts of Japan: *judo, karate, aikido, kendo,* and so on. They all still flourish in Japan, and a surprising number of people I meet, including Kazu, have attained *dan*, or black-belt, status.

Clowder reunion

She's there!

'... i want to come to japan'

'You can! Do so! Now!'

'excessive punctuation but lovely sentiment, leo'

'I'm rather proud of my lovely sentiment, actually.'

tyger laughs. 'so you should be. 'tis a fine specimen. but seriously...'

'Hmmmm?'

'i think a visit to the land of the rising economic dominance would be very good for tyger. what does leo think?'

'You need to ask? Of course it would be good for tyger, Leo *and* the LOTRED.'

'gosh, rather a good acronym, isn't it?'

''Tis so. You can have the copyright.'

tyger bows. 'if you seriously don't mind, i will initiate peregrination interrogations'

'Can't imagine anything better, to be honest.'

'oh leo, imagine a winged hug flying towards you'

'Ditto.'

tyger sighs 'i've rather a lot of bridge modelling to do...'

Leo weeps. 'And rather a lot of bridge-crossing too. Does this mean we better say "hasta luego"?'

'si, si'

'Que sera, sera.'

'quite so, quite so'

A priest in ambiguous circumstances

Before I hear from tyger again, I make a few peregrinations of my own. With a small backpack and a couple of travel guides, I pick my way across Kansai, staying in business hotels and the occasional *ryokan*. I use the local buses and trains to get around. In each town I look for places that are not to be found in the guide books. I don't know why.

On one of my walks, near a place called Uchikoshi, I come across a large sign pointing the way to something big or fat (I recognise the character *tai* but can't read the whole message). This activates a vague memory of seeing a tourist attraction, marked on a sightseeing map, in roughly this location, so I follow the signs. A few minutes later I notice a towering replica of the Arc d'Triumphe standing beyond the rice fields. Other strange stone objects lurk among the trees behind it. Separating me from these curiosities is a manned gatehouse and ticket window. No one at the gate speaks English and the staff tell me they have no English leaflets. I now see that the name of this place is Taiyo Park, but nothing else makes any sense. Looking at the prices, which range from 500 to 2,000 yen, I wonder what to do. I opt for the cheapest *koen dake* (park only) ticket, figuring this will let me see if it is worth spending more to see more. The park contains stone copies of pyramids, both Egyptian and Mayan, the Statue of Liberty (a decorative favourite in Japan, especially with love hotels and pachinko parlours), the Easter Island statues, North American totem poles, Copenhagen's mermaid, Singapore's merlion, Belgium's Manneken Pis, graven gods from South America, the Middle East, and the rest of Asia. Huge stone copies of coins from all over the world lie in the grass, or lean against other carvings. They are the size of cartwheels. A British One New Penny coin is present but I find no stone George III cartwheel penny. It is as if some itinerant stonemason had travelled the world and copied anything that took his fancy, regardless of theme, quality, or importance.

Further up the path, to one side, are three large sheds painted red, white, and blue. To my astonishment they contain a full-scale reproduction of Xian's terra-cotta army. For a minute I think it might be the real thing. The exhibition is truly gargantuan. About four-hundred statues are arranged in lines, surrounding three horse-drawn chariots. One line of statues has fallen like a row of dominoes, and lies smashed on the ground. A man beside me tells his companion this is the work of an earthquake, but does he mean this is a replica of damage done by an earthquake in Xian, or real damage done by an earthquake here in Hyogo prefecture? The exhibition is crudely carved, ineptly staged, badly looked after and dusty, but the scale and madness of it is impressive. Whatever can be its fascinating story, I wonder.

Reaching further up the hill are several mausoleums, also copies. Lining the paths, hundreds of sculptures of figures in traditional oriental dress are arranged in rows. They are almost identical, but not quite, having been carved rather than cast. Who would go to such effort to make so many, and for what reason? On two of the surrounding hills thirteen-storey pagodas stand. A monumental seated Buddha is carved into a hillside. Even more incredible, running up and down a line of hills is an attempt to replicate the Great Wall of China. This wall meanders for some way into the distance. I get tired walking on it, so without having found out how long it is I turn back to the centre of the park.

The park is made more inexplicable by the fact that homes for the elderly and handicapped are dotted around the grounds. I struggle to find a satisfactory explanation for what is here, but none comes.

In the warmth induced by exercise I later roam around the more remote parts of the grounds. At the top of a longish slope a Buddhist temple sits on a small level patch of ground. Real or replica, I do not know. While investigating some old-looking gravestones nearby I'm surprised to hear, in clear English, 'You are very welcome to come inside.' A priest walks towards me, broom in hand. He wears the traditional two-piece working clothes of Japan, in an attractive umber, and his head is shaved to a shiny golden brown.

He ushers me inside, where he shows me around the temple altars. We ply each other with questions. He tells me that his predecessor, a priest named Moguchi Kenzo, established the park some thirty years ago. The temple we sit in is part of the park, but the real (*aha!* I think) temple is situated further up the hillside – another twenty-five minutes climb away.

The *raisons d'etre* of the park still puzzle me. When I try to learn them, my questions fail to bear fruit. I must accept that the park was created, and it is here. The priest and I exchange cards. He is Okamoto Sondo, and he has been a priest since he was fifteen. He tends the temple at weekends, while during the week he teaches Social Studies at a high school in nearby Kakogawa. While we talk two women approach from the valley, and when they draw close to the temple Okamoto-sensei introduces them as his wife and daughter. I am invited to join the family for tea at the *kotatsu* in the corner of the temple. I sit with Okamoto-sensei and his daughter, Maya, whose English is careful but animated. Okamoto-sensei's wife busies with the tea and cakes, and says nothing, though she laughs at all the right places in the conversation. I tell them that I would like to climb up to the other temple, the 'real' one, and they respond by suggesting that we all go together. We arrange to meet the following Sunday at 1 PM. Maya also suggests that I might like to return at a later date for a fire ceremony.

When I get up to leave the family follow me out onto the veranda of the temple and all kneel to bow. Maya's mother presses her head to the floor several times.

I walk down the hill, past the many incongruous statues and other oddities, and after a few minutes turn to look back at the temple. High above, all three Okamoto family members are still waving to me. I wave back and then turn the last bend and pass out of sight.

A few days later Okamoto-sensei calls to apologise that he cannot take part in the mountain climbing, but I return anyway for *gome*, the fire ceremony. The altar area has been rearranged so that a black cauldron is in the centre. People arrive in ones and twos. They take their places on cushions facing the altar while I sit at the *kotatsu* with Maya and she explains the proceedings. Following her instructions, I write my wish, my name, age and sex on a *soegomagi*, a small piece of wood. She adds it to a pile beside the cauldron. Like the others, it is to be fed into the flames and my wish thereby despatched to heaven for fulfilment, no stamp required.

Okamoto-sensei shows me his ochre-coloured robes and the book of instructions that he will follow. The book is like a craft manual. It shows him not just what to say, but how to move his hands, and how to pile the *soegomagi* in the fire.

When I ask where I should sit for the ceremony Okamoto-sensei suggests I join the others facing the altar. By now, all cushions have been taken, so I kneel directly on the *tatami*, wondering how long I'll be able to sustain the painful *seiza* position. Okamoto-sensei explains what will happen, and hands me a *shakujou*, a large metal rattle. Automatically I try to take it in my left hand but he tells me to use the right instead.

'Shake it. Fast is best.' he tells me.

I place it on the *tatami* in front of me, as other people have done.

Okamoto-sensei starts his incantations, sonorous at first, then rapid like a machine-gun, then casual, as if he is just having a chat with Buddha. He shakes his bell – the signal for people to shake the *shakujou* and begin intoning the sutra that has been printed out for us. The congregation repeat the passage over and over, in a fast droning monotone. Each *kanji* takes one beat, regardless of whether it has one, two, or three syllables. The passage itself is repetitive, and makes extensive use of the –u syllables, like *mu, ku, tou, sou*. As Okamoto-sensei adds the *soegomagi* to the fire, the interior of the temple fills with smoke. The rhythm of the incantation and *shakujou*, with Okamoto-sensei reciting a different chant, is intoxicating and I soon feel myself drifting away, despite the dysrhythmic woman with a sandpaper voice who chants disconcertingly beside me, and rattles her *shakujou* in twenty fractured rhythms, each stumbling into the next.

I alternate between a disembodied dreaminess and the harsh reality of pain in my ankles and wrist. We chant the sutra for over forty minutes, until the last *soegomagi* is fed to the fire by Okamoto-sensei. I want to shift my position, but it is not easy to do so without losing the rhythm of my *shakujou* – and I don't want to do that. Thankfully, exactly one hour after he began, Okamoto-sensei rings his bell again and we all fade to silence. The woman to my right has managed to work herself into a heady sweat. Drops run out of her hair and dampen the collar of her *kimono*. She smiles disarmingly at me and I have to forgive her the aural torture she inflicted on us. Many people step up to the altar to waft smoke onto themselves for good fortune. Instead, I stay on the floor and try to ease my legs back to life.

Maya gives us each a large packet of tea before we leave. It strikes me as a warm and simple gesture.

A week later, when I return, the Okamoto family welcome me just as effusively as before, and ask me to stop for tea and another chat. Then I make elaborate leave-takings and climb upward in search of the real temple that Okamoto-sensei had spoken of. The track soon fades away, so I scout left and right through the bush. I twist an ankle on the steep and uneven slope. By the time I reach the crest of the hill I am unsure of finding the temple, and tired from pushing up through the under-growth. First I search along the ridge to the right. Despite finding some encouraging signposts I see no temple. Instead I find a geological survey marker at the summit of the ridge and, just below this, a semi-circle of Buddhist idols in a small shady clearing. Turning and searching in the other direction I come across a path leading down the other side of the hill. This is not the direction I want to take, so I backtrack to the ridge and then follow a good path, the path I lost, which descends all the way back to the temple, where the Okamoto family are keen to hear about my expedition. Maya now tells me that there isn't really a temple up on the mountain, and that the collection of idols in the clearing had been my true destination, though I hadn't realised it. So my failure trans-forms into success, without anything really changing. The temple down here, far from being the sub-temple, is actually the only temple.

When I first saw Okamoto-sensei's temple I thought it was just an-other surface reproduction, nothing more than one of many park amusements. Then Okamoto-sensei's presence convinced me the temple was unique among park edifices in being a real building. Then his story of the 'original temple' further up the hill suggested that this one was a derivative, or a more conveniently situated substitute. And then the discovery that there has only ever been one temple here, and that this is it, made it seem real again. I wait in anticipation, half ex-pecting some other negating revelation to emerge, but reality appears to have reached a kind of stability, for now.

Then I remembered that as I walked up towards the temple this morning, Okamoto-sensei had hailed me from one of the mausoleums. I ask about this and he tells me he had been conducting a service for the dead. Far from being copies, these mausoleums actually do house corpses – mainly those of people from the nursing homes who had no surviving relatives to organise an alternative burial. Things here drift so easily across the line separating the real from the unreal that I won-der if there is a line at all. And if so, what is the line, real or unreal?

Excuse me, sir

Back in Tokyo, I call Satomi and suggest we meet up. She wonders if I would like to visit an *onsen* with her, which sounds promising, if also potentially expensive, and I agree. These days, she says, she is busy with both her guys and maybe we could meet in a few days. This sounds less promising, much less promising. Another plan that never grows firmer than a possibility.

At something of a loose end, I take the Yamanote line to Harajuku and wander the streets. It seems appropriate to cross the footbridge and revisit Meiji-jingu. As I walk across its courtyard I notice two young Japanese women watching me. Seconds later, one of them is at my shoulder.

'Excuse me, sir?'

I turn, and note that she is a short round-faced girl. In perfectly accented English she offers to show me around the shrine. At first I am cynical enough to think that this is a soft hook that will be followed, after the tour, by indignant suggestions that I pay the appropriate fee. Ah, but this is Japan, where we sometimes can take things at face value, and Akiko, as she introduces herself, is a volunteer guide who enjoys the opportunity to speak English. Akiko has an excitable personality, and is gaily dressed in a short red coat. Her legs look white with cold. Her flat features give her a strong Asian look, incongruously matched with the well-spoken English vowels.

By this stage in my travels I have accumulated a fair few questions about things I've seen at shrines and temples. Why, for example are so many pieces of paper tied to that tree? Ah, so. Yes, that is where the people put their fortunes if they are not what they wanted. People can buy a paper fortune at many shrines, and if it is a good one, they're lucky. If they don't like it, all they need to do is tie it to the tree and the Supreme Being will obligingly alter the course of destiny to make sure they get something better instead. Akiko explains the colours, the designs, the small wooden votive plaques in the shape of a stable (as horses are too expensive an offering nowadays), and tells me that these days she is officially no longer a volunteer guide, but came here today to relive pleasant memories. After forty-five minutes she has walked me around the shrine and answered all my questions. I've enjoyed talking to her. At the gate to the shrine she thanks me over and over again. I am almost speechless. 'No, no, no, it should be me thanking you,' I protest. She laughs and asks a man passing by if he will take a picture of us. Then we exchange numbers and email addresses and I bid her goodbye.

Afterwards, as I walk through the park, I realise I should have asked Akiko to have dinner with me tonight. I've been getting so tired of eating on my own. But it's too late now. *But hang on*, I think, *why not walk back and see if she is still there?*

She is. I ask. She accepts. We eat, in an Italian restaurant in Harajuku. Then we walk. The streets darken, empty, and grow cold. On the way to Omotesando station Akiko tells me that she is married. At the station entrance we stop and turn to each other to say goodbye. There is an awkward pause, as if she is waiting for something more, so I give her a goodbye peck on the cheek. She throws her arms around my neck and pulls my head down hard. Her lips are pressed against mine.

'Can I stay with you until the last train?' she begs.

I take her back to my hotel room and undress her quite unceremoniously. She is not particularly pretty, *un femme ordinaire*, but her youth and freshness is a turn-on. We lie naked on the bed, kissing and caressing for a few minutes. She gets up on one elbow and asks,

'Do you want to do it? I have a condom.'

So we do it, in a disengaged way. It has all the romance of meat-packing. Akiko steps into the bathroom and emerges to pull on her skirt and bra. It seems as if she is dressed in five seconds.

'I have to go,' she says.

'I'll walk you to the station.'

For the third time today we say goodbye.

'It was fantastic,' she breathes into my ear, as if it was expected.

The next day, unable to stop thinking about sex, I call Akiko and ask her out for the evening. We both agree that the best place to meet is in the hotel foyer – the unspoken reason being that this will be close to the bed.

I see her walking towards me before she sees me. She looks cold, her arms are crossed and she is walking quickly. Her face lights up brightly when she sees me. We go straight back to my room and make love again. She is an enthusiastic and energetic lover, but seems to be doing all this for me, not herself. We lie on our backs, panting and shining with sweat.

'Can you love me?' she asks.

The unexpected question completely floors me, and I cannot muster any adequate reply. I try to cover my silence by covering her in kisses, tracing her downy downs and running down into her gentle shady gullies. Her body is taut but also soft and aromatic. With my tongue I touch the light hair on her temples. She reaches down and holds me in her hand. I lie beside her feeling a whole body satisfaction; she seems to have merely had a pleasant time. Nevertheless, she suddenly turns and clings hard to me, trembling.

'Akiko, you're married...?' I say over her shoulder.

'I hate him,' said with finality.

To change the subject I explain my travel plans, which will be keeping me away from Tokyo for quite a while.

'I will wait for you,' she says with a smile so trusting it shakes me.

Later we eat noodles, slurping but otherwise silent in a noisy shop. She slips me a present, a book of Japanese poetry. I sheepishly offer her a cheap pair of opal earrings I've carried for just such a surprise gift-exchange.

The unexpectedness of my encounter with Akiko is somehow fitting in this strange city. Akiko has basked in a heat stoked by Satomi. It is Satomi I think of as I eat.

Kyushu connections

It is a long trip from Tokyo by train. The *shinkansen* takes four-and-a-half hours to reach Kokura, where I am to change to a local train that takes a further five-and-a-half hours to reach Miyazaki, on Kyushu's south-east coast. At Kokura I have an hour to kill between trains. As the train slows I collect my belongings, obedient to the recorded voice, and allow all the other passengers to alight first. I have plenty of time so I dawdle. I'm standing beside a bin on the platform slowly emptying my pockets of rubbish when a vague feeling of unease starts to grow. Something is wrong. The feeling intensifies and then suddenly the thought hits me like a blow: *I've left my suitcase on the train.*

The train is still at the platform, and the doors are open. Instinctively I grab my backpack just in case I can't get off the train in time, though I know carrying it will slow me down. I look up towards the end of the train and see the guard. I want to ask her to wait but both Japanese *and* English desert me, and instead I just shout 'Aarrrrgh!' I jump back through the door and rush down the compartment, grab my suitcase and head for the door, just a metre to go – and the door slides shut in front of me. The train slowly accelerates. Trapped.

I now have to travel all the way to Hakata station in Fukuoka, which is sixty kilometres away. I study my timetable to see what I can make of the situation. I also prepare a little speech for the guard, essentially confessing that I made a mistake at Kokura. The guard discovers my mistake when she sees my ticket, whips out her timetable, shows me that I'll have twelve minutes to change platforms at Hakata, then I can catch a return *shinkansen* and be back at Kokura with fifteen minutes to spare before my Miyazaki connection leaves. Such is the reliability and predictability of the *shinkansen*. My mistake is actually quite fortuitous, since now I will ride the entire length of the longest *shinkansen* line in one go, I have a comfortable reclining seat instead of a platform bench, *and* I can see a little more of the country. Though, actually, the *shinkansen* is a frustrating way to see Japan, because it spends half its time underground in a succession of tunnels, including a long one that passes beneath the straits between Honshu and Kyushu.

Miyazaki sushi

I had expected Miyazaki to be provincial but, while it doesn't have Tokyo's chic, or Kyoto's aloofness, it is no country town.

At the hotel I call Satomi and amuse her with my adventures over the last few days. I tell her, not very seriously, that she's mad if she doesn't fly down to Miyazaki to join me. To my surprise she agrees to come, and calls me back within the hour to say her plane will arrive in Miyazaki early in the morning.

That evening I find dinner choices a little limited, since the hotel is a long way out of town. There don't seem to be any other foreigners in the hotel, and on entering the restaurant, I cause a bit of a stir. The chefs and the waitresses all look at each other as if to ask *what can we do with him*? I run through the standard greeting phrases and the tension relaxes. As everyone settles into their role, things ease up still further, and the staff even start to ask me a few questions. My stumbling

Japanese is attended to with undue respect. Once again, being Australian scores points, since one of the chefs went to Sydney for his honeymoon. 'Very good place,' he announces in English, looking at the waitress for admiration, which is duly given. He warms up a few more English *non-sequiturs* to try on me, as I discuss the weather with the waitress who is now treating me like a long lost son, standing in a half-bow at my elbow, asking me, after every mouthful, if it is *oishii,* delicious. I'm sure I've won them over now. They will probably conclude that some southern barbarians are almost human. The English-Japanese dictionary is pulled out of a cupboard as their conversation becomes more adventurous, and we try to find the English word for all the ingredients of the meal. One such ingredient, which I'd never even considered a foodstuff until this evening, is gold leaf.

When I leave, I return to standard phrases, as do the chefs. Then one of them blurts out 'Good vacation!' breaking the spell a little, but impressing the waitress, no doubt. I call back 'See you later,' as I duck under the *noren* curtain. While I am settling the bill in the foyer, I hear the chef confidently explaining the meaning of this phrase to the attentive guests.

Before going to bed I head for the men's baths in the hotel basement, and notice a young father washing his only-just pre-pubescent daughters. Everyone is, quite naturally, unconcerned. I try to be too, wishing I didn't inherit peculiar moralities from my culture.

Seagaia

My reason for coming to Miyazaki is to see Oceandome, an indoor seaside. The idea that things cannot be improved upon is anathema to many Japanese, and though the real seaside is just a couple of hundred yards away, across a golf course, billions have been spent here to make something even better. Just think about it, there are so many awful drawbacks that a seaside holiday is better off without: tsunami, North Korean submarines, rip tides, sharp rocks, dumpers, sharks, jelly fish, broken bottles, sunburn, sand flies, jet skis, even sewage. Holidays can be hell. Oceandome protects us from all these horrors, and its ovoid form says it all.

At breakfast, I ask the waitress if she has ever been to Oceandome.

'Once,' she says, 'but I didn't swim.'

'Was it enjoyable?'

'Certainly,' she replies, diplomatically. The hotel and Oceandome are all part of the same huge complex, Seagaia. She was probably taken to Oceandome as part of her training.

Satomi arrives at the hotel in a flurry of luggage and sunglasses. We spend almost half an hour at the front desk, rearranging my account with the receptionist who, while quite accommodating at a moral level, is completely unprepared at the procedural level. Three of her colleagues join her to assist in the complex accounting manoeuvre. Upstairs Satomi unpacks her several bikinis and *wampiisu* and then we catch the shuttle bus to Oceandome.

The Oceandome brochure is a marvel of compressed information. I count forty-five different prices before I give up. And it is all unnecessary, because as soon as I am spotted in the vicinity of the dome a brisk young man in a baby blue suit comes out and immediately begins briefing me on what to do, where to do it, and how much it all costs, regardless of the fact that I have a conspicuously pretty and perfectly good Japanese interpreter on my arm. The simplest thing is to just follow his program. We soon find ourselves in a foyer, made strange because outdoor shoes and bare feet cross paths here, and then I temporarily part company with Satomi to go into the men's changing room, and thence to the pool area. Several people, predominantly women, glance at the thin matting of hair on my chest. As is usual these days, I am the sole *gaijin* present. Emerging in a bright blue, yellow and pink bikini, Satomi looks gorgeous, and makes me feel quite proud. I slip my arm around her deliciously bare waist as we take a look-around, but she is not comfortable with it and after a few minutes takes my hand away.

The room that contains the pool is large – probably as big as two football fields, end to end. The huge vault of the ceiling is high overhead, the biggest retractable roof on Earth. The back wall has a sky painted on it, reminding me of the scene in *The Truman Show* where Jim Carrey's boat runs into a similar wall. As in Venusfort, the lighting changes so that the wall appears to mimic the daily changes of the sky. The waves issue from the back of the pool and come in different varieties; they can make left and right hand breaks, or break in the middle. They can even make a half-decent tube for a second or two. The waves are tailored for surfing or body boarding, depending on the time of day (these things happen according to a strict schedule). The surfing waves seem to be made by first releasing a smallish wave to create a backwash, and following this with a larger wave to break over it. The one unnerving feature of the pool is the large and malevolent maelstroms that form at the back when water is being sucked up into the tanks, in preparation for the next wave. These vortices froth and swirl viciously, and all swimmers are kept a safe distance from them by a floating boom and lifeguards who patrol on surf-skis.

The beach is made of small white pebbles, not sand. They stick rather comically to anyone who sits on them. Near the beach line these pebbles are actually held in place by plastic sheets, to stop the waves sucking them back into the pool and destroying the gradient. As we wade out we pass over these plastic sheets and then feel the concrete floor underfoot. Satomi finds this distasteful, and wrinkles her nose to show it. The water doesn't appear to wet Satomi's naturally hairless skin, it just rolls up into droplets that fall off her. I've never seen anything like it, but she says her father and brother have the same skin, so it must be an inherited characteristic.

Fake rocks, islands, palm trees, caves, streams and an active volcano complete the illusion. Music plays continuously, on a ridiculously short loop. A muzak version of Peter Frampton's *Baby I Love Your Way* is repeated five or six times. Announcements are in English, Japanese and Chinese. One of these announcements is an invitation to join 'us' for a show.

The show is vaguely Rio de Janeiro *mardi gras*, and features a small troupe of Caucasian dancers moving desultorily and miming to well known songs. *The Girl from Ipanema* should have been included, but wasn't. An old white-haired man occupies a table, not eating, and forces a small family to eat standing up. A waitress asks him to move to seats at the back but he refuses, buying a cake instead. A few moments later two of the singers walk out to shake hands with the audience. As one of them nears his table he bolts and stands at the counter until she has passed.

In the afternoon, a concert starts up. It is an Okinawan rock band, who sound like stable mates of the Gipsy Kings. Satomi and I want to swim while listening to them, but this mix of sensations is not permitted, for some reason. A lifeguard sternly points us back to the beach with his paddle. There is no need for dry ice, the place is so balmy it steams already, even though we are still in the middle of winter. Large raindrops plop down from the roof – the result of heavy condensation. The band divides the audience into halves and encourages them to cheer in competition with each other. The audience, to its credit, remains indifferent to such hackneyed tricks.

While we listen to the band, a strong odour of coconut oil wafts our way, evoking 1980s memories of Reef Oil, which in turn evoke strong memories of dangerous days on Sydney beaches, dodging the sharks while trying not to swallow the dead seaweed and raw sewage.

In fact, there is a whiff of something rotting at Seagaia. The complex was built on 1980s euphoria and megalomania, rather than sound planning and risk management. Of the project's $4 billion cost, $2 billion is still owing to creditors, and attendances are falling. No one entertains realistic hope of merely reducing the debt for at least five years. Banks have started to defect, so that the local prefectural government has had to start making financial contributions, and the three thousand workers have all had to accept wage cuts. The heady dream is suffering from being too much of just that in the face of unpredictable financial realities.

We return to the hotel room and shower. Before we go out to eat, Satomi is keen to have sex. We do, once. She grudgingly concedes this is sufficient until after dinner.

At the restaurant I make a meaty mistake, ordering what I take to be a baked potato but is actually a ball of hamburger meat. The plastic models of food at the door are deceptive. I leave the meat and pick at everything else. I stifle a little annoyance at Satomi – she should have warned me that the food I pointed at was a meat dish – but I realise that to her vegetarianism is slightly incredible and something of an eccentric whimsy on my part.

Our waitress is like a robot. Everything she says has the tone of a public announcement, and it is all straight out of the *keigo* handbook that is given to employees who deal with the public. She is so loud and expressionless that I can't help feeling that she is a machine. I feel like doing something outrageous to her, just to see her automaton façade crack, but don't. I reserve my outrages for a more appreciative Satomi, with whom I have a long, drunken and salacious evening in the privacy of our hotel room.

Kumamoto strolling

The next morning we catch a bus to Kumamoto, both of us in a sleepy fuzz. The bus is just as comfortable as the *shinkansen*. It has a small self-service kitchen area, music channels in the seats, and a video screen at the front. The road passes through some dramatic countryside, almost completely covered in concrete cladding and pine plantations. Satomi spends an inordinate time looking after her manicure and fiddling with her hair in the window's reflection.

Our hotel is conveniently situated beside Kumamoto castle, which we explore immediately after dropping our things in the room. The castle is a particularly elegant building, even by Japanese standards. It is immediately obvious to any visitor that Japanese castles were not built to withstand artillery. If they had been, they would no doubt be the solid lumps of masonry that most European castles are. While the surrounding embankments and walls were built of stone, all *donjon* were made of wood, and their design offered many jutting and protruding sections that just beg to be knocked off by a few well-aimed cannon balls.

I am amused, inside the castle *donjon*, to find a golden cherry pattern headpiece that was worn only at times of crisis at field headquarters. Pausing at crucial moments to change into one's special crisis gear does not seem particularly military-minded, nor good for morale. The concept is too Pythonesque. Satomi laughs, too.

My main purpose in Kumamoto is to visit Suizen-ji garden, since it is based on wood-block print scenes from the Tokaido, main link between Kyoto and Tokyo. Suizen-ji garden is not large, and the representation of Mount Fuji is easily identified, but not much else is. Perhaps I will find a book explaining the source of each view. I hope so. We look around the dozens of souvenir shops but none of them has anything remotely informative, in either Japanese or English. Perhaps there are signs in the garden itself, I think. Satomi sips tea while I go off to investigate. I do indeed find a sign and, full of hope, start decoding it, but all it says, in rough translation, is 'keep off the grass.' This is rather disappointing. There simply must be a book somewhere that links views in the gardens to specific wood-block prints, and thence to actual scenes. If not, there is an excellent opportunity for someone to write what would surely be a popular item.

Japanese gardens are as controlled and artificial as classical European court gardens, despite lacking their overt symmetry. Japanese gardens are meant as evocations of an idealised nature, peaceful and perfect, just as romantic European gardens are attempts to evoke an imagined form of nature, with intentional wildness and drama.

The nature of stroll gardens like Suizen-ji, which make allusions to wood-block prints, is more complicated than the creation of an idealised nature. In suggesting particular well-known images, such as scenes of Mount Fuji, or Lake Biwa, the gardens are setting themselves up as references, and wood-block prints as referents. But a print, in depicting a scene, is already a reference in its own right, and the actual scene is the referent. The garden's meaning is now twice displaced, as is the reality it symbolises. Could this chain of reference ends with the actual scene, or is there a further layer of symbolism? In the case of Mount Fuji there certainly is. The mountain is a symbol of Japan, even to the Japanese, and has been for some time. How appropriate that this mountain, with the simplest, most elegant lines, lonely, restful and serene, but at times dangerously unpredictable, should be in Japan, of all places. And so, here in Suizen-ji, a small grassy mound of earth, a symmetrical cone, *is* Japan.

Many kinds of junk are on sale in the garden; packs of postcards, confectionery, plastic toys. Fortunes for the gullible are also available. For 100 yen one selects a piece of paper according to one's gender, month of birth, and blood group (A, B, AB, or O). Satomi, who is inexplicably happy that we share blood group O, pays for two slips of paper and spends many minutes studying what they have to say about us. I remember none of the details, only that it was generally pretty good stuff.

Satomi is obligated to visit family this evening. Kumamoto is her hometown. I see her off at the station and wander in search of somewhere to eat, secretly pleased to have the opportunity to do a bit more solo exploration.

After last night's disastrous meal, I want to make certain of eating vegetarian food this evening. I have the name of a restaurant (Annapurna) and its location, but no telephone number. The general area is easy enough to find. I scout around for fifteen minutes, then start asking for directions. I always approach women, because men often wave me away when I try to talk to them. First I ask a group of teenage girls, and though I ask in Japanese they struggle and confer among themselves to put together a response in painstaking English. After a few exchanges they suddenly realise that I have been speaking in Japanese. At first they are struck dumb by surprise, and then helplessly overcome by giggles. In the end, they can't help me, and everyone else I ask later sends me in a different direction. While I am crossing and recrossing my tracks I assure myself it will all be worth it. I imagine a cosy restaurant décor with world music in the background, a laid-back style, bowls of lentils and eggplant and, if I'm really lucky, a cold beer too. After an hour, I am no closer to finding the place than I had been at the start. The one compensation is that I stumble upon writer Lafcadio Hearn's house hidden away just south-east of the north end of Shimo-tori. It is a large house by Japanese standards. Hearn moved here from his more famous house in the shadow of Matsue castle.

Just across the road from the house I stop yet another innocent passer-by, who has the first constructive idea of the evening. She takes me to the local *koban*. Inside four policemen are on duty, and three youths are there to drop off a lost mobile phone, all in a room not much larger than my bedroom. My guide and I make it nine people in there. The police show me, on a large map on their wall, where I need to be. My guide waits until everything has been explained to me. I confirm that I understand and we say goodbye. Again, I miss the opportunity to ask a woman to dinner, but having developed a detailed knowledge of the surrounding streets I now know exactly where to go. It won't be long now.

Four minutes later I arrive at the artlessly concealed entrance to the restaurant. It is closed. I am hungry, tired, frustrated, and now just plain disgusted as well. Utterly defeated, I fill up on McDonald's French fries, regretting a fine day turned bad. At least tomorrow, I tell myself, I'll remember only the pleasant parts. I turn in for an early night. Some time much later I let Satomi into the room without fully waking.

Aso-san gas

Up before dawn, I open the curtains an inch and see the slim crescent moon and Venus form a perfect symbol of Islam over this Shinto-Buddhist land. Is it really only two weeks since I was at Kashikojima on the Shima peninsula, looking out over Ago-wan, with the full moon at my back?

Satomi and I have a strained discussion about when to get started. She is immune to the argument that we must catch the early train if we want to see Aso-san, Kyushu's biggest volcano. When I ask her what she wants to do instead, she says 'sleep' and rolls over. She won't talk and I won't stay. I announce that I will go alone and meet her back at the hotel later in the day. She neither agrees nor disagrees.

It must have been cold last night, because outside a deep chill hardens the air. I wonder what it will be like on top of the mountain.

While the train moves into the interior of Kyushu I recoup some sleep. Soon the mountain is dominating the landscape. Its outer slopes look grassy from a distance. It is indeed a kind of grass that covers them – bamboo, in dense, impenetrable thickets, but shimmering in waves as the wind runs over it. In heavy mist, the train crosses over the rim and moves down into the base of the crater. At the centre of the huge caldera of Aso-san I must change to take the bus. In the bus station is a sign:

> Warning!! Please don't go near Nakadake because
>
> of gas emission. Thank you for your co-operation.

Nakadake is the active core of Aso-san – just where I wanted to go, in fact. The mountain is known to misbehave periodically, occasionally throwing a fit, and it looks as if it is in a bad mood today.

The ground is frosted at this high altitude, and mist still hangs in the air. It is hard to see the ring of the enormous outer caldera that now surrounds me. I wait for my bus in a café, entertaining idle thoughts. Funny how many cars share people's names here: Gloria, Laurel, Cedric. I propose Mark (mark I) as an appropriate marque, but we are just as likely to see Arthur or Gladys used first. Japanese magazine articles, I note to myself, are often strong on opinion and soft on facts. Even in translation, an earnest seriousness, redolent of high school essays, is evident. Western writing is not always strong on fact either, but often compensates for this by being funny, irreverent, controversial, or clever. Perhaps these characteristics are being lost in the translation, but my intuitions tell me they are not, because what comes through in Japanese writing is a heartfelt call either for a return to the good old values of the past, or a march towards some bright inspiring future state. And what is it I wonder, looking out the window again, about *gaijin* that allows us to identify them from their walk? I consider starting a *kanji* notebook, or perhaps a cup of coffee. And so it goes, my mind wandering hither and thither, hence and thence.

The bus climbs steadily away from the floor of the crater. It lifts me and the few other passengers out of the mist and soon we catch sight of the surrounding crater rim. A deep purple haze glows above it, as if the air here has a different constitution. It cannot be photochemical pollution, it is the wrong colour, and there is not enough industry here. Could it be due to the emissions of the volcano?

We pass over grassy uplands on the slopes of the central cone. From bus I now transfer to ropeway. The girl in the ticket office at the bottom of the ropeway warns about *gassu*, while selling me a ticket. A sign on the counter says:

> Beware of the volcanic gas. Now Mt Aso is in strong vulcanism
> and is ejectting (sic) sulfurous acid gas but we will warn those
> who have the asthma. The trouble with the respiratory organ
> not to go.

At the top of the ropeway, they have a better go at it:

> Warning. Now Mt Aso is strongly activating and
> producing sulphurous acid gas We will warn
> those who have the asthma or trouble with the
> respiratory organs "not to go near the volcano."

I venture as near as I can towards the abyss of Nakadake. Under these conditions it is no surprise that people are being kept away from the edge today. There is nothing to do here, so after a quick look around and some daringly deep inhalations of the sulphur dioxide for medicinal purposes, I set off towards a geological museum the bus passed on the way up. It takes only twenty minutes to get down there and it is a pleasant mountain stroll.

The museum makes a welcoming first impression by playing Crowded House's *Don't Dream It's Over* as I enter. Inside, a large moving georama demonstrates how the sequence of mountain building and collapse created the circular geology of the area. Despite being some of the most dynamical geological features on Earth, mountains are often thought of as symbols of permanence. Rivers, symbols of fluidity and transience, can be much older.

A fifteen-minute video shows how red-hot rocks the size of cars are gaily tossed all over the surrounding landscape when the volcano erupts. It brings to mind Milton's dramatic lines in *Paradise Lost*, describing the fall of Satan, Beelzebub, and their host of hell's angels:

Hurled headlong flaming from th' ethereal sky

With hideous ruin and combustion.

Cameras have been placed inside Nakadake and they are controllable from within the museum. Panning down, an entire lake, boiling violently, becomes visible. It is downright sobering to realise that such massive physical forces are so close at hand.

I try calling Satomi from the train on the way back, but all I get is long confusing announcements from the phone company. With the rattle of the train in my ear I cannot tell if they are telling me there is no connection, or that the phone I am dialling has been switched off.

Back at Kumamoto I discover that Satomi has gone. No note on the bed, no message at reception, no clothes in the wardrobe. I sense I've somehow caused offence. My first reaction is to mutter 'damn!' a few times, but I soon get over it. I briefly wonder what will happen between us now, without reaching any real conclusions.

The only thing to do is go for a walk. At the nearby craft gallery I watch in fascination as craftsmen make baskets, cups, chopsticks, jewellery, brushes and tea whisks out of bamboo. Is there anything that cannot be made out of this wonder material? The adjoining art gallery has an enjoyable ambience, and the enthusiastic way the staff supply me with Japanese leaflets and explanations of the exhibits is quite touching. The art gallery has a branch dedicated to calligraphy. I must concede that after looking at hundreds of items of calligraphy my interest starts to wane, but middle-aged and elderly Japanese women find much to discuss in the exhibition. Attempting to eavesdrop, I wish I could understand everything they say. Is it ever possible for a person still learning Japanese as a second language to share the associations and connotations experienced by native speakers when they read calligraphy?

In one gallery there are several large *hiragana* scrolls. I can read a few of them. They encapsulate positive ideas; bright heart, country morning rain, *fuji-yama*. The classic test piece *to ten go shiki no kumo* 'in the eastern sky five coloured clouds' appears more than once. These scrolls are the work of children.

Later I walk to Annapurna restaurant again. Still closed.

Nagasaki

In overcast conditions, I take a bus from Kumamoto to Nagasaki, misty aerial perspectives softly shrouding the more distant mountains. The rain worsens as the bus pulls into the station. My hotel is a few blocks away, and when I arrive, tired and drenched, the receptionist tells me she has no record of my reservation, and I must pay a higher rate. I show her the reservation confirmation I received by email, but it turns out to have not originated from here.

On checking later, I discover that it came from a hotel in the same chain, but in Sasebo. The Internet travel site I used obviously had some of its links cross-wired. Just last night an Internet pundit on CNN had expounded how easily one could book an entire two-week holiday in twenty minutes on the Internet. The truth is naturally somewhat different. It took me several evenings to find hotels of the correct type, location, and price range, make the reservations, await their confirmations, then rebook when the initial confirmations turned out to be just useless automatic email replies, sent regardless of whether the room was actually available. In fact, I left Australia with several holes in my itinerary, and had to leave the repair work to a real, live travel agent. She was able to find rooms in hotels that had told me they were full.

My room is a typical business hotel affair. The bathroom is by Hitachi, the overall design Lilliputian. I stash my belongings and walk out into the light rain, looking for somewhere to eat. At Hamanomachi a loud scraping sound shatters my reverie. I turn to see two people and a motor scooter sliding along the wet street. The girl gets up and limps to the pavement, the boy lifts his scooter and, after a couple of tries, gets it started again. He hops on, and I expect to see the girl take the pinion seat, but she doesn't. He rides off. I look back at her, she is still limping, but speaking on her mobile phone. I assume she had been a pedestrian trying to cross against the lights. The impersonality of this sequence and the absence of apologies, of any words at all, strike me as thoroughly surreal.

Huis Ten Bosch

Huis Ten Bosch is easily reached by bus from Nagasaki. The highway cuts across steep-sided valleys and runs for several kilometres alongside Omura bay, where islands float like clouds on a glassy formless sea. Why one would make this trip, to visit a contrived Dutch theme-town, is difficult to say, but millions of people come here from all over Asia. On arrival, the trip immediately feels more justifiable, because the first buildings one sees, despite being mere hotels, are dramatic simulacra of period Dutch architecture.

Curiosity now combines with admiration, and so the attraction of Huis Ten Bosch begins to work on me. The size, detail, and overall niceness of Huis Ten Bosch are quite affecting. Japanese cleanliness combines with true urban planning, and a fundamental desire to create a place that is simply a pleasure to occupy.

Everything in Huis Ten Bosch is expensive, and by any good European standard of cool, it is just all too twee. *Yes, but in a cool way*, I think. All the town's windmills are spinning, magically in the solid stillness of the air, but at least they point in the same direction. Huis Ten Bosch proves you can get away with anything, as long as you do it with sufficient style, or the courage of your convictions.

Not a single overhead cable mars the scene. No dogs bark. Hallelu-jah. No traffic, no discernible pollution. In fact, the canals are so clean that white mollusc shells can be seen growing on the submerged parts of the canal banks (I *hope* they are not replica seashells).

'Do places like this really exist?' asks Greta Scacchi.

'Only in movies,' answers Tim Robbins.

Occasionally a replica veteran car glides silently by, adding a 20th century anachronism to the 17th century dream. But let not anachron-ism be an obstacle. If you are wealthy enough you can buy a house here, with canal frontage for one of your boats. That makes it a real place, doesn't it?

Here is a teddy bear museum, which features the world's largest, at 500 kg. Why it is here, I do not know. I suppose there is no right place for a teddy bear museum. Another one is situated just as inexplicably in Stratford-on-Avon, famous more for its playwright than its Pad-dingtons and Poohs, I always thought.

I eat a late breakfast in the Chocolate House, then stroll further into the town of Nieuwstad. The drizzle drives me back into another restaurant, just beside the Franz Hals cake stall. I stifle a patronising smile. Here at least, I really do forget that I am in Japan. I look out of the window and am momentarily surprised that there are so many Asians around today.

The flags droop damp and lifeless in Maurits Plein. Feeling the need for art, I hurry through the puddles towards the museum in Paleis Huis Ten Bosch. It hosts an exhibition of posters by Toulouse-Lautrec, who worked at the time of the first great love affair between Japan and France. Under the central dome of the palace is a large mural by Rob Scholte that stylistically links Bosch (Heironymus, not Huis Ten) to Dali, to Peter Greenaway, to wartime newsreels. Just beside the door is an image of the unfortunate boy who is having this nightmare.

From the windows there are good views of a formal baroque garden, designed over two hundred years ago by Daniel Marot for the original Paleis Huis Ten Bosch in Holland, but never built there. It is artfully tapered to enhance perspective and give an impression of space – an interesting counterpart to the Japanese technique of using 'borrowed' scenery to achieve the same end. However, above the trees the humdrum makes its presence known: neighbouring factories and apartment buildings.

One room of this museum replicates another in the Rotterdam Historical Museum. Among its authentic touches is one that is particularly thought-provoking – some Japanese Imari ceramics, once exported to Holland, now back home in Japan (of a sort).

The European rooms are dark and oppressive by Japanese standards, and it is a relief to once again be outside, under a now brightening sky.

A little white rabbit character appears all over Huis Ten Bosch. For the purposes of professional journalism, I want to identify it correctly, so I stop three women and say, 'Excuse me. This animal, who is it?' 'Miffy,' they reply in instant, smiling unison. I thought so. I smile back and thank them. They tell me I am very welcome. I wonder if they know Miffy is Dutch.

Various national stalls have been set up in a kind of marketplace. Boomerangs are on sale at the Australian stall, and they actually work. It's gratifying to know we make such a valuable contribution to world culture. Items are being sold from one of the stalls by a process of auction, but it is of neither Dutch nor Japanese type. Here, the seller displays an item and sets a high price for it, then slowly lowers the price until a buyer, driven by the fear that someone else will bid first, snaps it up.

Here, again, several people are giving me long enquiring looks. Now, I've been mistaken for Dutch many times, even by Dutch people, so perhaps people think I am just another authentic touch, Hollandman, a decorative automaton. Perhaps they are waiting for me to do something typically *Nederlands*. I can't think of anything to oblige.

Mountain ghosts

Within a few days, Satomi and I are on amicable terms again. She is vague about where she went after leaving the hotel in Kumamoto, but I gather it was to see an old boyfriend, and that she stayed with him for a night or two – that would seem the most plausible explanation. None of this really bothers me, and so another trip together still seems like a good idea. Satomi says she can borrow a car from a friend in Osaka, and we settle on a few days drive around the island of Shikoku.

We take turns in driving and paying the heavy highway tolls. The outrageously long and high bridge at Akashi is our route from Honshu to Awaji Island. The central span of this bridge was designed to be 1,990 metres but then the Kobe earthquake intervened and stretched it another metre. Another large impressive suspension bridge spanning the Naruto Straits makes the final link to Shikoku. From this bridge we see the sea tearing at itself far below. We are lucky to be passing just as the Naruto whirlpools are active. These are well known, and regularly visited by tourist boats venturing out to give sensationalists a closer look into the maelstrom, far more real and carnivorous than those of Oceandome. As the powerful local tides try to force great quantities of water through the straits at speeds up to twenty kilometres per hour, the turbulence becomes intensive, and great ten-metre-wide holes form. Some say many lives have been lost to these watery jaws.

As the day wears on we stay alert for good places to stop, finding few. We keep driving, inland from Tokushima now, hoping for something that will compel us to stop, and perhaps stay for the night. Neither of us know it, but we have been lost ever since we left Tokushima. Instead of heading west through the great valley of Tokushima, we are heading south-west, into the mountains. An evening gloom descends. The roads narrow, and begin to wind into woods and up hills. A light rain falls. Now that we need help, no one is in sight. The sun sets and the dark of the sky adds to the shadows of the forest. Slowly I steer the car along what are now only mountain tracks. The headlights illuminate the trunks of tall trees, and sheets of loose leaves being blown between them. A small wooden sign says that one way lies Kamiyama.

'Ghost Mountain.'

'Oh, don't say that.' Satomi shudders.

The feeling that we may be heading into a dead end at the top of a mountain starts to worry me. I take great care not to let the car slide on the leaves and mud that lie over the twisting tarmac. The lights of the car cast confusing shadows into the trees. There are no other lights in sight. Satomi wants to hold my hand, but I grip the steering wheel.

Then a light looms off to one side. It seems to keep pace with us, travelling through the trees for some minutes, then it disappears. The road turns left, towards where the light had been and seconds later we find a lonely convenience store cum supermarket at the side of the road. Famished and thirsty, we stock up on food and canned drinks. Satomi asks for directions while I clean out the car. After a surprisingly long time she returns with a map and the explanation that we must continue the way we are already going.

'Where are we?' I ask.

'I didn't ask.'

'Then what good is the map? What *did* you ask him?'

'What you said,' she replies, defensively.

'Did you tell him we were heading to Oboke?'

'I said we wanted to find a main road,' she says, '... yes, to Oboke.'

At this point, though I've learnt nothing new, I stop questioning Satomi. How she now feels and how I feel are completely different. She is suddenly happy again, no longer anxious about being lost, and apparently clear about what to do. I don't feel any of these things. The conversation she had with the storekeeper obviously reassured her, but that reassurance cannot articulate itself convincingly to me. Unsatisfied, but also intrigued, I resolve to drive on.

We start to descend and soon find ourselves with other traffic on a straight road running between parallel ridges. We are back on track, in the Tokushima valley – although it is now eleven o'clock, and we'd planned to be here about five hours ago. It is time to find a place to stay. Satomi doesn't see it until I've turned the car into the driveway. When she realises that we are about to spend a night at the neon-illuminated Favorite Hotel, set back from the road in what appear to be cattle pastures, she slaps me twice and tells me, with a smile, that I am bad. Our arrival causes a flurry of activity around the side door of a farmhouse adjacent to the hotel block. Two women step out and simultaneously shout instructions to Satomi, being on her side of the car. There is much pointing and bowing, repetition and gesticulating. We are shown where to park and 7,000 yen is gratefully taken from my hands.

Like most love hotels, the Favorite Hotel is a theme park in miniature. The theme in question is 'hunting lodge (half-hearted)'. The room is cold and uninviting, but we pour a deep hot bath and lie together drinking tea and Pocari Sweat until fully relaxed and ready for bed.

Shikoku highlands

The following day, Satomi and I drive into the centre of Shikoku and visit all the tourist sites. The country is wild and rugged in a way that I haven't seen elsewhere in Japan. Rope bridges span the gorges. The gorges are great wounds carved out of the rock by thrashing rivers, and hemmed in by oppressive mountainsides. I feel unsafe. Some places leave one with a feeling that great violence has been done there. For me, this is one of them, and I am genuinely relieved to get out of the area before any violence is done to me.

Shikoku Mura

Alex Kerr, in *Lost Japan*, bitterly suggested that Japan's love of the artificial and indifference to the fate of her own culture would lead one day to 'Japan Town' where the modern disassociated Japanese will go for the safe thrill of enjoying a realistic Japan experience without the trouble of actual sightseeing or cultural self-enlightenment. It may already be happening. Historical buildings are already being relocated from all over Japan, and collected according to themes.

Shikoku Mura is one such collection. It preserves many old buildings that would otherwise have been sacrificed to progress. The cost of saving and transplanting them has been significant, but worthwhile. The place is an open-air museum, providing a walk-through, hands-on, recreation of old Shikoku life and work, both of which were pagan, primitive, unrefined, unromantic, cold, and exhausting.

It appears only delighted tourists and bored schoolchildren come here. Satomi and I wander the recreated villages and draw giggles from young children, one of whom asks Satomi if I am her brother.

We drive back to Honshu over another impressive set of bridges, the Seto-Ohashi, spend a few hours in the pretty tourist town of Kurashiki, and then head for Osaka to return the car. Tomorrow, Satomi leaves for Tokyo, and I plan to investigate other ghost towns like Shikoku Mura.

Meiji Mura

North of Nagoya, near the town of Inuyama ('Dog Mountain,' I think, though both Emi and Satomi say that I must try to cure myself of the habit of spontaneous literal translation of place names and surnames), is a place called Meiji Mura. It is a large collection of buildings transported from their original sites all over Japan to a lakeside where they have been artfully arranged in a leafy village-like setting. The theme that links them is that they all date from the Meiji era, marked by its strange confluence of European and Asian architectural styles. Victorian solidity and grandeur try to get along with Japanese airiness and understatement. Juxtaposed styles of roofing and fenestration can sometimes be seen in a single building.

There are few people here today, and the warm colours of autumn that persisted through winter are still strong enough to create the illusion that it is not really that cold. I happily wander from building to building, trying not to get annoyed at a lady who keeps dialling my telephone number and asking for Okamura-san.

Tomatsu was an oil merchant, one among countless forgotten minor Meiji era capitalists. But he is not forgotten. His house, carefully reassembled here, is a looming three-storey affair, split by several half-staircases, mezzanines and a full-length hall, which itself opens up to a full-height atrium, from the top of which the lord of the house, leaning over a small balcony adjacent to his bedroom, could survey and no doubt direct all the domestic and commercial processes of the premises. A long and precarious ladder, rising from the main hallway at ground level, reaches his housekeeper's bedroom. Presumably she was forced to use this to get to her room – rather than the staircases, which would have taken her through the family quarters.

Next-door is the Nakai *sake* brewery, primitive but ingenious, with underground furnace, an indoor well, and a small tearoom in the corner for those rare contemplative moments.

The toilets in the park are so designed that when I stand at the urinal I am in full and clear view of a small group of women who walk past the doorway. Hearing them, I briefly look over my shoulder; they look at me, but show not a glimmer of amusement or horror.

In Soseki Natsume's house a ceramic cat sits on a cushion by an open *shoji*, an obvious allusion to his novel, *I Am a Cat*. I am surprised to hear a cat's miaow come from the room. I look around and then realise that, this being Japan, there simply *must* be a sound effect to enhance the experience. This is a feature of many of the buildings. St. John's church, authentically sited atop a small hillock, just as it might be in England, rings to a recorded choir.

The bank has a teahouse behind the counter. At first all I can read on the menu is *keki setto*, which I order, but after a few minutes study I realise I can actually read much more, so when I finish my cake set I order and eat a proper meal. I tell the waitress this is the first time I have eaten lunch in a bank. She is unimpressed, surely having heard this a thousand times.

Also here is Frank Lloyd Wright's faux-Mayan monstrosity, the entrance to the old Tokyo Imperial Hotel, as ill-fated as the Titanic, being destroyed (deservedly, I think) by the great earthquake of 1923, the day after it opened. All I can say for Wright's design is that it is a mishmash of suburban brickwork, coarse mouldings, and over-decoration. It looks fine in photographs, but the reality of it I find a little repulsive. It is everything Japanese architecture is not: careless, heavy, unnecessary, and dated.

After walking to the far end of the park I catch a miniature train and a miniature tram back to the entrance, past wide views over the lake, which is unusual among lakes in, inexplicably, having no water in it at the moment.

I came expecting to find much of Meiji Mura quite laughable, but like Huis ten Bosch, its evident care, professionalism, and the quality of the exhibits eventually wins me over.

Ogata-jingu and Tagata-jingu

My guidebook claims that a country walk will take one from Meiji Mura to Ogata-jingu, a shrine dedicated to female fertility. Amazement ripples through the staff at Meiji Mura when I ask for directions. A conference is called. The spokesman assures me that walking to Ogata-jingu is not possible and that I should either call a taxi or first get a bus to Inuyama and then a train from there. In fact, all kinds of alternatives are suggested, but none includes even a token amount of walking. I won't stand for this, of course. The Japanese are as well known for their unnecessary incredulity as are Americans when it comes to the suggestion that two places can be linked on foot. To save them further anguish, I ostensibly agree to the suggestion that I go via Inuyama, and pretend to wait at the bus stop. But then I nonchalantly dawdle across the car park, sidle away around the corner, and then march fast down the hill, hoping to be well out of earshot if they discover my 'mistake.'

Despite using a GPS unit I get lost in the switchbacks across the tops of the intervening hills, and probably walk three times as far as necessary. An old man cutting wood offers to drive me to the shrine in his miniature truck. Aware that evening is fast approaching, I accept.

I am led to believe that Ogata-jingu is replete in representations of female genitalia, but what I find is far less vulval than I'd imagined (or hoped). The crest of the shrine is made of three (or nine, depending on how I look at it) pairs of labia, but otherwise the sexuality of the place is not evident. I'd expected to see vaginas in all states of receptivity, from the apricot-like to the cavernous. No such luck. I don't have the guts to ask the *miko-san* where the objects resembling female genitals are kept.

At Tagata-jingu the male genitals are, of course, proudly displayed in all forms: erect, floppy, arched, straight, helical, and peculiar asymmetric shapes. Penises stand in the flower beds, and lean against walls. Some are obviously 'found' objects, others have been carefully crafted. A huge five-metre wooden penis looms menacingly in the dark of one of the side-buildings. There are pictures of the local festival held on 15 March, when this monster is taken out and pulled around the streets. Ogata-jingu has its festival on the same day, and every five years they hold them together, so to speak.

That the Japanese people have such shrines is not so much a peculiarity of theirs, rather, given our own widespread (but furtive) veneration of genitalia, it is more peculiar that we don't. Nicholas Bornoff documents a great deal of the erotic in Japanese society in his fascinating book, *Pink Samurai*. Japanese sexuality displays a unique mix of down-to-earth paganism and fetishism. A mother's natural wish that her daughter will be fertile can often be expressed by her sitting the little girl astride a giant wooden penis at a fertility shrine. In *Empire of Signs* Roland Barthes makes the interesting observation that in Japan the sexuality is all in the sex, whereas in the United States it is in everything but sex. He could mean almost anything (that's the trouble with Barthes) but something about this statement rings true to me.

Across the road from Tagata-jingu the video store, whose hours are advertised as 10:00 to 25:00, caters to all the passions aroused in the shrine, by offering hundreds of videos in the appropriate genre.

Leaving Tagata-jingu at about five o'clock I encounter the local rush hour, which consists wholly of like-attired women (black coats, black boots), cramming themselves into the railway station. I share a carriage with two other men and sixty to eighty women. The average working male in Japan is still hard at it at 5 PM. In fact, he appears never to stop. I wonder if the delicate, refined, and sometimes cutesy nature of much of what is offered in Japan is due to there being a predomin-antly young female audience for it. The legend has it that the Japanese male is a rarely seen nocturnal visitor at home, is interred for all hours of daylight in his office, then submerged in the floating world until it is time to sleep. Never seen outside, he is unable to influence anything public. Hardly able to influence much at work or home either, he is the sacrificial drone of Japanese society.

A female land

I can't help feeling that there is something female about Japan itself, though I struggle to explain why this is so. It has perhaps something to do with the emotions Japan creates in me. This is hardly an explana-tion, but I am not alone in thinking this way. Pico Iyer seemed to make the same observation, and cites Kazantzakis expressing a similar idea, the femininity of Kyoto. In *The Idea of Japan*, Ian Littlewood claims that Japanese aesthetics are, apart from anything else, also fem-inine. It is hardly surprising that Japan exerts a stronger attraction on the foreign male than it does on the female – but perhaps this is be-cause the male role in Japan is easier to adapt to.

Britain II

Even the British qualify as models these days. The Times of 22 October 1999 reported that Ishiya Chocolate Factory in Hokkaido was to be given a mock Tudor façade. The façade (a street scene from Elizabethan England) is being constructed by a British company, Border Oak, then shipped to Japan and fixed to the front of the factory. The façade is modelled on Warwick's Mill Street and Chester's Eastgate. John Green, managing director of Border Oak, is reported to have said 'The Japanese want to learn about the English way of life and English history, without the graffiti and the skinheads.' It's an appealing idea, certainly.

In 1993, Border Oak built a complete English village in Fukushima. It is called British Hills and consists of thirteen country cottages, a tithe barn, a craft workshop, an 18th century castle, tearooms and a pub, and employs a butler called Stansbury. Local university students go there to learn about the English way of life. Shakespeare Dream Park in Chiba is the work of the same company.

The British Empire strikes back with butlers, not bombardiers.

Ghost towns

So what is Japan? An empire of signs, dreams, senses? Land of the chrysanthemum or rising sun? A wonderland or a tragically broken fantasy? Have globalisation and recklessness overwritten the delicate sketches of a local culture with heavy brushstrokes? What is Japan?

My head is so full of half-ideas I feel urged to write things down, if only to fix a point in my evolving thoughts. In the *shinkansen* I practise phrases and sentences to myself as I stare blankly at the land rushing past the window. Getting nowhere I wander up to the cafeteria car and order something to drink and eat. A *gaijin* girl who comes up behind me asks for help with making her order. She is English, chatty and big-breasted. We talk for a while then I gesture with my hands, full of my dinner, inviting her to come and eat with me at my seat. She humps a ridiculously large and grimy backpack onto her shoulder and follows me.

Her name is Isla. Inevitably we discuss Japan. Isla has studied the Japanese language for years, she says, but now she is here she cannot work up the courage to use it. Rashly I mention my desire to write down my thoughts and impressions, even talking about perhaps attempting a book. This unleashes a kind of tirade from Isla. She starts by deriding the very idea, listing the standard clichés: the doll-like woman, the star-crossed love affair, charmingly simple at first, hopelessly complicated at the end, clichés about the electric toilets, the public baths, the tea ceremony, the *sashimi*, jokes involving swapped *r* and *l* sounds, the concept of face. Next she warns me not to use the words 'inscrutable' or 'exquisite' and not to include a character called Boon. She asks if I've read *Bicycle Days* by John Burnham Schwartz, or *The Art of Being Japanese* by Robert Dunham. She talks about writers who say all things about Japan are different, but imply that all things about Japan are inferior. I suggest we had to wait for Alan Booth before we had an author who was capable of being funny about Japan without demeaning either himself or his subject. Maybe, she says, and continues...

Eventually, bored with her own talk, she dozes. I steal hungry sideways glances at her breasts, swelling high, and imagine what I might do if we were alone on the train together. When she wakes I ask her if she would like to stay in my room tonight, but she declines.

We say goodbye at Tokyo station and in the concourse I walk past a train loony wearing huge headphones. A pair of binoculars tucked under one arm, he's flicking a torch on and off, grinning widely, cackling, shaking his hands in excitement, making shapes with his fingers, and constantly checking for the headphones even when they are not on his head. I am strangely annoyed at him. Frustrated at being turned down, I want to chase after Isla and explain that she has just made a big mistake, that she doesn't know what she is missing, etc.

I check into my hotel and fall asleep with the television on. In a half-dream I try to make sense of the discussion on TV, which has been recreated for me in a conference room. I sit at the table with several other people, but they never let me get a word in. As soon as one pauses, another starts. I have interesting points to make, but no one knows I am there, and thoughts keep swimming away from me anyway. Noises from the corridor, where two hotel guests are talking loudly in English, gate-crash the dream and bring me back to my senses in a state of mild alarm. Unable to sleep now, I run a bath.

The Face of Another

Japan's fictional Elmyr de Hory

ELMYR DE HORY WAS A MASTER FORGER. In 1968 it was revealed that over a thousand paintings and drawings that were thought to be originals by Picasso, Matisse, Modigliani and others were in fact the work of de Hory. He was imprisoned on Ibiza for this. Such notoriety surrounded him that it became fashionable to openly acknowledge that one's fine art collection included the odd de Hory (unless one represented a museum, of course). Elmer de Hory had operated under many names, possibly as many as one hundred, and became the subject of as many imaginative myths. A 'documentary' about his exploits entitled *F for Fake* was produced by another great blurrer of the real and unreal, Orsen Welles. Elmer de Hory paintings now change hands for about $20,000, so much in fact, that there are strong suspicions that fakes of these fakes are in circulation.

In *The Counterfeiter*, by Inoue Yasushi, an arts reporter is asked to write the biography of the artist Onuki Keigaku, but becomes far more interested in the shadowy figure of Hara Hosen, who passed his own paintings off as those of Keigaku, and, it turns out, was once a friend of the artist. After finding several forgeries by Hara Hosen, the reporter comes across a work bearing his signature and, suspicions primed, immediately wonders if this is also counterfeit. The more he learns of Hara Hosen, the more tragic the forger's life appears. Daunted and overshadowed by the genius of his best friend, Hara Hosen trips haplessly from one failure to the next, eventually dying alone and impoverished.

The reporter's turning away from the world-class success story of Onuki Keigaku and his fascination with Hara Hosen are more than just the typical Japanese sympathy for things that fall short of success, the quiet and the unnoticed, or the tragic sadness of being. They are emblematic of the Japanese obsession with fakes, substitutes, replacements, replicas, simulacra and representations. In short, the unreal.

What does it matter? At the end of the story the reporter remembers a mountain hamlet he visited during World War II. Here he had discovered two forgeries by Hara Hosen. He chose not to expose them as fakes and as far as the villagers were concerned, they were genuine works of Onuki Keigaku. Looking back, he says:

> Life held one small reality which was irrelevant to both Keigaku and Hosen: in that mountain hamlet originals and forgeries had no meaning.

Gibson, greetings, oil

Noticing an Internet café I drop in to see if I can catch tyger at her desk. It is early morning in the UK. Sure enough, she is there when I materialise...

```
Leo roars in.
''lo leo'
'Hi tyger.'
Leo licks tyger's ears.
'awwwwwwww'
'What are you working on this morning?'
'bridge designs. in fact, i think i have
unravelled the secrets of the uberbridge, the
bridge that rules all bridges, the essence of
bridge'
'Sounds impressive. It's clear I've got a tyger
in my thinktank.'
'that's less obvious to me'
```

I spot the string 'ess o', and give that line a tweak.

```
'She'll always be my muse,' muses Leo.
'oh, leo's mental mobility, his physical
agility!' mews tyger.
'If I were truly mobile I'd fly to you like an
exocat missile.'
'that's a sort of anagram pun, not a hidden word,
leo'
```

Leo nods sheepishly. 'It was the best I could do.'
'i doubt that very much. um... um...' tyger
misses her cue eight times.
'Gosh, tyger, brilliant! BTW, is Branson in this
game yet?'
'not when i checked this morning. probably is
now, though'
'All he has to do is drop olive.'
'extra too possibly, but would that upset or
please popeye?'
'Dunno. Wonder who would win if Branson and
Popeye had a fight over Olive.'
'nobody'
'Change of subject?'
'aidoru? since you are in nippon?'
'A Gibsonian discussion?'
'william today, not j.j.'
'You know J.J.?'
'only professionally, of course'
'He was a bit of a way from image-processing,
more up the psychology neck of the woods, wasn't
he?'
'he was interested in landing aircraft'
'Ah, yes.'

We are touching on her Ministry of Defence work, so I change tack
slightly.

'William *and* J.J.? I wonder if the Gibsons are
a particularly talented family.'
'there's also josh, mel, and les paul'
Leo fends off the thought that tyger knows
everything.
tyger ricks her back trying to evade leo's
elaborate fending.
Leo rubs tyger's back, 'Sorry, little cat.'
'dat's awright,' tyger purrs, 'you're a muso'
Leo smiles, 'you are amuso.'

THE FACE OF ANOTHER

I lose the telnet connection suddenly. Then the prompt comes back and I log in again. Everyone else is reappearing. Evidently the whole talker went down and everyone was thrown off. But it takes a good twenty minutes before tyger reappears.

```
tyger bounces in.
'a new me!'
'tyger! How is my most esteemed cat?'
'small, but perfectly morphed. how is my lionised
lion?'
'Ummmm, magisterial today, thank you.'
'i'm pleased to hear that'
tyger pecks leo on the whiskers.
Leo bats his long lashes.
tyger cuffs leo playfully and flops down beside
him.
```

Things always feel so right when I converse with her like this – aimlessly, childishly, and in complete confidence that whatever I say will be given the most amusing and sympathetic reading. It is the feeling of being accepted.

```
'Always a pleasure, tyger.'
'i know. so strange isn't it?'
```

We talk for a couple of hours, rambling from one subject to another, sometimes serious, sometimes flippant, always deeply rewarding and memorable. I wonder what makes this relationship so satisfyingly intimate without it ever having to become anything more than it already is.

Meanwhile, during the telnet delays, I catch up with the news on a few online newspapers from England and Australia, check the state of the test match at Cricinfo, fish around unsuccessfully for something interesting in my mailbox, and run Lycos searches for anything that takes my fancy.

Information overload

Satomi told me that there was 'too much information' in Tokyo. At the time I didn't really understand what she meant, but now I do. So much is happening, and there are always so many messages in the ether that just trying to keep abreast of what is going on can become a full-time preoccupation, and yet still be doomed to failure. I feel this condition plays upon the Japanese propensity to be great absorbers of information. I see the connection between their minds and the ins and outs of operating complex electronic products, and it is a high band-width connection that locks in fast and stays locked in. A strong pref-erence for logic-based digital user interfaces is evident everywhere. A pervasive process is fast underway in Japan. Things are being replaced by virtual substitutes. We no longer operate machines, large or small, we instead deal with them through user interfaces, and are thus at least twice removed from the physical world that the machines deal with. We are reducing the intractable physical world to a tractable lo-gical world. We are creating, in fact, an information processing world for robots.

Japan, as itself

Michael, the irritating pragmatist in *In the Empire of Dreams* by Di-anne Highbridge, observes that no place is more real than any other. Yet, it is curious that so many writers have talked about being in Ja-pan as if they were onstage acting out a part in a story. Peregrine Hod-son says, of a character in *A Circle Round the Sun*:

> Something about her was artificial, as if she was playing her-
> self and everything she said was remembered from a film
> script. Perhaps she'd been too long in Japan.

In *Ransom*, by Jay McInerney, the narrator says 'These days it was difficult, he thought, to live as if you weren't in a movie.' Ian Little-wood reveals, in *The Idea of Japan*, how several writers, including Rud-yard Kipling, in the days before cinema, had repeatedly compared Japan to a picture. He also cites Oscar Wilde's amusing claims that the Japanese are works of fiction. Pico Iyer, in *The Lady and the Monk*, con-stantly casts Japanese people as actors playing their roles perfectly, places as pictures, events as scripts.

A man, a woman, and two cats

I sit on the floor in Emi's house, and wait while she makes some tea. It is mid-afternoon. I have a slight hangover from last night, spent with

Emi in Kyoto. As for Emi, she is impervious to alcohol. Her mother will be at work until 8 PM, she says, so I have plenty of time to look at their two cats, one real and the other a robot. My love of cats and my professional interests in robotics have led Emi to arrange this meeting.

Emi's real cat, Wapiko, a Japanese bobtail, comes in through the cat-flap, sees me, panics, scrambles frantically on the slippery floor, runs in a circle and leaps back out through her flap. All this happens so fast I re-member only a white and orange blur. Later, having forgotten that I am in the house, Wapiko jumps up to an open window from the outside, turns around, and delicately steps backwards into the room like a Lip-itzana. On turning round, she sees me once more, thumps to the floor, scuttles across to the cat-flap and, obviously terror-stuck, disappears again. It looks like I have seen my last of that cat.

'Wapiko is very excited that you are here,' says Emi.

'Hmm, maybe,' I say sceptically. 'Did you notice the strange way she came in through the window, backwards?'

'Yes. She always comes in that way. You are so observant. No one else sees that.'

I notice how Emi manages to weave compliments into nearly everything she says. Her friends do the same thing. In the evening I was with them I was told 'you are so smart,' 'you look good,' 'you are an ex-ample to me,' and, with no hint of irony, 'you are excellent.' Initially, my vanity soaked this up, of course. But I suspect these things are said not just to make *me* feel good. The exchange of compliments within the group created a pleasant, warm, social atmosphere with all the cosiness of a feather-lined nest. I felt I could lay my head in any of their laps and softly drift off to sleep. Indeed, Katsuya nodded off two or three times during the evening, eliciting only sympathy from the girls.

After kneeling and placing the tea things on the low table Emi swivels around and pulls the robot cat from a cupboard behind her.

A year or so ago I saw a Japanese pet robot cat demonstrated in Madison, Wisconsin, at the biennial International Joint Conference on Artificial Intelligence. This rather sleepy-looking creature had slowly stretched and slid about on a tabletop. Its minders had to guide it away from the edges. I picked up a leaflet in which there was a photo-graph of the cat with the caption 'Pet Robot wearing a cat costume.'

The researchers kept on referring to the robot as 'she,' which indicated plenty of fascination with what they were doing, but little objectivity. The leaflet went on to detail the relationship between the robot's sensors and actuators, but devoted much space to the robot's 'emotion model.' The emotion model encompassed satisfaction, anger, uneasiness, disgust, fear, and surprise. These are standard categories used in several ways by scientists. Machine vision researchers attempt, for example, to get computers to accurately distinguish between the facial expressions that are most associated with these categories. The cat also had desires: to sleep, to be stroked, to be held, and so on.

The express goal of the cat robot was 'to provide users with happiness and peace of mind by living together.' The idea was that animal-assisted therapy, which is taken seriously by psychologists, might, perhaps, be performed even better by robot animals.

It was not clear that any of this was working at the time, either from the behaviour of the robot, or the results in the paper. Yet the demonstrators were so obviously in love with their creation. I felt sorry for them – Sony's new robot dogs were drawing much bigger crowds, just around the corner.

Robot dog, robot cat

In the late 1990s Sony development engineers started work on a robot pet. The project was designed to lay the foundations for design, manufacture and marketing of future robot toys. The first of these toys reached the market late in 1998, and sold out in about twenty minutes, over the Internet. They were called Aibo, a Japanese word for 'companion,' but were known to many people as the Sony dogs. About the size of a toy poodle, and looking a little like beagle pups with their droopy ears and cute waddle, the Aibo cost about $6,000 a head.

Sony applied their highly developed manufacturing abilities to the Aibo hardware, and wrote a new operating system for it. A few kitsch demonstration programs were released too, but key aspects of the development of intelligent behaviour fell to a few universities who were engaged in an annual Aibo soccer competition, the legged robot division of Robocup. Sony released a team of four Aibo to each university, and provided basic support. The role of the universities was to develop the best algorithms for vision, locomotion, orientation, ball-tracking, goal recognition and ball control.

The rules of the Robocup competition were well defined, and each university was supplied with a standard Aibo soccer field, slightly smaller than the standard ping-pong table, sporting colour-coded goal mouths and coloured orientation posts at the four corners and at each end of the centre line.

The first of the tournaments took place in August 1998, at the biennial IJCAI conference. I was there with others of the Artificial Intelligence Department of the University of New South Wales and, like everyone, was amazed at the basic abilities of the dogs. We had for years been struggling just to get legged robots to maintain a reasonable walk. Sony's dogs could fall over, roll on their backs, sit up and do a hand jive, or get up and dance. They were programmed to gracefully kick a ball while standing on three legs. The articulation of their legs was far beyond anything we had been able to achieve with our home-made 'heath robinson' wire and plastic robots.

The dogs had been programmed to search their visual surroundings for the standard Robocup orange ball. This procedure starts with a scanning routine, then for as long as a patch of the colour of the ball is perceived, the head of the dog is continuously reoriented to keep that patch of colour in the centre of the dog's field of view. The effect of this is that as the ball is moved, the dog's head moves too, and appears to follow it with puppy-like interest.

I was watching the dogs ball-tracking abilities being demonstrated on the little football pitch when one of the demonstrators picked up a dog and cradled it against his chest. Someone else picked up the ball and walked past with it. The puppy in the arms of the researcher kept its 'eyes' on the ball as it went by. I had never seen this kind of vision performance in such unrestricted confusing environments. All of us were struck with the same thought – we simply had to persuade Sony to include us in the university development programme. The head of the department successfully convinced Sony that UNSW was a real contender for both research and football stardom and within a few weeks the equipment started to arrive from Japan.

In less than a year we were ready to compete. The next tournament took place in Stockholm. During the preparations our team was encouraged to see that their vision and locomotion programs compared well with those of other universities. The atmosphere at these competitions is collegiate. We are, after all, all on the same side. The teams made friends, shared tools and learnt from each other.

Our team was the smallest and least qualified in the whole competition. There were two undergraduate students who were undertaking Robocup as their honours project, and an experienced robotics engineer to help with the inevitable hardware problems. Other teams were as large as twelve individuals, most of whom already had PhDs.

Despite difficult draws in the early rounds, UNSW were able to get to the final, pitted against the formidable Carnegie Mellon University, which along with Stanford and MIT forms the top three AI research centres in the world. It was a close match, but UNSW lost, and had to be content with second prize.

Our team were happy with their result, since all the other teams had a great deal more robotics experience and a previous competition to learn from. And there was always our encouraging result in the shoot-out competition...

The shoot-out competition was simple. A team was given the field to itself, and places were awarded according to how fast they could score a goal. There was a time-out of ninety seconds. It is an indication of the embryonic nature of robotics that no team actually scored a goal within the time limit, and places were instead awarded on how close the teams managed to get the ball to the goal. UNSW won this more controlled competition, which indicated that our dogs had a good repertoire of skills. So, with a first place and a second place under our belts, we felt successful and even started having qualms about how we were going to follow this success.

The third competition, and the second for us, was held in Melbourne in 2000. Our competence had improved. No phrase other than 'complete dominance' describes UNSW's performance in this tournament. Other teams had intimated that they were so nonplussed by the speed and deadliness our dogs demonstrated in a few informal practice matches that they merely hoped to score a single goal against us. As it was, none of them had the chance. We finished the competition with a record of forty-eight goals for and one against. The one against was an own goal caused by our goalie knocking the ball as it turned around. We walked off with the shoot-out title as well. Perhaps the most important factor in our success was a walk that had been developed by postgraduate student Bernhard Hengst. The walk was low, almost a crawl. This brought the dog close to the ground and allowed it to roll the ball forward with its chest, keeping the ball centred, trapped almost, between its forelegs – exactly how real dogs dribble a ball. Once one of our dogs captured the ball it became hard for the opposition to even see it, partly because it was moving so fast, but also because it was difficult to visually separate it from the outline of our player.

In Japan, everyone knows Aibo. It is iconic of Japan's cleverness and they know it. I visited an Aibo display at the Hankyu department store. The dogs were performing modest tricks on the floor in front of crouching children, who were delighted and completely captivated. Interested parents stood back and smiled indulgently. Aibo merchandise was on sale for those who wanted the image but couldn't afford the reality. I tried to explain to the shop assistant that my university was Aibo soccer *yokozuna*, grand champion. She had no idea what I was talking about, and I probably shouldn't have been boasting anyway.

After each Robocup competition the algorithms developed by the universities are given to Sony, who have rights to incorporate them in future revisions of the operating system or applications software. So everyone wins. Robotics researchers have a supply of thoroughly reliable test platforms, Sony gets free research, and the public gets fifteen seconds of entertaining news reports every year, and smarter toys. Perhaps it is only real dogs that are the losers.

Among the winners are the lonely. People treat Aibo dogs rather as they would a real one. It starts with a name. Then the children of the family realise that if they wear bright colours the Aibo will follow them around. The Aibo fires their imagination in a way that a real dog wouldn't, because a real dog needs no imagining. Adults find that they develop surprisingly emotional relationships. Rumours of travelling businessmen taking their Aibo along for company in lonely hotel rooms are circulating on the Internet. Families take them on vacation.

Sony have noticed that the owners of faulty Aibo call into their service centres at a much higher frequency than customers of their other electronic goods. They liken the effect to people calling in to the vet to see how a sick pet is faring. It has for a while been acknowledged that pet ownership has therapeutic effects. The American National Science Foundation has now granted money to support the study of whether Aibo have similar effects.

Nearly 100,000 Aibo have been sold, three-quarters of them to men. While the installed base of any hardware increases, the range of available software is also likely to increase. It is said that software now in development will enable Aibo to recognise playing cards, and be able to play card games, to recognise printed words, and read them out for its owner.

As Emi crouches on the *tatami*, playing with her robot cat, which can walk, miaow and move its tail, I watch her, rather than the toy. She is the more feline, particularly in the limbs and eyes. In her black designer jeans and sweatshirt she presents a delicious picture. Her nestled feet, in sheer black stockings, have the softness of a cat's paw, and I feel a strong desire to touch them. A faint cry from outside indicates that Wapiko is unhappy. Emi gets up to call her and I am left with my thoughts.

A real pet is a complex of advantages and disadvantages. On the credit side of the ledger we have trainability, affection, defence of the property, companionship, and so on. On the debit side there are the smells, chewed books and furniture, need for constant care and attention, unnecessary barking, daily pooper-scooping duties, etc.

Can the net balance be improved? To the Japanese mind the answer is yes, there is always a better way. Removing the unpleasant characteristics of real dogs is relatively simple – we just don't bother to program them in. Tasks such as the guarding of property are already within reach of today's AI methods; machine vision programs already provide surveillance for military and civilian applications. Once a 'suspicious' situation has been identified it is a simple matter to produce a bark in response.

Trainability is not an intractable problem either. Most AI programs involve some degree of learning. Machine Learning, neural networks,

adaptive systems and genetic algorithms all provide their own defini-
tions of learning, and all can be brought to bear on the problem of
getting a machine dog to respond properly to its name or commands,
or to learn to patrol its surroundings.

It is the companionship that is the hardest characteristic to create.
But perhaps it is less difficult than it seems. Under all human characteristics there are a range of 'behaviours' of varying tractability. Take
affection, for example. We can easily make a dog's tail wag when it
sees movement inside the house, or has its head patted. Other behaviours, such as the quizzical, head-on-its-side, big-brown-eyes-and-
raised-eyebrows look of a dog who finds its owner crying, for example, may be harder to achieve, because the triggering stimulus, the
owner crying, is harder for the dog to identify. It is not difficult to produce the behaviour; it is programming the dog to know when it is appropriate that is hard. When we deal with other people, and animals
of a sufficiently sophisticated behavioural repertoire, it is the appropriateness and timeliness of their responses to our inner condition, sadness, happiness, confusion and needs that makes us feel close to them.

If this appropriateness can be achieved, the result, already seen in
several experiments, is an instinctive anthropomorphisation of the machine. Thus we can be programmed by our machines. We do not just
choose to see the machine as a personality; it actually becomes harder
for us to act as if the machine is 'just a machine,' and easier for us to
respond as we would to a flesh and blood interlocutor. At this point,
we will consider the discrepancies between the real and the artificial
animal to be insignificant. The extra convenience, however, will be significant and undeniable. Ultimately the artificial world might so fill
our perceptions that all discrepancies will be forgotten. Without the
opportunity to make comparisons, the felt need for them diminishes.
And it is not just one layer of insulation that is being drawn between
us and nature in the raw, it is many.

Machine on machine

Most species of animal interact with the world in a direct physical
sense. In order to manipulate prey, predators, mates, offspring and
shelters to their own ends they must rely wholly on their own bodies.

It is only by advantageous bodily contact with the objects of their lives that they survive.

A few species, including Homo sapiens, have learnt to use intermediate devices called tools. These species wield their tools, and the business ends of their tools affect the world. Humans may be alone in using tools as sensors as well as effectors. The simplest form of sensory tool may be the blind person's walking stick. The world acts upon the stick when it is moved around, and by the vibrations and movements transmitted to the other end of the stick the blind person is able to form a spatial representation of the world as prodded.

At some stage in their evolution, tools became complex. By this I mean that they developed both effector sub-systems and control sub-systems of their own. Prior to this stage, the tool simply translated a human's effort into something smaller, more distant, more powerful, or more reliable. But in the new phase the human did not have to put effort in at one end (such as tightening a screw or pulling a lever), but instead could issue a command of some kind, which would itself then initiate an action. For example, the engagement of a gear allows a windmill to turn its millstone. The effort of the operator is unrelated to the output of the machine. Instead, it simply *permits* the machine to work.

Later, as the complexity increased, the controls of machines began to be grouped around the operator, and consisted of both effector and sensor types. Thus were born control panels, dashboards, switchboards, and keyboards. Now, not only were humans often separated from the objects or materials that their machine worked on, but they were further insulated from the machine itself, by the control interface.

The process of intermediation has continued even further. The next important development was the digital interface, which dispensed with the need for physical control, and replaced levers and switches with a means for issuing information to the machine through a medium that translated it from a human-understandable form to a machine-readable form. The advent of the information age has enabled complete separation of the machine's effector parts from the human controller. This is called 'fly by wire.' The physical laws that govern the operations of a machine do not apply to a digital human interface, and so a new kind of unreality has become real. It is the commonplace self-representation of machines.

Many machines now manage themselves, the human simply stands by to react if something unforeseen happens. The next stage might be to remove the human from the process completely.

O B Hardison wrote of this, and other related phenomena in an intriguing book called *Disappearing Through the Skylight*. The cover note says, 'Today nature has slipped, perhaps finally, beyond our field of vision.' The thesis of the book is that we have, in many aspects of modern life, created nested layers of representation, and cemented our dependencies on them. Our known world is now a world of information or messages *about* the exterior world that our animal cousins still scratch and bite at.

The familiar digital interface was developed on computers, and has since spread to many other electronic devices. Around the world the same basic function may now be found in several stages of development. The old mangle-topped washing machine may look advanced next to the scrubbing board and bowl, but it now shares the market with the electric washing machine, and the push-button washing machine, and, in Japan, the washing machine controlled from its own touch-screen. It is not that Japan is the only place where digital interfaces and other kinds of world-distancing intermediate systems exist, it is just that Japan has more of them per square metre, and loves them with a depth and madness not yet seen elsewhere.

Matsumoto Ukiyo-e Museum

Emi makes dinner for us. It is rice made in the rice cooker, and a kind of sauce, containing meat and vegetables, which she heats, still in its plastic packaging, in the microwave. I lean against the cupboards and tell her about tyger, about the strange way that all the computing and telecommunication intermedia have both facilitated a relationship between us and simultaneously guaranteed that it remains completely mental. Emi doesn't see what I am getting at. I change the subject.

Emi gives me both a fork and chopsticks, but uses only a fork. We watch television while we eat. Or rather, Emi watches television, and I watch her. After she clears up, and is standing at the sink I spend a minute straightening my aching legs, then walk up behind her and put my arms around her waist. She curves away from me with surprising determination. I am at a loss, so I weakly thank her for the meal and act as if I had not been making a pass. After her formal *do itashimashite*, addressed, apparently, to the sink, I resume my place at the table and pretend to watch television. Something has gone wrong, but I don't know what. Later, when Emi gives me a lift back to the hotel, we are silent and uncomfortable.

The following day we meet at my hotel early. It is still dark and we have a long way to go. In Emi's little car we do 80 kph in a 40 zone, 150 kph in an 80 zone. So does everyone else. It feels absolutely helter-skelter, and makes me so tense I have to ask Emi to slow down.

I am the navigator. It is a difficult assignment, as I have to match the unfamiliar *kanji* on the map to the *kanji* on the street signs, and cannot pronounce them to tell Emi which town to head for; I can only point 'that way' when I see a character that matches one on the map. My reading speed is often too slow. Signs pass by before I have a chance to check them.

Our route goes east through mountainous country. We negotiate countless bridges, innumerable tunnels, and uncountable switchbacks. Evidence of landslides, long vertical gashes through the steep forest, show that this is active mountain terrain. The mountains here are precipitous. In places, the dark dense forest looms vertically over deep blue or milky white lakes.

We discover our chosen route is closed due to landslides and are forced to make a long detour, as the roads are literally few and far between. Everywhere rain is falling. The brooding dampness worsens my mood. My relationship with Emi is still unconsummated. I thought that once she agreed to come travelling with me we had an unspoken understanding that this was to change. Her rejection of my advances last night scuppered that idea, and now the prospect of chaste nights, sharing a room but not touching, is dispiriting. I don't yet know what to talk about, or how to act with her.

In many places the steam from hot springs rises dense and white against the forest green of the mountains. Clouds drift both above and below us. Sheets of mist hang against the valley walls. Rivers crash down the mountainsides and fall vertically into lakes. We are surrounded by water in all its forms, a water world, a floating world. Appropriately, we are about to visit a metaphorical floating world...

At the Japan Ukiyo-e Museum in Matsumoto we settle down to a long visit. Wood-block printing was influential in propagating visual ideas through Japanese society, since multiple prints could be made from one design and, consequently, prints were cheap enough for many people to afford. As with many popular art forms, *ukiyo-e* are notable for both the beauty of the design and the craftsmanship of the technique.

The artistry of *ukiyo-e* is so elaborate it can be described only inadequately or at length. Firstly, one notices the purity of line. In mathematical terms this purity can be expressed as lines having a constant second derivative, in aesthetic terms it is a fluidity, and naturalness that only the most skilled can capture – particularly by a method as unforgiving as wood-carving. Next, colours co-exist in fine balance, technically difficult to achieve, given the irreversible printing methods. Then there is the humour and subtle eroticism of the content. Many of the prints have such a lively feel that one has a sense of being there with the characters, of knowing what they are thinking or trying to do.

Many prints are of courtesans with mirrors, cats, and glorious flowing *kimono* falling open suggestively. These prints often served as a form of advertising, helping to enhance the desirability, and price, of the woman concerned. The sexuality of the images serves to remind me of the vexatious stalemate that seems to hold between Emi and I.

Emi calls me over to look at a print in which a society girl is being prepared for her wedding night by other women of the court. The ideal preparation will leave the girl neither too surprised, nor too knowing, when her husband first enters her. To achieve this perfect balance she takes part in a dance with an older woman who has a long wooden implement in hand. At some moment in the dance this implement is pressed into the girl, enabling her to get some idea of what sex will feel like, without actually having to practise it for real. I try but fail to read between Emi's lines.

In a sub-genre of *ukiyo-e*, known as *shunga*, sexual intercourse is depicted explicitly, and often with great exaggeration. This form of *ukiyo-e* has many adherents in the west, but to me *shunga* have curiosity value only and today with so many other riches on display I do not want to look at any of them.

The three most revered masters of the art of *ukiyo-e* are Hokusai, Utamaro, and Hiroshige. Hokusai is known for his landscapes, such as images of Mount Fuji and the stations along the Tokaido. Utamaro is known for his endlessly repeated images of women, all of whom have the same face – approximations of his ideal, it is supposed. Hiroshige is known for outdoor scenes depicting the struggles of common, often faceless, people.

Once the design of an *ukiyo-e* has been drafted, it is traced many times onto sheets of transparent paper. Each tracing is glued backwards (this reverses the design) to a flat piece of wood, to form a template. The wood surface is then meticulously carved away so that only parts of the design remain in relief. These raised parts are inked with a single colour, though it may be applied in varying strength to create shading. The block is then pressed onto a piece of paper (reversing the design once more) to transfer the colour. This whole process of carving, inking and pressing must be repeated for each colour. It is not unusual for there to be a dozen or more blocks for a single image. The alignment of colour blocks is crucial to the final composite print. Any misregistration of colours renders the print worthless.

The carving must be of impeccable quality. This is especially evident when the design contains, as many do, clothing of complex patterns and textures, since each tiny detail must be carved into the wood. And since carving is a subtractive technique, a single slip of the chisel can ruin a whole block.

For each multicoloured print, there once existed a set of original wooden blocks. In some cases, the complete original sets still exist. This means that occasionally trusted contemporary masters of the craft can reproduce the classic prints of the great artists of the past. This is an exciting prospect, since it means that 'new' originals can be made. They will differ from the old originals in colour, since the inks of the originals have inevitably faded, particularly in the blues, which tend to be the most fugitive of colours. The only drawback is that the blocks, like anything else that is used repeatedly, will continue to wear away and eventually lose their usefulness.

So, let us imagine that we wish to obtain a print of the most famous of *ukiyo-e*, Hokusai's *The Great Wave off Kanagawa*. The costliest option would be to negotiate with a current owner of an original. This will set us back at least five million yen.

The second option, which would be less expensive, but still not cheap, would be to find a 'new' original, as just described. It will differ, not in design, since the wood-blocks used would be the same, only in the vibrancy of colour. It will look the way the originals did when Hokusai made them, rather than how they look now. The thrill of this is that, like the great shrine at Ise, which resembles itself at any point in its own time because it is new and has always been new, a new print from old wood-blocks leaps through time and brings the past to the present.

The third option, which will cost about 10,000 yen, is to buy a *ukiyo-e* made from a new set of blocks copied from the old. This will be a true *ukiyo-e*, in fresh vivid colours, but there will probably be detectable differences between the design and the original, particularly, in the case of the Hokusai, much copied, in the drops of sea-spray. The differences may be exceeding difficult to detect, if the intention of the copy was to deceive. Japan's most notorious forger, Takamizawa Enji, duped many a collector by cutting new blocks of formidable accuracy and printing 'faded' ink colours with them. Some art historians believe Takamizawa even went to the extent of reproducing the woodgrain patterns of original blocks.

The final option, at about 2,000 yen, is to buy a photographic reproduction of the original. This will look like the original in detail and colours, but it is a photographic print, not an *ukiyo-e*.

I desperately want to take prints away with me, but manage to quell the materialist urges, and enjoy the prints as fleeting experiences rather than as possessions. I have too many possessions already, and feel I need to train myself in the Japanese experience of *aware* – sympathy for the transient, the helpless, instead of desperately trying to hang on to everything that is important to me.

Late to the inn

We leave the museum late in the afternoon. The sun shines through low cloud windows in the west, but the rain still falls. We drive in and out of the rain clouds, and eventually find our inn, tucked in the bottom of a large v-shaped valley filled with cloud, and deep in the shadow of the surrounding mountains. The weather has eased a little; just a cold thin rain, common to mountain areas, persists. The mist is thinning.

Our welcome has the flavour of an admonition. We are late for dinner. We arranged to arrive at 6 PM and it is now nearly 7 PM. Some of the food may be ruined, we are warned, but it cannot be cooked again. It is our fault. We should have told them we were going to be late, they could have waited a bit longer before starting the preparations.

I listen to this and try to look sorry, but inside I am wondering why Emi, who is being pathetically apologetic, did not let me know it was so important to be on time.

We are shown to a ten-*tatami* room with a view over the pond and rock garden, and a wonderful aroma of fresh straw rising from the mats. The room is spacious through deliberate emptiness. It contains only two small cushions and a low table, upon which we are served tea. Noticing my height, the maid rushes off to bring a longer *yukata*, and bigger slippers. I am glad about this.

Once the maid has left us with our tea I ask Emi why she had not hurried us along today. She is evasive and talks about how enjoyable the museum was. I bite my tongue. I realise that she did not feel it was her place to rush me, and that she had been suffering silently, torn between upsetting the *ryokan* staff on one hand, and me on the other, and she had chosen in my favour. I try to establish that it is all right for her to take charge, as I often know so little about what is going on. I tell her that I think one is often reduced to a child when travelling in a new country, depending on others, missing the nuances of what people are saying, talking only of simple things. She laughs sweetly at this but I can see that nothing will change.

The maid comes back to guide us to the room where we will eat. I, no doubt, will be blamed for the lack of punctuality. It is a distinctly *gaijin* trait to ignore the proprieties.

Japanese clock, Japanese time

Punctuality is, of course, a modern phenomenon in Japan, just as it is anywhere. Clockwork was introduced to Japan by early European visitors, perhaps in 1551. Some think that Portuguese sailors arriving at Tanegashima on Kyushu in 1542 were responsible; we cannot be certain. All we know is that at some time all the evocatively-named components of European clockwork: foliots, pirouette escapements, pendulums, hairsprings, crown wheels, contrate wheels, wheel arbours, counterweights, striking trains and going trains, circular balances, pillars, bridges, verges, and plates, were forced into marriage with an altogether incompatible partner: arcane Japanese horology.

Since at least the 10th century, and perhaps even as far back as the 7th century, the Japanese, following the Chinese way, had used the twelve terrestrial branches, familiar to us from Chinese astrology, to divide the times of day. Noon was given the sign of the horse, after which followed the sheep, monkey, cock, dog, boar. At midnight came the rat, then the ox, tiger, hare, dragon, and the snake, each marking a Japanese 'hour' or 'watch' of roughly two hours. Temple attendants marked the hours by beating drums or clapping sticks. There were nine beats for the horse, eight for the sheep, and so on to the boar, which received four beats. The number of beats then started again at nine for the rat, descending to four for the snake. We have only one dubious explanation of this peculiar beat sequence, in *Japanese Clocks* written in 1932 by one N H N Mody. I am more attracted to the idea that the downward counting is a way of seeming to approach zero, or nothingness, but never actually getting there.

What complicated the union of clockwork and Japanese time was the unequal and constantly changing lengths of Japanese hours. The six hours of daylight were lengthened and shortened during the year so that they always coincided with the period from sunrise to sunset. Consequently, daylight hours stretched long in summer and grew short in winter, and night hours were compensatingly short and long. The sun always rose, by definition, in the hour of the hare and always set in the hour of the cock.

European clock mechanisms had to be substantially modified to fit the Japanese horology. This was done in two ways: either the hand (there was often only one) was made to turn at different speeds during the day, or the hour markers on the dial were moved. The first Japanese clocks, *yagura-dokei*, required their owners to alter the speed of the hand twice a day, at dawn and at dusk, by moving weights suspended on a foliot. Later, the *shaku-dokei* appeared. This was the more unusual of the two clock designs, since the time was given by the position of a pointer attached to a weight, which slowly fell on a chain. The pointer passed down a vertical scale on which the unequal hours were marked, and was rewound to the top each day. Every fortnight a different scale was used to ensure that the position of the hour markers properly agreed with the seasonally changing times of dawn and dusk. Thirteen such scales were necessary to cover the year, each being employed twice. On some clocks all thirteen scales were permanently present, but other designs necessitated a fortnightly visit from the clockmaker to change the scale.

Japanese clock-making eventually became so sophisticated that the original cumbersome timekeeping systems were replaced by mechanisms that could be accommodated in watches small enough to be hung from an *obi*, an affectation probably more cosmetic that useful. Orreries were also produced. Later clock designs incorporated small automata: a little hand that turned, or a butterfly that moved in a circle against a floral background, items serving no purpose other than to delight.

In time, all such horological whimsy had to yield to greater pragmatism. In 1873, soon after the Meiji Restoration, western timekeeping practices were decreed. There was dissent and remonstration, and so the original hour system was allowed to persist alongside the occidental invader until 1910. Special clocks were produced during this time, showing both Japanese temporal hours and western equinoctial hours. Not for the first time, attempts to simplify things had made them more complicated, but eventually the western system prevailed.

It is tempting to read into the temporal Japanese horology a more naturalistic, or relativistic approach to time than that of Europeans. However, this would be a mistake, for the first Europeans to arrive in Japan would not have been surprised to find a temporal system, one had also been in use in Europe. The temporal system had originated in the Middle East and spread both east and west, wherever it suited the agrarian societies it met. It was the demands of science, particularly astronomy, and hence the art of navigation, that had forced Europe to change to an equinoctial system, and later it was for essentially the same reason that Japan changed too.

The Japanese did take a relativistic approach to time on a larger scale, numbering their years according to three separate systems. Under one system, years were counted from 660 BC, the start of the reign of Jimmu, the semi-mythological first Emperor. Under the second system, years followed a sexagenary cycle developed in China, using the twelve terrestrial branches and the ten celestial stems. The stems were the five elements, namely wood, fire, earth, metal and water, each of which came in two forms, younger brother and elder brother. But it is the third system, still in common use, which is the least systematic. Under this, the number of the year is reset to one on the occasion of a *nengo*, some noteworthy event, usually but not necessarily the enthronement of a new Emperor. The last such *nengo* occurred in 1989, when Emperor Akihito ascended to the throne, and the Heisei era began. The year, which had started out as Showa 63, instantly became Heisei 1 instead.

Like most calendars, the original Japanese calendar was often revised – in 1684, 1754, 1798, and again in 1843, when the principles of western astronomy were adopted. In 1873 the Gregorian calendar, a fourth system, was introduced alongside the *nengo* system. It is the Gregorian calendar that is now used to determine New Year's Day, instead of the first dawn of the second new moon after the winter solstice. The old oriental New Year was placed exactly halfway between the winter solstice (22 December) and the vernal equinox (23 March), which is how it comes to fall in February. So, for the sake of metrical precision, a solid grounding in astronomical events that any peasant could easily observe was forsaken.

In English the months have names, and the days of the months are given ordinal numbers. In modern Japanese, it is the months that are numbered and the days of the month that have special terms. These terms are better thought of as day counters, functioning like the other special-purpose Japanese counter terms for people, thin things, and so on, but ordinal as well as cardinal in use. The first ten days are *tsuitachi, futsuka, mikka, yokka, itsuka, muika, nanoka, youka, kokonoka, touka.* After the tenth, the numbering system is conventional, except for the fourteenth, *juyokka,* and twenty-fourth, *nijuyokka* (analogously, in the European names of months there is also a veiled Latin numbering system from September to December).

The numbering of months in Japanese is a 19th century innovation. In the venerable lunar system, months were given names evocatively descriptive of the seasons. For example, the first month, which roughly coincided with February, was *mutsuki,* meaning harmony or happy month. this was followed by seasonal change of dress, grass grows dense, plant rice, rice sprouts, watering month, month of letters, month of leaves, long month, month of gods, month of falling frost and, for January, poor-looking.

Months were also divided into thirds, *jun,* of ten days each: *shojun, chuujun,* and *nenjun.* The twenty-six fortnights of the year had names inherited from China: spring begins, rain water, excited insects, vernal equinox, clear and bright, grain rains, summer begins, grain fills, grain in ear, summer solstice, slight heat, great heat, autumn begins, limit of heat, white dew, autumnal equinox, cold dew, hoar frost descends, winter begins, little snow, heavy snow, winter solstice, little cold, and severe cold.

What wonderful arcana.

Ryokan evening

The maid leads Emi and I to our dining room. In the middle of the floor is a sand-filled fire-pit. In the pit glows a neat charcoal fire, around which are small fish, potatoes, and rice cakes, all impaled on sticks planted in the sand. Around the edge of the pit are arranged the various bowls and plates containing the rest of our food. The maid brings in a huge platter of yet more food, which is to be cooked over the charcoal. At one side, the screens of the room are open onto a small mossy rock garden lit by a lantern, but a plate glass window is there to keep the cold out. The little fire warms us gently as we settle down beside it, me cross-legged, Emi on her knees in classic *seiza* pose. The room is cosy and the expectation of delicious food makes my mouth water.

We consume *sushi*, carp *sashimi*, wild grape juice, crispy *tempura* leaves, beer, tea, fruit, carp soup, various meats and vegetables all cooked over the fire. Some delicacies are presented to us covered with small sheets of diaphanous sparkling *washi*. The owner of the inn drops by to welcome us and explains a little history of the place.

After dinner we change into *yukata* and head for the baths. The inn is a large rambling big-beamed building, running alongside a mountain stream. Water is drawn off the stream and mixed with that of the local hot springs to create a pleasant temperature.

Only one other man is using the bath, and he leaves before I immerse myself. After a few minutes in the indoor bath I walk out into the garden dimly lit by one small lantern, and slide into the pool there. The rain has stopped. I wonder where the women's pool is. I wonder what Emi looks like sitting naked in the water, and I wonder what she is thinking.

Looking up through the trees, I see Cygnus appear in a hole in the clouds. I move around the pool, walking my fingers on the bottom. Two Japanese men join me in the semi-darkness but don't stay long.

Back inside, I give the electric massage chair a try. It is better than I thought it would be, but no match for a real massage, and not really relaxing. I find Emi back in the room. She is surprised I took so long in the bath. We grab some drinks, including Pocari Sweat, which I like, at the vending machine in the corridor and try to replenish the fluids we have lost. Sitting together by the window, overlooking the garden pool and listening to the sound of the stream nearby, it is all deeply relaxing. I mentally run through my other senses, one at a time. I can feel my *yukata*, slightly damp. I can smell the *tatami* and something else. I think it is our bodies. The frustrations of the last twenty-four hours are lost memories and all I feel for Emi now, as she talks drowsily about the stars and the stream, is an indulgent affection.

I sleep well on my *futon* and wake feeling bright and keen to move on. Emi is already dressed, which is probably a good thing. She has tea ready for me.

In the daylight, we can see that much of the architecture of the inn is rough-hewn beams filled in with carefully carpentered walls and frames. The inn has the feel of a mountain lodge, and I can imagine it is wonderfully cosy in deep snow. We have breakfast in the room we used for dinner last night. I cannot adjust to traditional Japanese breakfast food so easily, but eat most of what is offered.

Toilets with interfaces

The inn offers a variety of toilets including both extremes in sanitary equipage. Last night I had used the 'Washlet' arrangement, which includes an electrically heated seat and an electronic control panel for washing functions. I'd been stricken with anxiety when I had first seen one of these. I'd been afraid of doing something wrong and getting squirted with water, or being unable to flush the toilet and having to call for help.

Here I am free to experiment in private. What's more, an English instruction card has been thoughtfully placed on the wall beside me. The control panel has little diagrams of water being squirted at bottoms. I am relieved when I see the flush operation does not require logging on through the cryptic user interface, but works just like an ordinary one – a chrome plated lever on the side of the tank. First I turn on the 'Rectal Cleaning' function. Mechanical growls issue from the toilet bowl and a most pleasant sensation ensues. Until you have had a stream of warm water gently squirted at your rectum you don't know how agreeable it can feel. Next I try the 'Bidet' function, which is essentially more of the same thing except the stream moves around a little, so you don't have to. There are controls for water temperature and pressure, and other unidentified things. I spend a long time playing.

In the morning I use the old-style squat toilet. It is a short porcelain trench set into the floor, with a splash-control hood at one end. Having nowhere to hang my *yukata* in the cubicle, I hold it across my knees. I worry about it draping into the trench. It's hard to keep my feet in the undersized toilet slippers, and I get pains in my legs from squatting, but eventually all goes well.

The Japanese are fanatically serious about cleaning and hygiene, and obviously spend much creative time thinking about how to improve the processes. I'm glad they do. Too often in the west the bathroom is the last of the architectural priorities, and is a bit of a trial: cold, smelly, cramped, inconvenient. Even though the toilet is often more pleasant in Japan, it is usually considered too dirty a thing to be placed in the bathroom, the epicentre of Japanese cleanliness. Indeed, they would rather have the toilet near the kitchen than near the bathroom.

The bathroom is the most sacred place of all in a Japanese house. It often has the best view of the garden. This makes sense when you value cleanliness so highly. Evidence of the importance of cleanliness is found well beyond the bathroom. Homeless men, who live under tarpaulins in parks or along riversides, routinely wash their nearest stretch of tarmac every morning. I am now slightly ashamed of the level of litter and dirt that routinely decorates Australian streets. It is not excessive, but why is it there at all? Japanese streets, even back alleys, all give the impression that they have been hosed out in the last half-hour. People in Japan do drop litter, just less often. People in Australia clean up litter, just less often.

Replica envy

Replicas enjoy a high status in Japan. Most historical buildings are actually replicas of originals long lost to fire or bombing; yet this doesn't diminish them in Japanese eyes. I would even venture to say that replicas are sometimes given a higher status than originals in Japan. Alan Booth tells an amusing story in *Looking for the Lost*, in which a display, consisting of an autograph and handprint of Konishiki, a famous *sumo rikishi*, is being discussed. Someone suggests that the display might be a manufactured print, rather than the genuine article. After the ensuing debate, in which everyone offers their verdict on the display, a test is performed. The signature turns out to be printed. Its owner beams with pride. Everyone is delighted. *How artful*! they seem to think. For them, the manufactured print represents the *rikishi* no less than an autograph. Or perhaps it is that an original, whatever it might be, is nothing but a dream, or could only ever be a dream, and any dream is as real as any other.

There is a telling passage in *A Japanese Mirror*, by Ian Buruma:

> What meets the eye in Japan is often all there is. Japan is, after all, as Roland Barthes observed, the empire of signs, the land of the empty gesture, the symbol, the detail that stands for the

whole. The fetishist ikon is so powerful that the real thing becomes superfluous.

Buruma is discussing a fetishist coffee bar, decorated with inflated
condoms and female underwear, and crewed by naked waitresses. One
of the points he develops is that there is often no connection between
the appearance and an underlying intent. Thus men can happily sit
and drink coffee in such an environment, or read explicitly sexual and
violent material in public, without shame, and without others suspect-
ing them of prurient or deviant leanings. Their activities are not being
'read into.' Equally, the performing of religious rituals (or any other
kind) implies no actual beliefs, and only the virtues of conformism
and appropriateness. When Emi suggested, during one of our trips
around Kyoto, that I perform the purification and prayer ritual at
Fushimi-inari shrine I demurred, saying that I felt it would be hypo-
critical to go through the act when I didn't believe in it, and that it
would be a rude parody of those who do. 'It doesn't matter.' she said,
'No one believes.'

Booth also mentions the Japanese predilection for the superficial.
He describes Daruma's nine-year meditation during which his arms
and legs atrophied from lack of use: 'as a result the Japanese, being in-
finitely more comfortable with outward appearance than with inward
illumination, associate him not with piety, but with roundness,' (that
is, with limblessness).

Many of the religious icons of Japan are replicas. Often, the reason
for this is that the original probably never actually existed. Examples
include the objects supposed to reside at Ise-jingu, Atsuta-jingu, and
the Tokyo Imperial Palace – the belongings of the gods. The existence
of replicas of mythological objects is itself often questionable, but it
doesn't really matter whether these things exist or not, whether they
are real or replicas, because they will never be seen anyway. Kobo
Daishi relics, such as calligraphy and seals, are found at many temples
along the *junrei no tabi* (pilgrimage) taken by Oliver Statler in *Japanese Pilgrimage*. It is obvious that opportunities to see putative Kobo
Daishi relics actually motivate pilgrims, and so many temples promote
objects of clearly dubious provenance. Yet even when the inauthenti-
city is readily admitted, pilgrims don't seem at all troubled.

Other objects have been replicated for different reasons. The whole of Heian-jingu in Kyoto is actually a replica of a larger building, Byodo-in temple at Uji. That one is Shinto and the other Buddhist is just one of the many curiosities in the relationship between these two systems of belief. The reason for the replication has never been clear to me.

Replication is nothing new in Japanese architecture. During the Heian era the Hall of Cool Breezes in the imperial palace compound was replicated, down to tiny details, but at a reduced scale, in the west wing of the Sanjo Mansion. Many of the people of the court moved between the two buildings, and must have found the shift in scale marginally disconcerting. The reason for this replication, as far as any-one can tell, was nothing more than great admiration for the original. The replica enhances the importance of the original, and *vice versa*.

Sometimes the object being replicated, and the replica itself are only a few feet apart. The image of Amida in the Jodo-in of Enryaku-ji is a replica, but the original is in a box just behind it. The same is true of the image of Shaka in the nearby Shaka-do, and the image of Yaku-shi in the Kompon-chu-do. The concealment of the originals may well be for the protection of valuable religious art, but has the paradoxical effect of rendering the valuable objects quite useless, and possibly without value. If we cannot see art, does it have any value?

In *The Lady and the Monk*, Pico Iyer recognises this Japanese tend-ency towards appearance and surface, but from his position, that of a romantic outsider, it is not easily understood. To such a person, the veneration of perfection in tiny things will be seen as a preoccupation with details, niceties, protocols and fastidiousness. No words can ex-plain how satisfying such superficial qualities can be, regardless of whether they accord with inner feelings, seething or serene. More-over, Japanese writers praise appearances, not essences, because they know essences don't matter, or even exist. Iyer, by contrast, maintains that 'good souls' are important, but finally admits it is hard to argue the point. His suggestion that Zen is suitable to people not prone to deep introspection is surely his own superficial reaction to Japanese attitudes towards appearance – he's still lost on the assumption that something more real exists below. I feel that the sham of his position is exposed in the passage in which Sachiko is probing the possibility of leaving her husband, obviously looking for some honest passion from Iyer, a westerner full of romantic ideas, but ultimately arid, lifeless and cerebral in a passionate sexual Japan. Iyer is too careful about being true to himself to plunge in bodily, whole-heartedly, with reckless abandon to the moment. How graphically the tables of self-restraint are turned on him!

Briefly virgin again

My entire tour of central Honshu *ryokan*, with the often naked and always delicious Emi, was perfectly chaste. I had been looking forward to the trip as something of a erotic fantasy: Japanese girl in *yukata*, fresh *tatami*, soft *futon*, cold country nights and gentle rain outside the *shoji* screens patterning the rhythm of sensual gasps inside. The reality had been much less to write home about – or more, in fact, given my mother's social mores.

However, back in the urban drab of Otsu, away from all the suggestive power of nature, things take an unexpected turn for the better.

At the house, Emi gets a big bottle of beer out of the fridge and brings two glasses to the table. We kneel on cushions, at ninety degrees to one another.

'Do you still love tyger?' she asks, as she pours.

'I never loved tyger.'

'Maybe you do. You think about her all the time.'

'Hnnn.' I am not sure whether I have said yes or no, but whatever it was, it seemed the right thing to say.

Emi takes a sip of beer and begins to tell me one of the most surprising stories I've heard for many months.

It transpires that her marriage was called off for more than just reasons of her prospective father-in-law's fraud conviction. Her intended, with whom she had slept five or six times (and not too pleasurably, she adds, conspiratorially), had detected that she was not a virgin. Why this took him so long to confirm I can only guess. However, Emi's lost virginity had been the first impediment to marriage, and the wedding plans were consequently already unravelling by the time the Takegawa family's detective dug up the fraud. The resulting stand-off led to a typically civilised and cooperative cover-up in which the official version was that the 'young people' had simply decided that they had conflicting careers, would marry for love, were not ready, anything, in fact, except the truth. At first Emi had been shamed and devastated by the break-off of the engagement, though knowledge of the fraud had helped to spread the blame a little. However, she still felt that being 'opened inside my body,' as she put it, was a liability, and that she should do something to rectify it. She proceeds to tell me, with the frankness one would expect to accompany a story about a saucepan or a lawn-mower repair, about the operation she underwent to restore her hymen. I can only listen in stunned silence.

It turned out, as I discovered through my own baffling experiences, that the operation had been a little more thorough than intended, and that her new hymen had formed thick scar tissue, and had been, to all intents and purposes, unbreakable.

'So that is why we couldn't make love?' I ask, for confirmation.

'It was.' She nods.

'But now,' she smiles, suddenly brightening, 'everything is fine!'

'How?'

'I had another operation.'

This, and its implications, are a lot to absorb at once. I ask questions about cost, hospital time, pain, doctor's liabilities, her mind-set, who else knows, regrets, etc. At the back of all my questions is an uncertain suspicion that this hymen preoccupation is something I would have expected of the Strict and Particular Baptists, not the Japanese. It doesn't quite ring true. Emi fetches another bottle of beer to replace the empty one, and fills my glass. I fill hers.

We talk some more, and then she carefully places her glass on the table, shuffles a little towards me, puts a hand on my shoulder and leans in to my ear, kisses it and whispers into it in her peculiar brand of English.

'Maaku-san. Let's be excited!'

There is no mistaking the message now. So we move to the upper floor of the house, where folding screens partition a single large *tatami*-covered room. Emi and her mother both sleep here, but today we have the floor to ourselves. I am shaking with excitement as I help Emi undress, And this time everything goes well. Our lovemaking is the way

I like it: abandoned, blacked-out, plunging, then subsiding and resurfacing all at once. With the groans of a small delivery truck moving down the street and the muffled sounds of the television next door coming through the window, we snuggle under her *kakebuton* and I muse on how much effort one puts into the pursuit of women, and how little is sometimes actually required. I don't for a minute think I've got to the bottom of everything that has been going on with Emi, but now is not the time to question.

'It is better to be real, I think,' says Emi, reflectively.

I nod. 'Do you still want to get married?'

'Of course.'

'Not to me though, eh?'

'You are just boyfriend.' she says, and taps the tip of my nose with her finger. 'Sex-friend, *ne*.'

Emi drops me off at the station, and then goes to pick up her mother. We have made arrangements to see each other again. She has just kissed me in public for the first time.

Overactive imagination

'i wish we could meet, leo'

'I would like that too, just you and I.'

'a man, a woman, and two cats'

'I love your apposite literary allusions, if I may be permitted to make such a gauche and direct observation.'

tyger curtseys and purrs in counterpoint.

'i've never had my apposite literary allusions so admired'

'Ogled, in fact!'

'leo!'

tyger twists coyly on one heel.

'i had a strange experience at work today, leo'

'What was that?'

'i thought there was a piece of string in my hand, when there wasn't. it kept coming back throughout the morning'

'That is quite strange.'

'sometimes it feels like a pen'

'Sometimes? You mean this isn't the first time?'

'nope. sign of an overactive imagination?'

'Sign of the constructive functions of your brain taking things a little too far in the piece of string direction.'

'what dat?'

'Well, there is no guarantee of isomorphism between what physically exists, and what we experience. We *construct* our experiences of the world, with or without evidence for them.'

'how do we manage to go about our daily business, then, i mean, without treating a cabbage as a king, say?'

'It is just that there is a reasonable correspondence between the sensory signals we receive, and what we construct out of them. And we constantly reinterpret or rewrite our past experience in terms of our current experience, to make sense of it, which really just means we try to make it fit together.'

'why do we try to do that?'

'Probably because reality is consistent enough, so that any system that aims for consistency based on small perceptual clues just might end up with a reliable picture of reality that, strictly speaking, isn't supported by the clues.'

'we fill in the gaps correctly, is that what you mean?'

'Sort of. It is probably truer to say there are no gaps that we can be aware of, but if the past and the immediate present don't fit, we usually change what we thought happened in the past.'

'is that why people's eye-witness testimony is so unreliable?'

'Yes, memory is an action our brain performs, not
a record that it retrieves from somewhere. And
the action is different every time.'
'i like that idea very much, leo!'
'You like it? I wish I could wrap it and give it
to you.'
tyger performs a little dance of glee, then sits
down again.
'It doesn't really make you feel less anxious
about the piece of string though, does it?'
'it does, a little. but i am still considerably
disturbed by it. why do i get pieces of string
when no one else does?'
'I think it is very wrong to expect your mind to
work like an ordinary one, tyger. It is a unique
and beautiful instrument.'
'thank you. i think yours is too'
Leo shakes his head. 'It's very average compared
to yours, tyger.'
'you're being awfully nice to me today, leo. it's
having the desired effect if you were after
cheering me up'
'I had no ulterior motive, but now that you
mention it, I've noticed that the people here are
awfully nice to each other. Perhaps it's
contagious.'
'you're not just talking about automatic
politeness?'
'No, automatic politeness exists aplenty, all
right, but what I am struck by is the almost
continuous streams of compliments that pass back
and forth between people in small groups.'
'is that so unusual?'
'Yes, the degree of it is. And anyway, most of my
friends at home pass a continuous stream of joke
insults back and forth. It can get tedious.'

```
'surely the compliments can get that way too?'
'Perhaps. It will be interesting to see if my
views change with longer exposure.'
'btw, what you were saying about consciousness
reminds me of 'consciousness explained' by
dennett'
'Have you read that?'
'yes'
'You really do amaze me tyger. So you knew all
along what I was trying to say.'
'yes, but i enjoyed your explanation more :)'
tyger hugs leo.
'You're very sweet, tyger.'
'mmmmmm, so are you'
```

Japanese space

In your mind you carry two maps of the world.
One is the map they taught you at school.
The other you see when you close your eyes.
It may not show famous cities, rivers, or peaks,
but upon this map the places you have visited,
and all your footsteps, shine like lamps in the darkness.
It is not rational, but it is alive.

So goes a poem by the painter Nakagawa Kazumasa. The relativist approach to space in Japan has caught me out a couple of times. The maps displayed in stations and other sites around Japanese cities never fail to include a 'You are here' sign, but they do not follow the convention of orientation in which north is up. Generally, Japanese maps are oriented so that the direction you are facing is up. This means that what is to your left in the world will be on the left of the map, and what is to your right will be on the right. I can see the advantage in this, but still I often assume north is at the top, and get led astray as a result.

Another spatial convention that has a unique variation in Japan is the series of advertisements often arranged along the roadside, telling us that we are 300 metres, 200 metres, 100 metres away from a shop, for example. The Japanese variation is that some places advertise themselves as being zero metres from where the sign itself is, and often without any preceding signs. It is another strange marriage of metrical and egocentric space.

Mann machines

I meet an Australian friend for lunch. Dr. Graham Mann, a robot designer and a lecturer at Murdoch University is in Japan for a robotics conference, again. Just last night he was featured on at least two television channels, talking about the current and future states of robotics.

'So where in the field of robotics is Japan?' I prompt.

'Japan? Japan is so far ahead on this they are in a different league,' he says excitedly. 'They are robot-crazy in every way. They see robots doing everything in the future and they aren't embarrassed about it.

'Robots are being designed now for all the floor-based activities in the home, like sweeping the carpet and washing the tiles. These things come creeping out at night when everyone is in bed, and get to work. You wake up in the morning and the house is clean.'

'What do they do if you get up in the middle of the night? Could you accidentally tread on one of them?'

'No, they'll scuttle away at the first sign of movement, like cockroaches. They even look a bit like big cockroaches anyway. And later there will be robots to take on what we call the 'fetch and carry' tasks. You'll say 'get me a Super Dry from the fridge,' and the robot will do it for you, or it will go down to the *tofu* shop and bring back your dinner. There are also robots in development to do the gardening. They look like big crabs with wheels on the ends of their legs, so they can clamber over rocks and uneven ground, but then skate along on smooth surfaces. Incrementally, robots will take over all the easy tasks, and progressively encroach on the more difficult ones.'

He pauses for a sip of coffee, but then continues before the cup has reached his lips.

'Japan is really worried about its ageing population. Soon over a quarter of the population will be over sixty-five years old. The plan is to create a race of humanoid servants to help old people. The government has called for this and the funding is already coming through for researchers. The big names, like Mitsubishi, Sony, Matsushita, Honda, they're all working on this. Tama from Matsushita is a cuddly robot cat with tiger stripes that is designed to provide company for old people living alone, but it is also programmed to remind them to take their medicine. It can even be contacted by the local health care authorities to pass messages to its owner. And the funny thing is that Tama doesn't move around, because old people said they didn't want to have to chase it around the house.

'What is the owner: pet lover or gadget freak? And what is the robot: little friend or big toy?' The questions, of course, are rhetorical. Graham continues.

'Robot pets are an amazing success now. Sony cannot make enough Aibo to keep up with the demand. Aibo user groups are springing up everywhere just like they did twenty years ago for microcomputers. And Sony is already developing the new generations intensively. They will be releasing male and female pets soon, and they will be less machine-like in appearance, rounder, and cuter.'

I remember the Meldog, a seeing-eye dog for the blind that was demonstrated in the mid-1980s. Robot dogs are nothing new.

'But anyway,' Graham continues, in his rapid manic style, perfect for calling stray thoughts to heel, 'even projects that start outside Japan are coming here because this is where the funding is. Robokoneko was the brainchild of Hugo DeGaris, an Australian, but he brought it to Japan to get the money. So far they have only made the brain for it, and the weird thing is that they have made this high-powered computer look like a thick slice of cerebrum. It is the shape of a cake slice with the cortex on the outside. Other companies are going to be coming into this pet market too. Robot toy designs are on drawing boards everywhere. Many are already lining up in the shops. The competition is going to be very interesting.'

I break in, 'The University of Hokkaido has a whole robotic menagerie, I'm sure you would like. They have robot water snakes, fish, even robot slime moulds. The water snake is wonderful. It was programmed to wriggle around but also to make its world brighter. What this meant was that any behaviour that took it nearer to a light source would be reinforced. Naturally people expected it to develop the sinuous movements of real water snakes, but the robot had different ideas. It hinged itself in the middle, and moved its two ends like the arms of a breast-stroker. It ended up swimming, very effectively, sideways.'

Nodding rapidly while I speak, Graham then continues, 'And there are robots that sit in parks, and they'll dance and tell jokes if you put money into them. If you don't put enough in they'll insult you for being a miser, but they'll do little extras if you put more in.

'Really advanced animatronics is also underway. Imagine artificial faces that can really smile and talk to you. People are working on ultra smooth skin and flesh substitutes for animated store dummies and displays. It is so easy to program formal Japanese behaviour into these things. And perhaps that is why the Japanese don't have a problem accepting robots.'

'Why, because they perceive much human behaviour as of an essentially programmed nature?'

'Exactly. Since so much of normal Japanese behaviour is quite inflexible the robot fits right in. The Japanese are not embarrassed by the predictability or inflexibility of it, perhaps they even prefer that. But put these kinds of projects in front of Australian or American AI researchers, and they will just scoff. They want general-purpose intelligence, not the acting out of scripts.'

'We want to get real jobs done in unpredictable situations,' I offer.

'Yes, yes, we do,' Graham nods, 'and so do the Japanese, actually. They are working on that side too. They have a robot that hangs from wires and builds the hillside concrete cladding that you see all over Japan now. It is too dangerous for people to work in places like that. They have also turned to robots to avoid a repeat of the disastrous Hanshin earthquake of 1995, which was more a disaster of inept responses than it was a geological disaster.'

The world has heard of Kobe, because of that earthquake. Looking around Kobe now, five years later, it is hard to see much evidence of the earthquake. But in 1995 things were quite different. During big earthquakes, solid things go liquid, objects ebb and flow across streets and floors, great tears open up in the ground, water, oil, and fire flow where they are not supposed to go, so all sorts of secondary things go wrong. Man-made islands, of which Kobe has a few, are the least resilient to earthquakes – the landfill that supports them has little integrity, and liquefies with the least encouragement. Some buildings twisted drunkenly, others leant on their neighbours for support, some simply crumbled into rubble. From the air, Kobe grew a blue haze, created by the thousands of tarpaulins drawn across broken roofs.

Graham presses on regardless.

'They have a complete virtual model of Kobe, into which tremors can be programmed, buildings made to fall down, and vehicles made to navigate through the resultant rubble. That is why "Robocup Rescue" was dreamt up.'

'What's that?' I ask.

'It's a new competition. We have the various Robocup soccer matches that many people have heard of now, but this new competition consists of a pile of rubble under which are buried victim dolls, and the robots have to rescue them.'

'How is that going to work? Will the dolls cry out? Will the robots just grab a foot and drag them out?'

'This is still being worked out. Apparently you cannot just lift masonry off people, because they sometimes go into a form of shock and die when the pressure is suddenly released. So the robots would have to be careful about that. And the issue of finding them, well, I heard…,' he pauses and drops his voice to a confidential tone, 'I heard that in real life they often use the smell of urine to locate people buried in rubble, so maybe the dolls will emit a chemical scent of some kind.'

'But aren't other countries also doing interesting things in robotics?'

'Not really. There is Cog at MIT but that is fixed and slow compared to what the Japanese are doing. The US Government is not funding robotics, and the Europeans don't appear to have much going on either. Their idea of a useful robot is something huge and strong with a truck attached to it so it can drive around and lift heavy things. Actually no, Lego is a great exception; people are making amazing robots with the Mindstorm kits. And the Australian robot research effort, well it is just too small.

'Japan's MITI not only officially sanctions robotics; it is actually in love with it. And so are other key figures in Japan. Visionary engineers pitched advanced robotics projects to the heads of both Honda and Sony. It turned out these execs were robot-mad too, and effectively wrote blank cheques. The research programs are huge and under the direct control of the corporate head offices. Aibo came out of Sony, and Asimo has come out of Honda. And in Japan robots are just plain cool. People have no technophobia, women like them just as much as men. It is not a geek thing; everyone likes them. The social milieu is altogether much more receptive to robots.'

Graham finally pauses long enough for me to formulate a thought.

'I remember reading somewhere that the Japanese are much happier with things that do not have personalities,' I say, 'I think it was Karl Taro Greenfeld in *Speed Tribes*. He quoted a *gaijin* academic who called the phenomenon *in-animism*. That was meant to account for the Japanese love of machines, but there is another side to this, because the Japanese go to great lengths to put personality *into* things that don't already have it. The phones say 'thank you' after you hang up. Buses and trains are given automatic voices, and there is Shinto animism itself. Toys talk, cars talk, practically every product has a face on it. Even the train to Kansai airport has been given a mask like Darth Vader – and his hissing sibilance.'

'Yes,' agrees Graham, 'but the opposite is also true. Every year in Japan more cats and dogs are destroyed because they routinely get discarded as if they are just unwanted toys.'

'So Aibo is not just a substitute for a real dog, it is actually the inanimate low-maintenance pet that Japan wanted all along. The real dogs were the poor substitutes.'

It occurs to me that it is not a question of whether on the one side personality is being attributed or projected into strange places, or on the other denied where it seems to belong, but that the whole idea of what has a personality and what does not is strangely blurred. And this result is just what would be expected if the concept of self, as reified in the west, were itself questionable. In the Shinto ontology, the soul is a less venerated entity. Just by virtue of being, things have a *kami*, or spirit. This spirit is as unremarkable in a robot as it is in a cave, or a fox, or thunder. As we make more sophisticated robots there will come a time – it may already be upon us – when people will simply cease to wonder whether the machines have personalities, consciousness, or even 'human' rights.

In *Inside the Robot Kingdom*, Frederik L Schodt writes:

> In Japan, the Robot Kingdom is part myth, part reality, and part state of mind. The robot itself is the crystallization of a mechanical dream.

Japan robot chronicles

We know that Japanese clockmakers mastered their art soon after the introduction of clocks from Europe in 1551, and we know that these days robots are a commonplace in Japan. Is there a link, and does Japan have a historical counterpart to the celebrated early European automata, such as Vaucanson's duck and Jaquet-Droz's androids? The answer to both questions is yes.

In the National Science Museum in Tokyo there is a small doll, about 35 cm high. It is a boy, hands outstretched, eyes downcast, head forward and low in a subservient position, body all but hidden by his *kimono*. This character is fairly well known in Japan. He is a *karakuri*, which means mechanism or trick. When wound up he will shuffle forward bearing a cup of tea. When the cup is lifted from his hands he will stop and wait. When the cup is replaced he will turn 180 degrees and shuffle back to where he started. His feet move, but he actually runs on hidden wheels.

Such *karakuri* date from the 17th century and are driven by clockwork mechanisms, such as governors, springs and gears. They were manufactured, as in Europe, by clockmakers and were used to entertain in a range of ways, of which the tea-serving boy is just one example. Records talk of mechanical fish, calligraphers, and acrobats. Bodily functions, such as urination, were also a feature, echoing the celebrated ability of Vaucanson's duck to defecate.

The art of Japanese *karakuri* endured for almost a century but, sadly, no original examples survive. The tea-boy on view in Tokyo is, perhaps not surprisingly, a replica. In the 18th century, craftsmen started building *karakuri* from standard mechanisms imported from Europe. Now, however, it is possible to buy, for many thousands of dollars, karakuri made to the original Japanese designs. The Tamaya family of Nagoya has been making dolls for seven generations, and in just the last few years has revived *karakuri* production.

In *Inside the Robot Kingdom*, Frederik Schodt describes several other forms of *karakuri* that continue to operate in Japan, mainly during festivals. Some are operated like puppets. The strings run inside their body, and operators sit below the doll's platform. Another variant so reliably reproduces the same movements every time that it can be set free to jump from bar to bar in a kind of trapeze act.

Whereas in Europe most of the great automaton engineers went on to design programmable machines, such as weaving looms, the Japanese designers were content to concentrate on the art rather than its application. Their designs indicate a much greater interest in entertainment than usefulness (which was a primary goal for the Europeans). In these early efforts, then, we already see differences between Japan and Europe that can still be found in contemporary electronic robotics research.

So, the Europeans are still hard on the heels of utility, but less inclined to attribute personalities to robots, and the Japanese are interested in the fun to be had, and don't share our reluctance to attribute personality. It is a curious comparison. I wonder what it tells us about our societies.

tyger, Tiger

I potter around all day, achieving little. Emi will not be home before 7 PM, which makes for a long day on my own. When I have something to do, like reading up on *karakuri,* these waiting days are convenient, but today the hours drag out slowly. I see a sign that says *intanetto,* Internet, so pop in for an hour online and the obligatory thimbleful of strong coffee.

```
Leo lands with aplomb.
'greetings, lord leo'
tyger bows, curtsies, wobbles.
'Lord, hah!' says Tiger.
[privately to tyger]: 'He a friend of yours,
tyger?'
[privately to leo]: ''tis so. his name's ghassan.
he's ok. i let him log on via my machine'
'leo, tiger, tiger, leo'
```

'hello Tiger,' says Leo.

'Hi,' says Tiger.

Tiger snogs Tyger.

'phewwww!'

'Is this normal?'

tyger thinks tiger is a bit of a handful and
ought to watch himself, especially when leo is
around.

'Yeah? Why?'

'can't explain now. have a surprisingly
interesting meeting to attend in a few minutes,
nay, seconds. i'll have to take my regretful
leave of both of you'

tyger shrugs, a picture of abject contrition.

'Bad timing on my part. Sorry, little cat.'

'i can talk again in two hours, if my lord so
pleases'

'Don't think I'll be able to today, tyger, this
was a spur of the moment thing. Perhaps tomorrow,
same time?'

'so hope so'

tyger kisses her esteemed leo goodbye, waves at
tiger, and disappears in a beautiful little puff
of blue smoke.

Tiger kisses Tyger goodbye.

'I think you were just a little too late there,
Tiger.'

'Yeah, so? Plenty where that came from.'

'Come again?'

'Too right!'

No point hanging around, now. May as well just surf in another
window.

'You still there, Leo?'

I notice this a few seconds later.

'Yep. Still here, Tiger.'

'Touch yourself often, do you?'

119

```
Tiger laughs head off.
'What?'
'Execrable communication, pal.'
Tiger logs off.
```

It doesn't take me long to realise that Ghassan has more than logging-on rights on tyger's machine. He has found a way to read her email, and he's clearly just been reading emails she and I have sent each other. He may have full access to all her files. I need to warn her about this but any of the electronic methods are likely to be intercepted by Ghassan. I will have to use ordinary mail.

A beautiful and seasonal postcard of snow in a rock garden catches my eye. I sit on a low wall and write.

> Dear tyger,
>
> Didn't see enough of you today, as you will know. And as if that wasn't bad enough, I now have some slightly unpleasant news. Ghassan has infiltrated your account and has been reading our email. I am sure you know what to do. Please send me an email using the words autoclave and praeterpluperfect as a sign that your system is secure.
>
> Much leonine love and gentle ear-rubbings,
>
> Leo.

I walk into the post office near Kyoto station and wait in line. The clerk tells me the card should reach its destination in four or five days. Meanwhile I shall act online as if I don't suspect a thing.

A Handful of Sand

A man and three women

WAITING FOR AKIKO, watching the people stream by, I speculate sexually about the women I see. It occurs to me that in the short time I have been in Japan I have begun sexual relationships with three very different women: business-like Satomi in Tokyo, hairless and highly-sexed; mercurial Emi in Kyoto, shaven and, until recently, impenetrable; and the forlorn married Akiko, also in Tokyo, downy, seemingly indifferent to sex but completely compliant.

Sex for Satomi is a kind of hobby, for Akiko I gather it is a kind of revenge. But for Emi – is it love? Only Emi could be prone to jealousy, I think. I wonder about her – is she my girlfriend now? Have we crossed some defining line that gives her special status? Do I love her? No, it is not love. Should I still be sleeping with the others? She wouldn't like it if she knew, but I don't yet feel my actions are automatically part of her business. I've always been troubled by these categories: friend, lover, girlfriend, affair, fling, relationship. Each has its own crucial etiquette. Satomi, friend and fling, I suppose; Akiko, affair and lover (for her at least); Emi, girlfriend and relationship? Thinking about them excites me, and I laugh at how easily my mind is entrained by sex. It colours all my time here.

Suddenly Akiko is at the tableside, dumping down her bag and greeting me breathlessly. We discuss what to do today.

Dance machine

Akiko wants to show me how she goes clubbing without raising her husband's suspicions. We enter an electronic games parlour and she heads for the Dance Dance Revolution machine. It is one of the largest machines there. A small guard rail protects a tiny dance floor. Akiko steps onto the floor and starts the machine. The huge screen before her jumps into action and a virtual dancer, who looks like Namie Amuro, starts to dance. The music thumps harder, and lights run in patterns around the screen and under the dance floor. Akiko and her virtual dance partner keep perfect time. They are both grinning like mad. The dance gets more complicated. There are twirls, crouches and jumps, deep bends and rapid shimmies. Akiko's hair flies out like a whip, and I can see small strands of it sticking to her temples. After a while the dance gets too fast and acrobatic even for Akiko, who falls back against the guard rail and steps off the floor. She is panting like a dog, wobbling on her heels, and the aroma of her body and perfume rises off her in a warm cloud. She is happy and tired, and bounces up and down on the spot.

'I want to do it again.' she cries.

She leans against my arm, and the heat from her body pours through my clothes.

Already another girl has taken her place on the dance floor and the thumping soundtrack starts again. A different figure is leading the dance and the new girl's friends are standing at the rail, clapping in time to the beat.

Akiko tells me she feels like a MTV music star when she plays the machine. She often has five or six dances in an evening, and has even made friends with some of the other girls she has met here. They have cooperated on working out the more difficult dance steps.

These dance machines have been exported from Japan to countries all over the world. The music selection and choice of characters is customised for different markets. In Europe, for example, the machine is called Dancing Stage Euromix I. Several selections of musical style are available on some versions of the machine, including rock, electronic, and pop. Dancing tournaments have been held in the United States and Australia. The biggest markets are Asian, even within non-Asian countries. Home versions, that run on Sony PlayStation, have also been sold in large numbers.

Before we leave, Akiko begs for another dance. She waits her turn at the machine, jiving to the music without moving her feet. When her turn comes she leaps back into the light, arms high above her head, abandoned to the music. The other girls smile at me, glad to see someone from another generation appreciating their hobby like this.

This kind of substitute for real activity is not unusual in Japan. Golf driving ranges vastly outnumber real golf courses, and can be seen in every city. Batting ranges, where mechanic pitchers pump baseballs at us, as fast as we can handle, fill in for real baseball grounds. There is even video horse-riding for horseless equestrians. We mount a mechanical horse by Matsushita, and kick it into motion. It will walk, trot or canter, using telemetric data from real thoroughbreds. The realism of the leather saddle and reins complement the video images of a country lane, beach, or pasture (we choose) that fill our field of view. These images are coordinated with the virtual movements of the horse. Speakers provide birdsong or perhaps the sound of surf.

One day on the Yamanote line I saw a fishing pool, looking just like a swimming pool, where anglers crowded elbow to elbow to capture already-captured fish that were never able to swim more than a rod's length away. Another virtual substitute. And on the way to Makuhari the train passes a massive and peculiar building. It looks like a giant worm rearing up 150 metres into the sky. Is it for loading ships, or is it some kind of launching ramp, I wonder? It turns out to be the Skidome, where Tokyo-ites can snow ski in the middle of summer, without even leaving town.

Cupid electric

A few years ago, so Akiko tells me, many of her friends played with Lovegety. These small devices could be programmed to transmit a signal which, when picked up by a similar device owned by someone of the opposite sex, indicated how sociable you were feeling. The range of the devices was about five metres. Akiko's friends all had pink Lovegety, the blue ones were used by boys. When the girls, who invariably moved around town in a group, came close to a boy with a Lovegety, all their Lovegety would start beeping. This was apparently hilarious in itself, but the embarrassment and confusion it caused the boy was even funnier. Faced with three or four girls, all jumping up and down, giggling madly, shouting 'choose me, choose me,' most boys were tongue-tied and anxious to disappear. The girls tired of this after a couple of weeks, and no more was ever heard of Lovegety. I asked Akiko is she still had hers, as I would like to see it, for research purposes. She tells me she doesn't know where it is.

The Lovegety came soon after the Tamagotchi. In retrospect, Tamagotchi were the herald of the virtual pet craze, which spread to the Internet, where it spawned mutants of various degrees of liveliness, and then to the physical robot pet domain, where Aibo is the leader.

Tamagotchi (from *tamago* for egg, and *tomodachi* for friend) were nothing more than a program that demanded a series of inputs from its user. A small primitive graphic display showed how the virtual pet was faring, and indicated its current demands. As long as the user, or owner, answered all the pet's demands it would thrive and eventually reach maturity, whereupon it would fly away! If, however, the user was negligent, the pet would whine, complain, fall sick, and eventually expire. It is reported that children in Japan and overseas (for Tamagotchi were a worldwide success) sometimes had to be treated for trauma when their pets died. Teachers complained that they could not get children to concentrate on their class work in the face of demands from Tamagotchi, but confiscating the pets simply created an even bigger problem, children were then so distraught and inconsolable that they were completely unable to work in class.

Inevitably, many parents were entrusted with the care of their children's Tamagotchi, as they often are with real pets. Many of them found something emotionally satisfying in this. The Tamagotchi conferred power and the opportunity to show compassion, without any distasteful animal behaviour to deal with. Looking after them was simply a case of producing the right response at the right time. Clearly, this was another case of the object programming the human, by simply appealing to the human in a way which would elicit the required response.

During our discussion of Lovegety and other things, Akiko's friend, Yumi comes and sits with us. She doesn't say a word, but smiles and imperceptibly nods in confirmation as Akiko talks. While I ply Akiko with questions, I feel uneasy about excluding Yumi from the conversation. Akiko doesn't make any effort, other than to smile at Yumi from time to time. When Yumi mouths something and returns to the dance machine I wonder aloud if she is always so quiet or just shy because of me.

'She is always silent,' laughs Akiko. 'She never talks.'

'Really? Doesn't that make her rather dull company?' I ask in all innocence.

'No, of course not,' Akiko retorts, offended. 'She is nice to be with.'

'Doesn't your husband mind you hanging out with girlfriends and using Lovegety?'

'Lovegety was before... but he doesn't care anyway.'

'No? That's unusual for a Japanese guy. Isn't he afraid of losing face?'

'He doesn't care. He tells me he doesn't care. He is never there. He has girlfriends.'

Her face is poised in a nameless shadow somewhere between nonchalance and sorrow.

The framed outdoors

Perhaps more than in any other country, here people travel simply to take photographs. Husbands retreat from the company of their wives and families by clasping camcorders to their faces. Thus armed or armoured, they can walk around and enjoy viewfinder images of their surroundings in place of something more direct.

Travel groups arrive at their destination and immediately assemble for the inevitable photographs. Sometimes everyone in the group will have a camera, each wanting their own picture. An innocent bystander will be supplied with one camera after another until the ritual is complete. By then it is time to hop onto the coach. They didn't have time to look around, but they are happy, they have the images.

Misasa Ryokan

Misasa Ryokan – the very name of it stirs envy in the people I talk to. Everyone has heard of it, and everyone wants to stay there, apparently. I have the good fortune to know someone who knows someone who knows the owner, so the charge for my stay is merely excessively expensive, as opposed to astronomical. The twenty-five-*tatami* room I am given is one of those used to illustrate the brochure. It is spacious and has sliding screens on three sides. Two sides open out onto little balconies, one leads to the ante-room and *genkan*. One of the balconies overlooks the courtyard garden, which other guests can only see from the reception hall.

After tea – served by our maid in the room – we take the first bath of our stay. As both the men's and women's baths are vacant we take the opportunity to bathe together in the women's. The washing area is supplied with a strange kind of raw salt that we rub into our skins. It has a wonderful abrasive effect on the skin, making it tingle with life, and feel deliciously clean in the hot water, but it stings the eyes and sensitive parts. We relax and talk in the water for about twenty minutes, so that our fingers and feet are looking puckered and whitish when we dry ourselves.

Back in the room we have time to cool down a little before the dinner is brought in. As usual in expensive *ryokan*, the food is an adventure in taste, variety, and presentation. Seasonal touches like chestnut paste are noted with appreciation. We feast hard and long and have to refuse the soup and rice at the end of the meal, we are simply so overloaded with food that another bath is called for.

But first, a walk in the cold lanes of the town. In wooden *geta* we clatter up and down the alleys as the shops start to close up for the night. Our *yukata* and *haori* are not really enough to keep the cold out, but feeling chilly just heightens the pleasant expectation of another hot bath. I somehow manage to snap one of my *geta* in half as I turn on my heel to look at something. Hobbling back to the *ryokan* for a replacement I get a blister.

Later we settle into the hot water again. Two women come into the changing room, but they disappear as soon as they hear my voice. Soon the manager is knocking on the door, so we dry off and emerge from the *o-furo* ready for our scolding. The manager tells us that he does not object to mixed bathing, but some guests do, so please inform him in advance if we intend to do it again. Chastened, we retire to the room, where our *futon* have already been laid out (I have two – to cater to my outlandish length). Off with the *yukata* and quickly under the *kakebuton* with a ready Japanese woman, the soft grassy fragrance of the *tatami* filling my nostrils, it is a sensory excess that only Japan can provide.

It should really be Emi I am with, but she hardly gets any time off work, and she has already used most of it to spend with me. Satomi, on the other hand, is able to take long breaks from work whenever she feels like it. It is Satomi I am sleeping with, Satomi whose hot velvety skin feels so good under the *kakebuton*, and Satomi who moans loudly beneath me in the dark. I know Emi wouldn't like it, but the monogamy she no doubt hopes I practise seems an unfair sacrifice at times like this. I prefer not to think about it. I feel both justified and guilty.

In the morning Satomi and I bathe again, separately this time. I have the opportunity to compare the men's and women's facilities and note that, as is usual in Japan, the men's are superior. Breakfast comes to the room at the arranged time, and we feast all over again. I have slowly been adjusting to Japanese food at breakfast. I can now eat it, providing I stop for a bit of toast and coffee soon afterwards. During breakfast the maid, now dressed in ordinary staff uniform instead of her *kimono*, asks me '*yukkuri neraremashita ka.*' This is an honorific style of address that I am not familiar with at the time, so I ask her to repeat it. She acts quite flustered and at a loss, and says 'did I say something?'

In set situations it is not unusual for people in Japan to speak so automatically that they are actually unaware of what they are saying. In particularly formal events such as funerals and wakes, where sentiments are not expected to be expressed in unusual ways, little active attention is paid to the content of one's remarks. Under these circumstances, mumbling and speaking under one's breath is more appropriate than speaking clearly and audibly.

Love hotel

The love hotels of Shibuya and other upmarket areas have been described by many writers – most of whom start their stories with the disclaimer 'I was stuck for accommodation, having missed my last train home, and had to resort to a love hotel for the night...' Well, I will attempt no such deception. I visited love hotels with Emi, Satomi and Akiko, and there was only ever one thought in our minds.

The out of town love hotels are less fantastic and more pragmatic than their fabulous big city cousins. People go to them to have sex. They do not need much help from the hotel designers to achieve this end, and little help is given. The bathroom is often glass-walled so that one can eye one's companion as they bathe or shower, presuming one isn't already in there doing this with them. The bed is usually large. In regional towns the love hotels cluster along the riverbanks, away from other buildings, but easily spotted by virtue of their neon and statuary. Only a pachinko parlour could be mistaken for a love hotel, and even that is not close. Country love hotels are just set back from the road among the rice fields, but identifiable by quietly suggestive names, such as 'Friend Hotel,' 'Delight Hotel.'

One drives into a garage and walks straight into one's room. In a moment the phone will ring and the duration and price of one's stay will be agreed. Moments later a knock at the door will indicate that it is time to open a little window and pass out the money. In some hotels they use the old pneumatic tube system to transfer money from room to office. Check-in time for an overnight stay is usually late: ten or eleven o'clock. Until then the room will be required for shorter visits, known as 'rests.' The compensating factor is that the check-out time is usually late too. The price for an overnight 'stay' runs from 5,000 to 8,000 yen, depending on the furnishings and equipment. If you can plan around the late check-in time, the price and availability of love hotel rooms is a good alternative to advance-booking hotel rooms, and certainly more entertaining.

Most rooms are equipped with television, offering both ordinary channels and a couple of sex channels that, even in these permissive surroundings, come with pixelated groins. This pixelation of genitalia even applies to the sex-anime movies with their gallons of gore and menageries of imaginary and well-endowed creatures. A karaoke machine is a common feature, sometimes too a pinball machine, mini-bar, and a couple of condoms ready on the pillow. A smell of cigarette smoke usually pervades. Quality varies, of course. A love hotel I visited near Izumo in Shimane, North Side Story Hotel, was reasonably tasteful. Its style could be described as self-conscious modern. A flight of pointless metallic grey concrete steps climbed one wall – to the ceiling. The love hotel Satomi and I visited in Shikoku was obviously once a barn, superficially and inexpensively converted. The bedroom suite was chipped and worn, full of plastic flowers and coin-operated gadgetry, and dominated by a giant box of a bed in red velvet and mirrors. Orgasms from next door were clearly audible.

The bathrooms are larger than the average Japanese affair. Two can sit in the bath without being squashed together like twin yokes, unless that is what they want. It is always fun to bathe together, especially after the forced separation of most *onsen* and *sento* bathing. I like to give myself a thorough soaping and scrubbing when I can, and if I have a willing companion I will ask her to scrub my back in exchange for anything she wants. Japanese girls are enthusiastic and compliant in intimate situations, and I imagine it is awfully easy to take this for granted. I make an effort not to, but sometimes with counter-productive results. A man who is perceived as spending too much time worrying about his partner's pleasure can be seen as lacking passion himself. Tread carefully.

Capsule hotel

I'd always wanted to try a capsule hotel. Having dinner with Satomi and three of her friends, Hanako, Shizuka and Miki, in Tokyo one evening I mention that I have made no accommodation arrangements, and ask if they know of a nearby capsule hotel. Satomi tells me there is one just around the corner from the restaurant, but asks if I am really sure I want to sleep in a capsule hotel. Other hotels are available. I say I really do want to see what it is like, and it turns out that the four girls are all curious too, so all five of us go to the hotel to see about booking in. Arriving with my entourage I make a memorable impression, but we soon get down to routine business.

I pay for my capsule by putting money in a machine and pressing the button marked *kapusuru*. I take my ticket to the desk where an attendant gives me a key on a plastic strap that attaches to my wrist. At this stage I have to bid a reluctant goodbye to the girls, who all wish me luck as they file out. The key opens a locker in the room next door. Inside are a towel, a hand-towel, toothpaste and brush, and a razor, plus a shortie *yukata*. I undress and put on the ridiculously inadequate *yukata* and take everything except my clothes, now in the locker, up to my capsule. Guests are not expected to have luggage when they stay at capsule hotels. So I will have to sleep beside my small backpack and my notebook computer.

At the third floor I get out of the elevator and look for my capsule. It is an upper bunk about one metre wide and two metres long. I can just fit inside, and with the backpack on my left and the computer on my right I can lie in near comfort as I watch television. I also have a light, an alarm clock radio and air conditioning. I'm all set. After flicking through the television channels a few times I decide to sleep, and do so, until about 5 AM.

Capsule hotels are often used by *sarariman* who have been out on the town and missed the last train home. Those who go straight back to the office the next day can probably get up later than usual, but those who want to go home first rise in time for the first train. The noise starts at five o'clock and lasts until about 8 AM. Then I go back to sleep for an hour, rising in time for a shower on my own, and a 10 AM check-out. I have so much time I could have indulged in the luxury of the *o-furo* bath. Apart from the early morning noise, the only drawback is the fear of fire. Captive in a small box, on the third floor of a small, tightly packed building, I worry about this. However, for only 3,000 yen, it is an experience I will gladly repeat. The staff ask me how well I slept, did I have enough room. Yes, it was fine, I enjoyed it, I tell them. They stamp my frequent visitor card and take pains to point out that after only fifteen nights at the hotel I'll qualify for a free night.

Christmas Eve and Christmas Day

Although Japan suffers the blight of Christmas muzak and gaudy decorations for just as long as any other place, when the day itself arrives that strange Japanese pattern of 'we're nearly there, we're nearly there, we're nowhere' reasserts itself. After over a month of preliminaries and expectation, Christmas day is indistinguishable from any other working day. All my Japanese friends, those who are not fortunate academics with much longer vacations than most people, are at work. They won't be giving each other presents, not as a rule anyway, and so a great retail opportunity goes begging. I suppose the Japanese department chains and other stores have tried to make Christmas the holy rite of consumption it is in most Christian places, but they must have failed. The people of Japan deserve a pat on the back for their powers of resistance.

But I am getting ahead of myself, because Christmas Eve came first.

Both Satomi and Akiko are already spoken for over the Christmas season, and Emi is in Kyoto. I want to use this opportunity to have a look at Tokyo nightclubs, so I plant myself in Roppongi. I find I can't set foot on the street without an American Negro sidling up to me and whispering the irresistible words 'Wanna see da best strip show in Tokyo?' or 'Wanna meet some sexy Japanese girls?' or 'Sexy massage.'

From my hotel window I have a good view of Tokyo tower, which is supposedly taller than the Eiffel tower. Having seen both I find this hard to believe. Perhaps it is the chunkiness of the tower in Tokyo that makes it look squat by comparison. The tower in Paris creates a delicate soaring effect that this one fails to achieve.

Tokyo is grey. Grey cars, grey buildings, grey clothes and grey sky. *Sarariman* uniforms are extended in view of the inclement weather to include grey trench coats. The press of bodies is one of the first things to strike foreigners coming to Asia, and I feel the need to adjust every time I come here. Apparently the first thing that strikes Asians when they venture to Caucasian shores is how fat everybody is. 'And they don't care!' they say. But I digress.

I start at the top when it comes to nightclubs. Just around the corner from my hotel is Velfarre – an awful set of consonants for the Japanese tongue. People have described this club to me as gorgeous, spectacular, enormous and extravagant. From road level I ascend a huge red-carpet staircase. The entrance fee tonight is 5,000 yen. This entitles me to descend in the lift back down to the level I started at. Stepping out of the lift I find a large dark room, high-ceilinged, tiered, with an gigantic mirror ball slowly revolving at its centre. Everything I see here I saw during my first forays into discos in the mid-1970s, so why is it so expensive? A singer called Anri is on stage and she is, I later learn, well-known. When I tell friends I spent part of Christmas Eve at an Anri concert, they say 'how romantic.' Indeed, the audience is made up predominantly of couples, most sitting quietly and watching the band. They can only be described as well-behaved. Anri is a pretty, confident girl, not brash or raunchy, not affected. She finishes with a tear-jerking version of 'Silent Night.'

The only other *gaijin* I see are two female employees both dressed as Santa Claus, whose function seems to be to create excitement by dancing and running around the club. My presence surprises a few people. One girl recoils from me as if I might contaminate her as I move past. After the show is over the two energetic *gaijin* females get up on stage and dance to KC and the Sunshine Band. One of them appears to be conducting a destruction test on a pair of white hotpants. Overall, the club is a disappointment, so I look for something else. The Gas Panic bar is not far away. I am sure it will be a little livelier than Velfarre.

Actually Gas Panic is not the dive I'd expected. Pairs of prim Japanese girls in cashmere cardigans sit at tables. Admittedly, two are squatting on the bar and revealing their underwear. The *gaijin* staff appear to have learnt their manners from the Japanese. They are all impeccably polite. It is really still too early to be here (only 11:30 PM). KC and the Sunshine Band blast out of the speakers. This time it is the original song. In Velfarre it had been a sampled and remixed version.

I am not interested in staying here either. Both clubs have unexceptional music, dress, décor, behaviour; nothing I haven't seen before. Whereas Velfarre's look is seventies disco, Gas Panic's is seventies punk. I've run out of enthusiasm for this evening, so I drop into Starbucks for a caffe latte. Upstairs I find a big armchair by the window and look out onto the street. Beside me a girl is alone but asleep in her armchair. Across the room another is doing her knitting. Christmas in Tokyo is really rocking. I can't wait for New Year.

I walk back to the hotel. At 1:30 AM I peer out of the window to see if it is worth going out again, but the streets look quiet. I realise it is Christmas day now, and fall asleep.

Later on Christmas morning, I go for a long walk around the city – to see what happens to normal people today. Nothing much, though at Takeshitadori I see a girl with long fire engine red hair wearing a *kimono*, looking like a cross-dressing underage *kabuki* dancer.

After dinner I go looking for another famous club, Yellow. I set off through Roppongi. Tokyo's finest women appear to be out tonight, and this drives my search, but all I find is many interesting and intimate little bars dotted around the Nishi-Azubu district – good for taking a girl to, not so good for taking a girl from. After crossing my tracks several times I realise I'm getting less interested in forking out 4,000 yen to listen to house and techno, so I trudge back, running the tout gauntlet once more, to my hotel.

New Year's Eve

Far too much has already been said about whether one moment or another actually constitutes the start of a new millennium. I will add no more other than to say that any event about which no one is quite sure when it occurs cannot be much of an event at all. Anyway, by popular decree, it seems tonight, 31 December, 1999, is the night.

I decided some time ago to be at Meiji-jingu for the New Year. I've grown tired of the sameness of this so-called event in Sydney and, put off by the more than usual degree of hype this year, wanted to be somewhere completely different.

For most of New Year's Eve however, I have no plans. I start the day by going for a short walk to Sengaku-ji shrine. All the graves are smoking with incense and a constant stream of families arrive on foot, by bicycle, and in chauffeur-driven cars to pay their respects and pray for a good year ahead. A sense of silent purpose hangs in the air along with the smoke. A few cans of water have been placed against the wall in case the fire gets out of control.

Inside the shrine museum the relics of the forty-seven *ronin* are blackened with age, but still inspire a certain awe. I imagine the *ronin* must have been a fearsome nocturnal apparition in their winged helmets and suits of armour.

Instead of going back to the hotel I continue to walk through the streets. They are all quiet. The sky is overcast. The day has a subdued and paradoxical 'day after' feel to it. I wander for miles through the Tokyo suburbs, past graveyards, apartment buildings, clothing boutiques, roadside shrines, all seemingly marking time just like me. Hours later I find Shibuya. There are now three giant outdoor screens here, and today one of them is showing scenes of… Shibuya. It even shows pictures of itself, but the temptation to incur infinite recursion is resisted. A camera crew, whose fellows must haunt this area on a full-time posting, is interviewing a pair of *ko-gyaru*. The cameraman is leaning left and right to ensure that necessary trendy *cinema verite* edginess. Photographers abound today. They appear at times to be taking pictures of each other, though this may be just an accidental side-effect of their local population density.

In contrast to the momentous nature of the day, nothing is out of the ordinary. Except, perhaps, things are quieter than normal. Many regular Shibuya shoppers will already be home with their parents in the provinces and prefectures, visiting their family shrines, or getting ready to do so. Heartful Town Shibuya is receiving the new millennium coolly. A few illuminated hearts hang here and there, and perhaps there are a few extra lanterns hanging over the subway stairs.

It is four o'clock in the afternoon; eight hours to go. I watch the inactivity from upstairs in Starbucks Coffee, then drift up to Tokyu Hands to look around. I'm delighted to see a miniature alarm clock that fits inside the ear, a portable bidet unit, a small tripod that can add a self-timer function to disposable cameras. I eat a pizza and salad at Charleston & Co, killing time.

I have another coffee. The café staff slur their 'thank you's' so they sound like *agzaimashta*. I realise I've run out of things to do, so I walk over to Meiji-jingu to see if anything is happening yet. At Yoyogi Stadium a huge crowd of teenage girls is gathering for a concert this evening. Many of them are wearing black and red vinyl, and a few are sporting explosive flaming red hairstyles, or wigs. I fail to find out why.

Three hours to go. Inside the shrine gardens there are hundreds of large lanterns where once there was a row of stalls displaying chrysanthemums. For reasons I cannot see, a giant screen and piped music complement the scene.

Hundreds of people are slowly walking towards the shrine, which is out of sight still, deeper in the park. There are parties of schoolgirls in uniform. *Ko-gyaru* scream at having to walk over the gently sloping bridges in their platform boots. I wonder how Louis Vuitton bags and Burberry scarves can retain any sort of cachet when every woman has them. Obviously the desire to possess them is not so that one appears exclusively rich, but to ensure that one does not appear exclusively poor. Squads of gloved police walk around with batons, loud hailers, and illuminated standards. A phalanx of scouts shuffles into position. Several people carry or wheel small Razor or Micro scooters, but I never see anyone riding one.

Inside the final courtyard I take my position off to the right, so I can watch the crowd as well as whatever is going to happen at the front. Already a few thousand people wait in the dark and cold. A dozen shrine attendants are wheeling around a giant *taiko* drum, as big as a truck, inside the building. The *taiko* is moved back and forth amid much gesticulation. It is so big it travels on its own cart. The drum skins must be about two metres across – I wonder what they were cut from, whales?

The piped music is so far away it cannot be heard here, so we all just stand and patiently wait in silence. There is no entertainment, nothing in fact, except a few police announcements. Now and again people throw coins forward. They sometimes fall inside the shrine enclosure, but more often flutter off course and hit someone standing closer to the front. No one seems to mind. The police practise a manoeuvre, holding aloft banners illustrated with cartoon characters. The manoeuvre completed, they marshal themselves to one side, inside a square of yellow tape. I am tempted to go away and come back later, but the fear that I might miss something keeps me where I am. It is so cold that I stand as still as possible, so no freezing air can slip inside my clothes. The crowd continues to grow.

Two hours to go. Inside the shrine dozens of attendants dressed in white begin to assemble beside the drum. This is it, I think. But then the attendants all walk away again.

A tall Dutch couple arrive and push through the crowd to the front and centre. It doesn't take long before an errant coin bounces off the Dutchman's head. Ping! He turns around angrily and demands to know who threw it. Everyone looks back at him blankly. When it happens a second time the indignant couple move away, still apparently under the misapprehension that they have been victimised.

Thirty minutes to go, and something happens: VIPs are shown to their places inside the shrine. It is now I notice that the steps and columns of the shrine are all encased in plastic, to protect them, presumably, from the coin storm. Cameramen scramble on the roof. One loses his footing and slides down the shingles. He is just about to tip over the edge and fall to the ground when he manages to catch hold of a ladder. That rates as an incident that almost happened.

Mobile phones are consulted regularly. The earth resonates as *kogyaru* clump past in their heavy footwear. The time is getting close now.

One minute to go and a young group behind me start a count-down: *roku-ju, go-ju kyu, go-ju hachi, go-ju shichi...*

A few crackers are let off. I can hear singing. *Now things are really starting to happen,* I think. The count-down comes to its climax: *san, ni, ichi!* The crowd manages a big cheer, thousands of coins thrown from further back rain down on us, a fluttering silver snowstorm, and a priest thumps the *taiko* with a heavy stick. Boom.

At the same moment, after standing for three hours in the cold and dark, everyone at the front runs, literally *runs*, away. The millennial moment arrives and departs all in the same instant, and now, apparently, it is over and people are keen to go. At the moment I had expected things to begin, it turns out they had just finished. I am astonished, dumbfounded, in fact. I stand aside and watch as human waves surge forward, and coins fall in a tinkling deluge (I realise why the police are wearing plastic face-guards). People moving up from the back press on and disappear off to the side – in a great rip-tide of citizenry. The police channel the flow with hand-held barriers, and the priest keeps beating the drum, boom, boom, to an ever-increasing cadence. I'm eager for something else to happen, but the millennial event, such as it was, has already passed.

A familiar idea starts to form. *Of course,* I think. What more appropriate way to treat an arbitrary second in an arbitrary timeframe? The sheer uneventfulness of the moment has made it, paradoxically, quite an event, at least for me. Later, when friends and I discuss what we each did on the millennial New Year's Eve, my story is the strangest and most memorable. Everyone else just saw fireworks and tasted alcohol to a greater or lesser degree.

A moment realised is a moment already gone. Tonight, a nihilistic culmination of 1,000 years. At a deeper level the way it turns out also seems essentially Japanese. A long and uneventful preparation endured, a sense of moving closer to the heart of things and finally, at the threshold and the moment of realisation, the revelation that at the very core there is... nothing. Let's all go home! It is like the central emptiness of Shinto shrines, particularly those at Ise and Atsuta which are supposed to house objects that no one has ever seen, or the void at the heart of Zen, or the space between the rocks in Japanese gardens, or the absence of the first person in Japanese language and thinking. The more I think about it, the more perfect it seems.

I follow the crowd away from the shrine. Two girls rush up to me and shout 'Hallo! Happy New Year!' It seems so, now, because an orgy of consumption is in progress (I knew that Christmas abstemiousness couldn't last). The path I follow is lined by stalls and it is here the hunger and cold that has been eating away at us is now banished by hotdogs, roasted rice balls, hot cocoa and warm *sake*. People are also buying up great numbers of charms and fortunes from the shrine shops. Everything is being pursued with a vigour at odds with the inactivity of the last three hours. I join in and come away with a full belly and a 'disease recovery' charm. The charm is probably unnecessary, but we can never be too sure about these things.

I make it out of the park at about 1:30 AM, and see the in-going crowd still slowly shuffling forward. Three million people will pass through here in the next three days.

I note that all the lights of the city are still shining, my phone still works, that the trains are running, that shops remain unlooted, and the sky is still in place. So what happened to the Y2K bug? It hit us and we didn't even blink. Later in the day the newscasters tell us the big Y2K story is that suddenly... nothing happened. They could have been talking about my evening. Many people on television seem genuinely upset that we have been deprived of all the anticipated disaster stories. It's so disappointing for the media and their advertisers.

Sento time

I pick up with Emi again later in the new year. We take another quick trip into the mountains – this time around the prefecture of Nagano, home of the 1998 Winter Olympics.

Mixed bathing is allowed at one of the *ryokan* we visit, so we sit in the pool in the garden and talk. Emi's world sometimes seems to me like a landscape of sensual impressions. She can talk for hours about how things look, how they sound, how they feel. I love listening to her when she rambles like this, I find it hypnotic. It is an aural massage.

This town features a circuit of nine public baths, all with different healing properties. Our next stop is one of the nine. It is situated under a small shrine. Emi wonders what kind of shrine it is, and I suggest it is a fertility shrine. She confirms this by reading the script, but wonders how I knew. Well, first, I say, here's a wooden statue of a man and woman, both dressed in such a way that they look like large phalli. The man's arm is also remarkably straight and stiff, and angles across the woman's body to her nippled breast, which forms a glans to the arm's shaft. She holds the arm in both her hands. The overall impression is strongly sexual. The script says the carving echoes a *ukiyo-e* by Hokusai. Later, inside the inn, we find the print in question. The man's face is a large wrinkled penis, and the woman's face is blank except for a long vertical cleft, complete with pouting labia. Also in the inn we see a small statue of a man with one hand clapped to the back of his head and the other firmly grasping his erect penis, and beside this, a ceramic phallus.

In the bath I wash using a small wooden bowl and then descend into the water. A Japanese businessman comes in later and strikes up a conversation until Emi calls me from over the wall dividing the men's half of the bath from the women's. We meet outside and head for the next bath. We are dressed in only our *yukata* and *geta*. I notice that Emi's hair is dry. She tells me a sign outside asks people not to wet their hair in the baths.

Bath number one is meant to cure stomach and intestinal problems, number two is for rashes and dermatological diseases, number three is where we go if we have open wounds. These are not the most plausible marketing concepts, really. The idea of sitting in the bath with someone who has diarrhoea, eczema, and sores doesn't interest me much. God knows what the other six baths will do for us.

In the next bath the water is simply too hot for me, and Emi has finished her bath before I have fully immersed myself. I quit and meet her outside for the short walk to bath number three. Here I sit in the water as three Japanese guys come in. They laugh at each other's jokes and shriek at the heat of the water. '*Atsui!*' the first one shouts. '*hai, chotto, chotto atsui,*' I say. They laugh that a *gaijin* sits comfortably in water that they find too hot. After adding a little cold water from the tap, they all climb in and the four of us sit close together. They try to chat to me, but give up when I reveal my understanding of Japanese to be a little rudimentary. I excuse myself and get out. They all start shouting good-naturedly as I make waves that send more hot water their way.

These public baths are not what I expected. I had in mind something like the classical paintings of luxurious Turkish affairs. The public *sento* are all tiny – able to hold only three to five people at a time. The surroundings are aged, sodden timbers, plain concrete walls. The water is grey. They are working people's baths, not those of the well heeled and leisurely, and are quite different from *onsen*.

Feeling hot and dehydrated, Emi and I head back to the inn and raid the vending machines once more. I spend a little time reading and writing before lying down to rest. Emi and I cuddle comfortably, her knees resting on my hip, her feet nestled behind my knees, our faces close together, our heads on bean-filled *makura*. Her unruly hair spreads over both our faces, and lifts a little each time I speak. It tickles my nose. Too languid to move my arm, I try to overcome the feeling by mental dissociation.

Word games

Puns are common in Japanese poetry, so I ask Emi if the Japanese like word games. I have in mind not just puns but anagrams, palindromes and other linguistic peculiarities. She nods and asks if I would like an example.

Emi suggests we play a game she calls 'new word on the end of old word.' One of us will think of a word, such as *moku* and the other has to think of a word that starts the way the preceding word ends, such as, in this case, *kura*. This could be followed by *rakugo, gomi, miya,* etc. Once used, words cannot be reused.

Emi leads the way with *neko*. I follow with *koban*. 'errrrr.' Emi makes a guttural sound like a game-show warning buzzer. 'That is not...', she pauses while she searches for the least offensive way to tell me I have done something wrong, '… not so perfect. You cannot start a word with *n*, Maaku. So you have made the game… impossible.' Of course. To a native Japanese speaker the terminal *n*, having no trailing vowel, is unrelated to the 'n' of *na, ni, nu, ne, no*.

We play the game for a while. Emi praises my every contribution. Then I ask whether Japanese has a tradition of playing with amphisbaenic words, ones that turned backwards make other words, such as *stressed* and *desserts*. Emi offers *kiku* and *kuki*, a fine pair, as it happens, but I almost demur before I again catch myself. Emi is reversing the words according to their *kana*, which are usually consonant-vowel pairings (*n* being the single exception). To her ears the words are made up of two atomic components, *ku* and *ki*. To my ears there are four: two *k*'s, one *u* and an *i*. Emi is thinking in *hiragana*, I am thinking in *romaji* (Roman) letters. It is then that I realise many word games are really visual rather than auditory.

We try to find a *kanji* compound that can be reversed, and discover a good one: *nihon*, made up of the *kanji* for 'sun' and 'origin' and meaning 'Japan,' and *honjitsu*, with the *kanji* for 'origin' and 'sun' and meaning 'today.' This is an example of how, in *kanji* script, the separation of the look and sound of a word can be quite drastic. I joke that there ought to be a newspaper called *Nihon Honjitsu*. Emi points out that *akuma*, meaning 'devil,' when reversed gives *maaku*, my name as pronounced in Japan. She says this shows that I am a devil; I say that it shows I am the opposite. She says that's just what a devil would say, and is then spooked when I point out that 'devil' is 'lived' backwards. Next we find *chuushin*, meaning 'centre,' and *shinjuu*, 'lovers' suicide.'

'So romantic,' sighs Emi, with a faraway look in her eyes.

Computer game

There are two interesting emails in my inbox. One of them is from the editor of MagA, an online magazine for *otaku*, who would like me to review a computer game. *Otaku* are technophiles who learn everything possible about the computer or machinery they own, and eventually identify themselves through it, forming user groups, constantly reading and discussing the niche literature with the similarly afflicted. The modern phenomenon of the *otaku*, ultra-geeks, is found all over

Asia. *Otaku* is one of the most formal forms for addressing the second person in polite Japanese; perhaps indicating the great distance *otaku* feel separates them and other people.

I presume the magazine got my name from Graham Mann or another colleague. Reading on, I discover that my eclectic mix of qualifications in fine art, cognitive science, and AI, and my experience in marketing, game interface theory, and smattering of Japanese have earned me the job.

In answer to MagA's request for a mailing address I give them Emi's. Only a couple of days later she calls me to ask if I am expecting a parcel. I let her open it and she tells me there are t-shirts, tickets to events and conventions, and a few CDs inside. She is animated and surprisingly excited by this development, and wants to know if she can install the CDs on her own computer. I don't see why not. I tell her she can have the t-shirts, too, as I only wear plain ones.

Game words

The other email is from tyger:

> evening leo,
>
> your beautiful postcard arrived yesterday. i'd just come in, arms shopping-laden, and went all shaky-excited when i saw from whom it came. the message, however, actually ruffled the legendary millpond that is my constitution. how did this agitation manifest itself? i wrinkled my brow in a small frown and told myself that i was upset. early this morning, our sysadmin (whose name you may remember, mr praeterpluperfect autoclave) and i restored my cyber-defences, and so on and so forth. a deserved, yet surprisingly mild, admonishment from the aforementioned mr pa followed, during which i stood with hands clasped before me, head meekly bowed and bottom lip aquiver. i'm so glad you discovered this pollution of the citadel. tiger 'phoned me today to ask why he couldn't log in, and i challenged

him over the matter. he pled guilty. he thinks it
was harmless, but it was far from that. sigh...
    sigh...
    sigh...
    but to other, infinitely more pleasing
matters. i feel even more strongly the need to
lay my reddened eyes upon my lionised leo de
leeuw. please tell me, dear leo, if i should not
appear at kansai airport (i'm told that's the one
for kyoto) at 5:40 pm on the monday after next,
aboard a shiny ba jet from heathrow. a possibly
disoriented and probably dishevelled tyger will
wobble off the aeroplane in great need of a
leonine hug and a virtually familiar face to kiss.
    ever your devoted admirer,
    lots of love and neatly knitted mittens,
    tyger the faustian postulator

In my reply I remind her, unnecessarily, to change all her pass-
words into talkers and other Internet services, and agree to meet her
at the airport when she arrives. I mentally assemble an itinerary for
us, starting with a tour of historic Kansai and moving to Tokyo later,
if time permits.

Jade cowboys

Emi and I pull into a car park outside the *Arumadiro* club. The neon
signs are lit but the silence is deathly. As we approach the door I take
a second look at the logo and suddenly the name of the club makes
sense to me: Armadillo. The interior is hot and cramped, and the band
is already playing. We order tequilas and nachos at the bar then cause
a seismic upheaval as we try to find a place to sit – half the people in
the club think it is necessary to shift about to make an enormous
space for us. Everyone is smiling and nodding at me, I feel that something I don't fully understand is being acknowledged.

Emi fishes around in her bag and gives me the package from
MagA. She tells me that the game has been confusing to play. She
doesn't know what she is meant to do, and hasn't found anything of

great interest in the scenario. She mentions that her phone has been receiving game-related messages that make no sense to her, and she has been receiving similar confusing emails. She thinks I have been up to something.

'But I haven't even seen it yet. How could it be me?'

'But these messages know many things about me. How is that?'

I shrug. 'I'll have a look at it,' I offer.

The guys on stage are tight and controlled. They wear the full country regalia: shoestring ties, blue jeans, oversize belt buckles, snakeskin boots, and Stetsons. Their equipment is all shiny and top quality: Gibson, Fender, Pearl, and Kawai. The lyrics are curiously accented, but comprehensible nevertheless. They play country standards. They are *Team Nashville.*

The drummer is a dentist, the singer is a mathematical linguist, Emi tells me. Their sheet music is laid out on music stands. They are all Japanese, of course. They are playing, having fun. They are playing, music. They are playing, at being musical cowboys. They are playing, in their own way, with our boundaries of identity.

I amuse and embarrass Emi with a few loud *yeeehaaa*'s and *arriba*'s when it is time to applaud. She stamps her little fist on my leg to make me stop, and lets it rest there.

During the intermission the band descends on me.

'Hello. My name is Masa. Are you American?' one of them asks.

'No, Australian,' I reply, and their disappointment is obvious and immediate.

'Ah, Australia very nice place.'

'Thank you. Yes, we have quite *a big country music scene* in Australia. Many *Americans* come over to enjoy our *country music festivals.*' My emphasis is a pathetic attempt to curry favour.

'Oh, really?' Now they are genuinely interested. The Australian country music scene is completely new to them. And so over the next half minute I tell them all I know about it.

'Do you like country music?' they ask. The killer question. I dare not lie and say yes, because the inevitable follow-up questions will have me tangled in the web of supporting lies I'll be forced to weave. I cannot say no, for reasons of politeness. I handle the dilemma in the proper Japanese way. I put my head to the side, suck my breath through my teeth and nod slightly.

'A little,' I say. They are able to accept this. 'I liked your act,' I add, truthfully.

'Oh, really?'

'Yes. Very professional.' They beam at me, but deny it.

'Please come and sing with us.'

'Oh, I cannot do that,' I say. As if they are offering me too high an honour. They offer once more and I decline. They excuse themselves and walk around the tables, chatting to their friends.

Another guest comes up to me.

'American?'

'Australian.'

'Ah.' He walks away.

Before the band resumes, their roadie gets up at the mic and cracks a few jokes. He sits in on a few songs, on *buruu gurasu baiorin* (blue grass violin).

Before the next set finishes, we leave. The doorman looks at me and asks 'American?'

'Australian,' I apologise.

Kan

There is a *kanji* whose meaning can be 'wickedness,' 'mischief,' or 'seduce.' It is *kan*, and it is made by writing the symbol for woman three times.

I know I am performing a doomed juggling act by sleeping with Satomi, Akiko and Emi. Something happened in the first couple of weeks in Japan, when all three of them literally took me to their bosoms. I must have been aglow with an exotic but short-lived sex-appeal. Since then, I haven't had the same effect on women. I don't know what changed, but I suspect that I may no longer have some special air about me: engaged, in wonder, enchanted by everything I saw. It was the same when I first visited the United States, two weeks of being invited to join women at their tables, being picked up on the sidewalk, and then nothing, as if I had so blended into the background that I had disappeared.

What concerns me is the fragile nature of my relationships with all three women. Satomi doesn't really care, Akiko on her own would not be enough, and Emi is unpredictable. I fear the present feast could soon turn to famine and wonder if I should make a commitment of monogamy to Emi, who has clearly emerged as the one who makes me happiest. My greed appals me, but I nevertheless applaud my lack of restraint.

Into this conundrum comes a great complication, one I fear will not leave my relationship with Emi unscarred: tyger's decision to come to Japan.

Another tyger-gram is waiting in Hotmail for me, and one part in particular strikes me:

    'let's finally consummate this cyber-dalliance.

    let's do the physical thing.'

Of course, it could all be word-play, it could just be referring to the extra intimacy of being in the same place, but I will soon find out. She expects me to meet her at Kansai airport in two days, and tomorrow I have arranged to meet Emi again.

The night of the torii

Back in Otsu, it is late afternoon, and the day has been unseasonably balmy. Emi bathes and I take a shower. In clean clothes and fully re-freshed, I expect us to sit and drink beer, as usual, but Emi lays on a little surprise for me. She grabs a plastic carrier bag and calls me out to the car. We travel up the west coast of Lake Biwa, which lies like a sheet of viscous oil under a low evening mist.

Somewhere along the shore, where the road runs right beside the water, we stop, and I see a large red *torii* out in the lake, looking much like the famous one at Miyajima. Evening has closed in and a few of the lights on the opposite shore are twinkling. It was here on the shores of Lake Biwa that Murasaki Shikibu wrote *The Tale of Genji*.

Emi takes the bag down to the water's edge and opens it. She's brought champagne, *sushi*, cheese, salad, savoury biscuits and Japan-ese pickles. We sit in the aqueous calm and sip the wine from delicate flutes. I take off my shoes and touch my toes into the water lapping in lazy slow motion on the shingle. Emi fondles me affectionately, and tells me about the ten-thousand *kami* that come through the *torii* every evening, wondering if we will see them.

The air is humid now, and our skins are moist. Emi's wet kisses taste of sweet pickles. Every few minutes a truck thunders past just behind us, unnoticed. Emi's eyes, so feline, are tonight huge and bottomless. I feel affection swelling up like a hard balloon inside me. When it bursts it drives a liquid warmth right down to my fingertips and toes. I'm left on an emotional high, unable to bear the idea of being separated from her. It is a romantic master stroke, timed to perfection, and probably driven by forces even she is unaware of.

Kansai airport

I catch the *shinkansen* out to Kansai airport, dulled by reluctance, not really sure if I want to see tyger just at this time. Last night has pretty well sealed things for me, and Emi is the only thing on my mind. I wander around the terminal, waiting for the plane to land. Its time arrives. I stand waiting for an hour, much more, but no tyger emerges. I pass the minutes by calling and engaging in small talk with Satomi, Akiko and Miho. I can't call Emi in case she wants to know what I am doing and when she can see me again. I make enquiries and am told that all the passengers on the flight from Heathrow have passed through customs. So tyger has stood me up. Oh, lucky man.

I log on to send tyger an email of equal parts reprimand and concern, but she has beaten me to it. She just bottled out, she says. A thousand abject apologies, she hopes the email gets to me in time. It would have, had I logged on last night, the night of the *torii* at Lake Biwa.

No Longer Human

China to Japan, laotai to gaijin

FLYING BACK INTO JAPAN after a brief working excursion to South China I expect to be struck by all the cliché contrasts: China chaotic, dirty, raw, mercenary, and brusque; Japan orderly, clean, refined, aesthetic, and courteous. Admittedly, I'd formed these impressions on little evidence, but it is stark evidence nevertheless. One night while walking a poorly lit city pavement in Xiamen, in China's Fujian province, I almost tumbled into an unmarked pit, about two metres deep and a metre in diameter. This recalled to mind an incident I'd experienced in Kyoto last winter, where a shallow depression about ten centimetres deep and fifty centimetres wide was protected by not only a black and yellow striped barricade but also a uniformed road worker who, with an illuminated baton, waved pedestrians in a small detour around the hole in absolute safety. I had once scoured the shops in Xiamen looking for a calligraphy set, but couldn't find one of merely adequate quality. In Japan, I had the same difficulty finding a bad one. These contrasts typified for me the differences between China and Japan, two countries so at odds I can hardly believe that as a young child I thought of them as just about one and the same.

Strangely, it is this childish misconception that is truer today. I board a plane in Xiamen, thinking I am the only *laotai* in a plane full of Chinese. Then, incrementally, I realise that one, then another, of my co-passengers is actually Japanese. This one reads a Japanese newspaper, that one chats with the flight attendant in fluent Japanese. The seamless racial transformation is complete as we descend into Kansai airport. I find I am now the only *gaijin* in a plane full of Japanese.

I take the *shinkansen* directly to Kyoto for a few days peace after the tension of work in Xiamen.

People not of this world

There was a time when Japan, having had a glimpse of the rest of the world, decided to have nothing more to do with it.

Richard Storry, in *A History of Modern Japan*, relates how a deputation from Portuguese Macau left for Japan in 1640. Their objective was to beg the Shogun for a resumption of trade between Japan and Portugal. This was soon after the beginning of Japan's 268-year-long self-imposed withdrawal from the outside world, an atypical exercise in resistance to change that resulted not so much in purity but in seizure, of the joints, and eventually by western trade interests. However, upon arrival at Nagasaki, the entire Portuguese deputation was beheaded, as were most of the crew of the ship that carried them. A skeleton crew was spared only so that it could bring back the most chilling of messages: 'let the people of Macao think no more of us; as if we were no longer in the world.'

To people of many other nationalities, the Japanese really are seen as if they are not of this world. Many Australians carry a confused image of alien extremes: orchidaceous *geisha* in *kimono* and sadistic sword-wielding soldier-fanatics, or robotic production line workers and brain-washed children. To counter this one might offer images of winter skiers, music lovers, parent-teacher associations, football fans, local mayoral candidates, bus drivers, and all the other familiar human pictures that really do illustrate Japan.

If not human, then what?

There was never a time when we were entirely sure about who or what we were dealing with in Japan.

I cannot imagine the shock to both parties when Europeans first discovered the advanced cultures of Japan and other Far Eastern countries. Until that encounter, the European assumption of superiority had had a relatively unruffled ride.

In early European colonial ontology there was a column of righteousness, the Great Chain of Being, headed by God and the nine orders of angels, closely supported by the decent Englishman, or dwellers of Christendom, and featuring, lower down, the natives of other parts of the world, and still further below them, the beasts. This stratification had remained intact through all contacts with Africa, the Americas, and the East Indies. In all cases, the technology and societies encountered by European explorers appeared less advanced than their own. Whatever particular advantages other cultures might have had, whatever fields in which they could demonstrate further development than that of Europe, were easily dismissed. And the beneficent spread of European civilisation and piety fitted perfectly as a rationalisation for the plunder and bloodshed that was intrinsic to most European colonisation.

But Japan presented a terrifying challenge to that set of Eurocentric assumptions and threw the happy world-view into disarray.

The Japanese, in European eyes, were not of the same lower echelon of other societies that had already been subjugated around the world. Here in Japan were complex cultures that were highly organised politically, militarily, and socially. Here were inventions that the west had never seen. There were arts and crafts so diverse and outstanding in their refinement they certainly rivalled and perhaps even overshadowed those of Europe. There were huge populations living in the world's largest cities supported by vast agricultural systems, there were powerful and elaborate religions, extensive histories, there was great wealth, great self-assurance, and great knowledge. And to top it all off there was the cleanliness, symbolically linked in European thinking to being *without sin.*

But the Japanese were also so unlike the European ideal of civilisation. Practices such as infanticide, mixed public bathing, public nakedness, sleeping and eating on the floor, frequent savagery, and decidedly non-puritanical attitudes towards defecation, promiscuity, homosexuality and other taboos of European society made the Japanese seem alien in the extreme. As Ian Littlewood says in *The Idea of Japan,* when civilised people start doing these things, we have to start revising our definition of civilisation.

The Japanese were clearly civilised, but they were just as clearly not one with Europe. So what does that make us? That was the shocking question that confronted Europeans for the first time. The Japanese could not be placed above, below, or even at the same level as Europeans in the Great Chain of Being. What Japan demonstrated, of course, was that the accepted columnar ontology of the Great Chain of Being was a nonsense, and this was disconcerting in the extreme. It seems that the European response was to place the Japanese in a vague parallel category all by themselves – neither man nor beast.

Ten thousand schoolgirls

Outside the Higashi-Hongen-ji temple I am surrounded, seized and interrogated by 10,000 Japanese schoolgirls. Their war-cries of 'Hi' and 'Hello' capture my attention, and by then it is too late. The blue wall surges towards me and I am engulfed. The girls extract from me the information that I'm called Mark, I'm from Australia, I'm 1.9 metres tall, and I'm going into the temple. 'We too!' they chorus delightedly. They also tell me they like playing soccer, that I come from the same country as koalas and kangaroos, and that I may join their party.

This is just the softening-up process before the serious interrogation begins. The two most precocious ones tell me their names and grab my arms. They call their English teacher over to display their live trophy. The bemused teacher says 'How do you do?' I nod and say 'Good afternoon' to him. They call another teacher over. She asks if she can help me and I say 'No thank you. They're just being friendly.' She rounds on the girls and reprimands them in Japanese. As soon as her back is turned they all make devil horn gestures at her and I can't help laughing aloud. The girls try to explain parts of the temple to me, but their English is not really up to it. We drift apart in the temple grounds. Later I see them all, literally hundreds of them, sitting in rows inside the temple, heads bowed, silently praying.

In the street a television crew is trying to lift the skirt of another schoolgirl. She won't let them, but neither does she move away. A small crowd of the curious gathers to witness her dilemma. I pause briefly, but see little of interest.

I have dinner with a couple of Japanese scientists, after a day of presentations and discussions on robots and machine vision. The talk adheres to the informal. I tell Kazuo and Akio I have some questions about the schoolgirls I see everywhere in Japan. Why is it that their uniforms look designed purely for sexiness? Why are there so many on public transport in the middle of the day when they should be at school, and why are so many in school uniform at the weekends? Kazuo chuckles and says he would also like to know the answer to these questions.

Kazuo tells me that schoolgirls in Japan are responsible for many new words and phrases, and fashions. I've no doubt they form a significant market. They all have miniature pastel coloured mobile phones, with dangling ornaments attached, many of them wear Burberry scarves, and many of them have access to too much make-up. White mascara is considerably more popular than it should be.

Schoolgirls also seem to have an inordinate curiosity about western men. I get many long open stares from them; they look deep into my face. They call to me across streets and overreact to any response I make.

Geisha glimpses

For dinner I walk to the Pontocho area and pick a noisy, busy restaurant beside the small river. After an eclectic meal of both Japanese and western food I walk to Gion to look for *maiko-san* (apprentice *geisha*). Why I do this is not that I have any particular interest in *geisha per se*, but a few people have mentioned that it is a rare occasion to see one these days. The young *maiko-san* wear more elaborate costumes than the older *geisha*, and are therefore considered more exotic.

I have been advised to find the smallest and darkest streets in Gion, and to just walk around and wait. If I'm lucky, I'm told, I might see one or two. The *geisha* avoid the lights and crowds, and try to move as discreetly as possible from one engagement to another. The engagements are private affairs, and apparently few westerners are ever privileged to take part. After only five minutes a *maiko-san* and an older *geisha* emerge from a doorway and walk away ahead of me. The daintiness of their steps means I soon catch up with them, just as they stoop to enter the low doorway of another house.

Their make-up, coiffure and clothing are immaculate, and of an extraordinarily high quality. As the *maiko-san* bends at the doorway I see that the white powder that covers her face continues far down her back and out of sight below the *kimono*.

A couple of minutes later two more *geisha* hasten from a doorway, intricate hair ornaments atremble and paper umbrellas aloft, and slip into a taxi. I feel I've seen enough for now, and head back into town with a sense of mission accomplished.

The experience of seeing these nameless celebrities is strangely hypnotic. The women are delicately beautiful in costume, but not necessarily in our conventional sense. The kind of beauty created by *geisha* is unrelated to the natural physical loveliness of the face or body, though obviously these characteristics can contribute to it. It is an utterly unworldly look of high artifice that uses a human body as a kind of armature.

Despite having made a little pact with myself not to buy any books while travelling (they weigh too much, and if they are around I tend to *read* rather than *do*) I head for the Maruzen bookstore on Kawara-machi-dori and buy *Memoirs of a Geisha* by Arthur Golden. It is highly praised as a recreation of the last great days of the *geisha*, which it may be, but I enjoy it for the simple fact that it deals with places I've been wandering through this week.

Hello, my paramour

hello, my paramour of the south,

i'm feeling significantly better now, if slightly snivelly. i had a good weekend... went out on friday night to spread my cold around, heard lots of really good music, remembered to take it easy on the pharmaceuticals front. then drove back to oxfordshire in the early hours of saturday morning. my health actually improved over the night. i have noticed this phenomemumenomenun before, but cannot explain it. later on saturday i went to my parents' house for a few hours, having still not slept. it went very well, funnily enough.

so you had a haircut, eh? what is the world coming to? a drastic one so your friends don't recognise you, or just a trim to keep your mane out of your eyes? as coincidence would have it (for it would be foolish to assign any more importance to it), i too have an appointment to get my mane managed. although not to get it cut. having been an orange and white stripy tyger for about two years now, i think it's about time to challenge peoples' perceptions of what exactly a tyger should look like. i am going to investigate some more possibilities on the dulux colour chart, and have a whole bunch of hairdressers running round with pots of noxious chemicals, making me cups of coffee and supplying me with magazines. cleopatra eat yer heart out. actually they love me at my hairdressers... situated as it is on the outskirts of a market town in the heart of true-blue tory land, they do a roaring trade in 'manageable perms' and 'blue rinses' on elderly wispy haired ladies. on the other hand, i have a large amount of very thick hair, and can be talked into doing remarkably stupid things to it. i am a boredom relief facility for jaded hairdressers. perhaps that's my vocation in life.

quite a scary incident this morning. remember i said a few days ago about having to have mri scans and e.e.gs to establish whether i'm schizophrenic or have something physiologically wrong with me, such as epilepsy? and part of the symptoms that might lead one to conclude that i've gone froot-loopy is various sensory hallucinations? well, normally these manifest themselves as people talking in the background, birdsong, thinking i'm holding pieces of string and pens, smelling chlorine and hay and stuff. like, peculiar, but not too distressing. with me so far? now, i'm a very light sleeper, and this morning i woke up hearing a mechanical voice repeat over and over "watch the gap", but

slightly muffled, as if it was coming from a
neighbouring bedroom. in the london underground
they tell you to 'mind the gap' in a very similar
way. and i got up to look for this noise... i was
in the living room before i realised that nothing
in the house was actually making that noise. now
that was quite distressing. doesn't really put
you in the right frame of mind for a day of work,
either. i try not to let these things get to
me... occasionally they're actively quite
funny... i turn around and agree with someone who
hasn't spoken for several minutes, or answer the
'phone when it's not ringing, but i felt like a
complete nutter wandering around the house
looking for a london underground announcer.

tell me about biggles.

i have bought you a nice thing i am going to
send you, but it needs to be treated before i
send it to you. i'd better do it soon, though,
because i'm getting rather attached to it. i
might have to buy myself one.

i do miss you, but ululations are not my
thing... i can manage a low moan, though.

take care. i have to go now if i want to do
any fencing tonight.

love and big juicy raisins to mix in your
cereal,

tyger the ineffably plant-like

Mizu shobai

One evening in Kobe, after several hours working at a PC in an Internet café, I am walking to Sannomiya station when I see a woman talking on her mobile and whatever I'd been thinking at that moment disappears for ever from my mind. Her tall elegant shape and the way she stands is completely arresting. Her feet are widely planted, all weight on one leg, hip jutting. It's a classic pose. I look back at her while I wait to cross the street, hoping her phone conversation ends soon, and that she will walk the same way I am. Just as I hoped, she soon joins me at the lights and I get a closer look at her. I still haven't seen her face, but every detail, her hair, her clothes, her carriage and posture is a statement of beauty. I feel compelled to approach her but she walks fast when the lights change.

I manage to remember that I had planned to go to a craft shop before returning to Kyoto, but I am not sure where the building is. I need to ask directions. It suddenly occurs to me that I have the perfect pretext for stopping the beautiful girl and talking to her. When she turns at the sound of my voice I find I am looking into one of the most captivating faces I've ever seen, physically perfect, but also animated and spirited. I almost fall into her eyes. I want to embrace her, kiss her mouth right here in the street. Besides looking radiant, she turns out to be utterly charming, taking my request for help so seriously that she waves down a taxi to get extra assistance. She seems anxious to make sure that I'm OK. Her concern for my well being is definitely heartening. We chat as we walk and look for the building. I am not a little disappointed when she points it out to me. I thank her and we say goodbye. I watch as she walks away.

Then I realise that I may have just let a great opportunity slip through my fingers, so I run after her and ask her if she would like to have dinner this evening. She looks crushed by disappointment as she tells me she is on her way to work, and cannot. I ask what her job is and she says she works in *mizu shobai*, the water trade, a euphemistic phrase that covers many forms of nightlife and entertainment, geisha included; hard-core prostitution; massage parlours; bath houses; and legitimate hostess work. It makes sense. A woman with loveliness and poise so devastatingly alluring could only have been born to, or shaped by, the water trade. I don't ask for details. She could be a nightclub hostess or perhaps an expensive call girl.

She looks at me helplessly, as if missing dinner with me is the greatest disappointment she has ever had to bear. Instead she tells me her name is Kayo and gives me her telephone number. While she is writing it down, I have to fight to stop myself from putting my arms around her and pressing my mouth to hers. Her perfume is intoxicating.

She programs my number into her phone. I take great confidence from seeing this. We part once again.

I try to call her several times over the next couple of days, but only ever get a voice message. I remember that she had had two mobile phones. This should have told me something. Confidence now on the wane, I have the feeling I was given her low-priority number. Still, the mere experience of meeting her has had a genuinely uplifting, if short-lived, effect on my spirits.

Thoughts of Kayo keep coming back to me. I remind myself that women are often, but not always, impressed by men who are persistent. I've tried to contact Kayo by phone and it hasn't worked. So I shall engineer another meeting.

The next day I wait outside Sannomiya at the same time we met. I try to watch in all directions, but focus on the short stretch between the station and the pedestrian crossing. I am dressed for the expensive nightclub that I guess she works in.

At 6:30 PM she comes into sight and I walk straight up to her. Acting pleased to see her is not difficult and the reaction I get from her is more than I expected.

'Maaku-san!' she squeals, and stiffly thrusts both her arms out to the sides, as if she has been transfixed by surprise and delight.

I tell her she looks great and she replies that I do too. She confirms that she is on the way to work. I tell her I have wanted to see her again. She thanks me. I ask if it is far to where she works, and she says it takes only five minutes. We walk along the railway line and then turn left into an alley. She asks me where I am going and I just gesture ahead. She stops at a door with a small white sign beside it.

'Is this where you work?' I ask.

'Yes, I am sorry. I must go inside now,' she says.

'I would like to come in. Is that OK?' I ask. I notice her fleeting, cornered expression.

'It's a little...' She shifts imperceptibly towards the door.

'Is it a nightclub? Is this the door for customers?' By flooding her with questions I try to avert any objections she may raise.

'Yes, a nightclub. But this is a door for staff. The customer door is on another street.'

'Oh, good. Is it just around the corner?'

'Yes, it is,' she says, with some hesitation. She looks slightly pan-
icked, as if the situation has just veered a little outside her control. I
tell her I will go inside, and will ask for her once I am there. I look forward to seeing her later in the evening. She agrees to all this but I can
see she is not entirely happy. I rub her arm reassuringly (I hope) and
let her close the door.

The front entrance is not difficult to find, but it is locked. I try
Kayo's number but she doesn't answer. Across the street is a restaurant from where I can watch the door. I ask for a table by the window,
and settle in for a long wait. Now I have sat down I realise that my
heart is fairly racing and my hands are slightly clammy. I recognise
the strange hard knot inside me as nervousness, but I have no reason
now to back off. Actually, I have an immediate and powerful sense of
purpose that makes capitulation impossible. Somewhere inside is a
feeling that this is important, and I need to acquit myself well. I need
to write a story of success, not failure.

After a while activity stirs around the door of the nightclub. The
lights come on, the street is washed down with water and detergent,
and a green carpet is rolled out from inside.

Soon men begin to arrive. I am relieved to see that they are ordinary-looking *sarariman*, in their thirties and forties, some a little older.

By the time I get to the door another group of *sarariman* has arrived, so I tag along as they pass through the door. The doorman bows
to me, with a look I interpret as slightly suspicious. The men ahead
are being herded through an inner door by the oldest guy in the
group. An elegant woman in a long black gown stands behind a steel
lectern and looks enquiringly at me. I ask what the door charge is, and
what the arrangements are inside. She tells me it is 5,000 yen to get
in, and as I am not with a party, I must sit at the bar, not at the tables.
This sounds fine. I ask if there is any music. Her impressionistic description suggests that it is going to be a showband. When I hand her
my money she launches into her routine: showing me my vouchers
for drinks and parking, telling me about their special offers, which I
decline, and then offering me a membership, which I promise to think
about. I pass through the inner door and wait in a plush red corridor

to let my eyes accustom to the darkness and the ultra-violet lights. Oil paintings, barely visible, hang on the walls. Then I put my head around the door and catch the eye of the hostess.

'*Sumimasen*, would you please tell Kayo-san that Mark is here to see her?'

'Ah, you know Ka-chan?' she asks, smiling and nodding like a little girl. 'Yes, yes, I will tell her.'

For good measure I ask the barman to pass on the same message, as he carefully slides a coaster in front of me and centres a tall bubbling vodka and tonic upon it.

I look around. The room is large and circular. Three tiers of booths surround the central area, which has a wide stage, two bars, and a sunken dance-floor. The air is cold and perfumed. Several of the booths are already occupied, and I can see dazzling girls in some of them. The girls are Asian and European, all tall or in radically high heels. Some are in long dresses, others in mini-skirts displaying silky toned legs. All the girls move around dreamily like off-duty dancers. The men are hard to see in their suits, only the glaring white V of their shirts are visible in the strange lighting.

I spot Kayo after a few minutes. She is sitting with three other girls and half a dozen Japanese guys in a large booth. The women are moving back and forth, as if they have other business to attend to. I try to catch her eye, but she appears not to be looking in my direction. I tell myself to stay cool.

My first vodka and tonic disappears too quickly. *Did I drink all of that?* I wonder. *I'll have to slow down, keep my edge.* A thin shiny-skinned guy comes in on his own and sits on a stool a few feet away from me. He orders, lights up, nods at me when his drink arrives, and is almost immediately joined by a tall woman with Italian looks and impeccable posture. They obviously have an arrangement of some kind. This is encouraging, because it shows that the girls will come and sit at the bar. All I have to do is to get Kayo over here now.

At about 9 PM she strolls over. She is sheathed in a dark blue satin dress. The neckline is cut deep down her chest, but the neck is narrow and topped by a raised collar. The effect is to invite curiosity but to reveal nothing. She composes herself on the stool like a cat, or a snake.

'You try hard to see me, Maaku-san,' she smiles. 'I am sorry I have been so busy.'

I tell her I like her, I want to see more of her. I don't know how long she can sit here, so I need to get straight to the point. I would like to meet her when she is not working. How long can she stay, by the way? About fifteen minutes, it depends, she says. I explain what I am doing in Japan, where I've been staying. I tell her my funniest stories. I get her laughing and swaying on her barstool like a sapling in a warm sea-breeze. Each thing I notice about her, the shape of her thighs, the way her hair swings when she laughs, is so perfect it excites me. It all seems to be going well, then she lays a hand on my arm and asks if I will excuse her.

It is an hour before she is back. I try to hide the fact that during that hour I felt lost, demoralised, impotent, unattractive and above all, frustrated. As Kayo slides onto the stool again I get seriously back into the job of entertaining her. She even returns the service. She has some brilliant stories of her own. They are self-deprecating, funny, and well paced. It is not the first time she has told them. She goes off to work the tables again. Her buttocks swing the dress in a tantalising way. I try not to be too obvious about staring.

The evening continues in this fashion until I realise that I must sleep, I cannot keep up the cheerful façade much longer. She looks as fresh as ever when she comes back the last time. It is nearly 2 AM. I tell her that I want her first priority telephone number, that I have to see her soon, that she cannot avoid me. She laughs and tells me I am crazy, but she gives me the other number. *Yes!* She even accepts that it is possible that we can go out together one day, perhaps.

I keep coming back. It is an uphill battle all the way, and slow, but we pass little milestones one by one. One evening she puts her arm around me as we look at phones in a shop window, later she turns down an invitation from her girlfriends because she thinks I may (*may!*) have something planned. One night we kiss, for a long time, but impassively on her part, in the back of a taxi between the club and her apartment building. I try to get myself invited in, but she won't do it. I sometimes wonder if it will ever be worth all the fraught groundwork I am putting in. I know what is going on. I have become infatuated by the idea of her, and far from being fun, my relationship with her is a source of continuous tension and anxiety, because I know she feels nothing for me.

Ko-gyaru

I briefly return to Nagoya. Groups of *ko-gyaru* like to hang out around Nagoya station. The look is ever-evolving. In the face of the current high temperatures and moist air, and the danger of sweating conspicuously, fashion makes concessions to practicality. But back in the crisp cold of December the only danger was that of frostbite of the thighs, and it seemed every *ko-gyaru* was willing to risk it. Skirts had risen to the point where the slightest movement revealed clean white underwear. Sitting down or negotiating stairs required careful positioning of the handbag. Boots were knee-high, revealing a few inches of black knee-stockings. Between the stocking tops and the skirts there was an acreage of bare skin, tanned, depilated, and goose-pimpled. The boot heels, once merely ludicrously high, became vertiginous. From wide curved soles they tapered upwards to chunky, round-toe uppers. The weight and size of these encumbrances forced many girls to drag them along the street in a peculiar knocked-kneed gait. Most girls wore short coats (short enough to ensure that all the bare leg remained visible). The coats invariably had *faux* fur collars and hems. Colours were white and cream. Materials were suede, leatherette.

Yet it is the cosmetic elements of the *ko-gyaru* look that are the most striking. In its extreme form they consist of silver-dyed hair (back-combed or dead straight), conspicuous and complicated nail decoration, a deep nut-brown tan, white eye shadow and lipstick, and black mascara. In *Egg* magazine, one of the *ko-gyaru* fashion bibles, we see creatures that embody this extreme and are held up as models to readers, but it is a look routinely and repetitively lampooned by everyone else. It defies any pre-existing ideals of beauty or attractiveness, and therein lies its significance. It is not just that most of us think the look is weird. We think it is especially weird for Japanese girls to look this way. It radically undermines our stereotypical preconceptions of the Japanese female.

In *The Modern Madame Butterfly* Karen Ma identifies two common western misconceptions of the Japanese woman: the submissive female who wants nothing more than to serve her master and look after his home, and the unfulfilled woman wilting in a loveless relationship with a domineering Japanese man and waiting to be romantically rescued by a western man, who better knows how to treat her. The archetypes can be seen in Katsumi in *Sayonara* by James Michener, and Sachiko in *The Lady and the Monk* by Pico Iyer. To these I would add a third: the enigmatically diffident beautiful lover, who inexplicably takes us in, shows us tantalising glimpses of the world she lives in, and just as inexplicably leaves us. Mariko in *Pictures from the Water Trade* by John David Morley is such a woman (and I wonder if Kayo is too).

The *ko-gyaru* defiantly shatters all these images. She emphatically says 'No!' to servility, subtlety, elegance, and mystery. She displays her loyalties by being seen only with her identically-clad girlfriends, or aggressively grungy boyfriends. I don't think I ever see one walking alone, or with a *gaijin*.

This radical reorganisation of values appears to offend the *gaijin* community. I do not think that many western men actually want girlfriends that look like pandas in negative, but what they do want is to know that they *could* have them, if they were so inclined. The resentment manifests itself as endless jokes about *ko-gyaru* in both print and conversation. In essence it goes, 'Aren't they weird?' 'Yes, too weird to matter.' It is a tiresome dialogue best avoided.

Where the *ko-gyaru* look will go next year, no one can say. I would not be surprised to find afro perms and filed teeth. Seriously.

Date date

The train came out of the long tunnel and into the station. Hundreds of people wait on the platform, fewer than I expected. As I walk out of the station I look up and see white clouds appearing over a grassy hillside. I stop and wait for Kyoko. This is where we arranged to meet. A large dark dog sits patiently nearby, apparently waiting for its owner. Over to the right is a river, silently rushing, shaded by trees, broken by boulders. A canned drink emerges from the water. Somewhere I can hear music, two different tunes. I hear Kyoko's voice before I see her. She sings along to one of the tunes and seconds later appears over the edge of the hill, before running down to meet me. Her face fills my vision. It could be twenty yards wide. I have a momentary flashback of seeing her in New York. I try to talk to her, but for several minutes she doesn't let me get a word in, she has so much to say.

We have lunch at the Ultimate Lounge, followed by coffee (for me) and tea (for Kyoko) at Planet Business café. Then we walk the streets for a short while, just chatting, or Kyoko answering my questions about the things we see in shop windows.

Outside le Moulin, a café, I suggest another cup of coffee, so we walk in, and find a booth by the window. We sit facing each other. In the booth behind Kyoko is another Japanese-*gaijin* couple. She is tall and willowy, with a child's face. He sits with his back to me, hunched and intense, black jacket, short grey hair, a creative type, I guess. Across the aisle, yet another cross-cultural couple. He's nervous and long-winded, she gives off an aura of tense dissatisfaction, frustration, barely contained by a mannered patience. No matter how accommodating she is, I sense, he cannot give her what she needs. I wonder why. What is his failing? Is it physical or psychological?

My eyes are involuntarily caught, and held for a while, by the breasts of a *gaijin* girl passing the window. Kyoko notices.

'Do you think my breasts are too small?' she asks me, with sudden directness. She looks straight at me, scanning my face for the give-away reaction before I compose myself for the diplomatic answer that she expects. So I give her the truth.

'No, of course not.'

'But they are much smaller than Australian girls'.'

'Well that's true, but shape is more important than size, and you have a nice shape.' I deliberately avoid smiling when I say this, to show I'm being serious.

'I sometimes think they should be bigger.'

I detect more than wistfulness in her tone. 'Kyoko-san. You're not thinking of breast enlargement, are you?'

'Maybe.' She looks down to assess the merits of the current situation.

'Don't. It's not worth it,' I tell her. 'They don't move right, they don't feel right, they don't change shape the right way. I don't like them. I can tell what is real and what isn't.'

'Do you think you could tell that with me?' Kyoko lifts her head and looks at me again.

I sense, in a way that cannot be put in words, that the scope of the conversation has just expanded.

'Probably,' I hedge, trying to sound judicious rather than non-committal. She pauses as if suddenly changing her mind about what she was going to say, and turns to look out the window. The Shibuya crowds shift unceasingly, back and forth, casting shadows on the glass.

'Maybe not,' she offers, smiling, playful and impish.

I sense what is being left unsaid. It is disturbing because it forces thoughts in too many directions at once.

She sits unmoving, with her hands out of sight in her lap. Her tiny teacup is nearly empty.

'Would you like some more tea?' I ask.

'No, thank you. I don't need more,' she replies absent-mindedly.

'What about the rest of you? Are you real?' I ask her.

Kyoko changes the subject.

'Have you had a Japanese girlfriend, yet?'

'What, already?' I laugh.

'You could,' she says, evidently warming to the subject, 'Japanese girls find western men very kind and interesting. They think they can learn many things from you.' She says this as if it is obvious and therefore should need no explanation. I suspect a faint smile is tickling at the corner of her lips. She takes a sip of tea, or pretends to. I wonder if she is teasing. I think about how to respond.

'I had a Japanese girlfriend a couple of years ago, in Sydney,' I tell her. 'She went to live in London.'

'Oh, really? What was her name?'

'Sakuko. Tsukuda Sakuko.'

'Did you love Sakuko-san?' she asks, forming each word separately and carefully, touchingly. She waits for my answer with her eyes wide, her mouth slightly open and her head tilted. She looks so concerned and empathetic.

'Yes, I was very sad when she had to go. It was a visa problem.'

'And you could not go with her?'

'At the time it didn't seem...' I search for the right word, unsuccessfully. I settle on '... justifiable.'

'And now?'

'I don't know. Maybe I should have gone, maybe not.' I shrug, uncomfortable with the turn in the conversation. 'I'm not even sure she wanted me to go with her.'

'I think Sakuko-san wanted you, but could not ask you to do that for her. She wanted you to make the decision without an... obligation.' Kyoko says all of this without taking her eyes from mine. I can only nod, and purse my lips as if giving due consideration to the thought. Somehow I am made to feel that I've misbehaved, and rather selfishly so.

'But now, Maaku-san, you are free to have another one, no?' The strange verbal forms, their changes of texture give me a slight pause.

'Maaku-san, I would like you to call me something else. Can you agree to that please?' she asks prettily, almost giggling.

I feel a little surge of pleasure, thinking she is about to ask me to change the form of address I have been using – Kyoko-san – to something less formal, something more intimate. *She trusts me*, I think.

'Yes, of course,' I answer. 'What is it?'

'Please call me Tsukuda Sakuko.'

'What! Are you serious?' I literally splutter, staring at her.

'Yes,' she says, in an even tone that reinforces her answer.

'You're serious?'

She nods.

A momentary wave of panic stirs my insides. *I'm in the presence of a madwoman.* I find them unfailingly. I give an exasperated laugh.

She gives me her level gaze for a moment then looks back down into her cup, almost sulkily. She withdraws her hand from the table and places it in her lap, nestled inside the other one.

This is ridiculous. There must be more to this. *It is some kind of test*, I tell myself, and one I am not interested in passing. I shake my head. I don't want to be drawn into it.

'Why can't you do that for me?' she asks, in a voice so quiet it is only sensed through the slightest of lip movements.

She drops her head further until all I can see of her face, framed between curtains of long black hair, is the tip of her nose and chin.

'OK,' I say slowly, 'Just please explain why.'

She lifts her head and turns to look out the window. Her profile is imperious and impassive. For a moment she watches the people walking outside, then says.

'Thank you.'

'But *why*, Kyoko?'

'Please don't use that name any more.' She shifts position uncomfortably, raising an arm to move the strap of her dress back onto her shoulder. The strong sunlight pours through the window, the shadow under her arm is so dark it looks bottomless. She is ready to leave.

Exasperated, I reach for the bill, and slide sideways along the seat. She watches me crossly.

'You told me about your friend in England who changed her name,' she says in an accusing tone.

'Yes, but her new name didn't already belong to someone else.'

'How do you know that?'

'All right, I don't know that,' I concede, 'but *I* didn't know anyone else with the same name, and she didn't adopt it *because* it was already somebody else's name. She changed because she didn't like her real name.'

'If you accept her reasons, please also accept mine,' Kyoko says, quietly, but at the same time suggesting that she indeed has very good reasons for asking. What they are, though, I feel I will never know. And frankly, I have lost interest. What started as a promising afternoon together has gone off the rails amazingly fast.

I let out a long sigh. Pausing on the end of the seat, I look straight at her. She looks back, unblinking – defiantly so, I imagine. It feels like we are having a fight. Her eyes are dark brown; so dark it is hard to see how large her pupils are. Her cheekbones are painfully sharp, and shadow her cheeks. Her soft shoulders are almost bare, and I can see most of her body, round the corner of the table. She looks so fresh and clean; *kirei* is the word. I feel that familiar burst of desire, a sudden shooting endocrine sensation, like fear, and imagine taking her, pressing my lips against hers. *What is there to lose?* I ask myself.

'Sakuko,' I say, 'let's go to a hotel.'

'*Hai*,' she says quietly, rising and taking my hand. She smiles briefly, and we walk to the cashier.

Just up the hill, the hotel is styled after a Greek villa. We choose a room from the display and find our way to the door.

In the half-light of the room, although we are uninhibited and earthy together, I know that much more than a gossamer thin rubber membrane separates us. Her face retains the profound calm of a graven Buddha.

I roll aside, lift myself up on one elbow and slowly draw down the sheet. Her skin is shiny, smooth, white, and flawless. She writhes a little at the touch of the cool air. In movement, her body is utterly, breathtakingly, beautiful. I put my face close to her stomach and breathe in deeply; funny, no smell, or just the smell of warm water. I feel her hand in my hair. I touch her skin with my lips. It feels unusually hard.

'Are you real?' I ask, raising an eyebrow.

First I see her lips smile, then her eyes half open and look down at me, only to glance aside when she sees I am looking up at her.

'I'm not real, I'm *cold*,' she says, in another attempt to change the subject, too obviously – no way to win the Loebner prize.

'Well, *are* you?'

A direct look now.

'Are *you*?' she asks.

'No, I really don't think so, actually.'

I essay a kind of joke: '*I* think the "self" is a bad idea,' I reply, but then I lose interest in the subject, suddenly aware that a post-coital *triste*, a vague sense of delusion, has enveloped me, taking away the last lingering aftertaste…

'Me too,' she says.

Waking up

Dreaming of Date Kyoko is as close to her as we can get. She is a dream girl, a virtual character only ever seen in digital pictures and animations. Date Kyoko was created in 1996 by a company called HoriPro Inc, who used the computer graphics software talents of another company, Virtual Science Laboratory, to create the images of her. Her name was deliberately coined to use the initials DK, for Digital Kid. Her purpose: to sell records, consumer goods, anything. Along with a name, she was given a brief family history, a friend, Adam Soft, a boyfriend, Yuyan, a birthday, a blood group, and an eye prescription (0.2 left, 0.3 right). Kyoko was elfin, with hair cropped at half-ear length. She was cute, but not particularly sexual. Her legs were long and often bare, but she could have been any age between thirteen and twenty-four. She was the first digital *aidoru*, the Japanese word for idol.

Aidoru had already existed in Japan, and still do, in human form (the actress-singer Namie Amuro is a well-known example). They are the manicured marionettes of the entertainment industry, and are just as strictly controlled by their masters as any digital character. Usually teenagers with malleable personalities, they are the commercial capital of mass media marketing operations. An earlier example of real flesh and blood *aidoru* is Matsuda Seiko, born in 1962. Her every trivial detail, including for example her body mass index of 16.61, was pored over and discussed by the Japanese girls who formed her target market. An indication of the slavishness of this audience is the fact that she had twenty-four consecutive number one hit singles in Japan, surely a feat that sheer musical talent alone cannot account for. In a Japanese TV poll, more women wanted to be reincarnated as Matsuda Seiko than anyone else.

In *A Japanese Mirror*, Ian Buruma captures the true function and *raison d'etre* of *aidoru*, also called *talento*:

> Talentos are the products of advertising companies using the most sophisticated marketing techniques. They rarely last long, but while they are around, their ubiquitous and inescapable presence makes them a major social influence. Everything they say is carefully programmed by the people who created them. It never veers from the most conservative morality: how wonderful it is to be Japanese, how glad they are for all the help from their seniors, how hard work is the prime virtue of the Japanese people and how finally they would like to get married and raise a family.

It is obvious, after reading this passage, first published in 1984, that when digital replacements for such robotic figures became feasible in the 1990s, it was inevitable that they would be created. There was never much a real person could contribute to the role of an *aidoru*. The *aidoru* was almost entirely in the hands of the management. With digital creations to play with, the control of the Svengali over the *aidoru*, previously merely enormous, finally became total.

Almost. *Love Communication*, Date Kyoko's first single, was released on 21 November 1996. The CD also contained video files that showed Kyoko walking through the streets of Tokyo and New York. She gained a small following. A fan club was set up. There were hundreds of love letters, there were even several proposals of marriage. The fan phenomenon took on a life of its own.

The demand for Kyoko spread overseas. Kyoko had to be made to appeal to the Korean market too, so a new version, called Diki (Digital Kid, again), was 'written.' Diki spoke Korean, but with a Japanese accent. She took holidays in Japan. There was a website that allowed the voyeuristic to look around her bedroom.

But problems lay ahead. Kyoko's attraction was her unreality, and it couldn't last. In feeding the market's need for her, Kyoko could only ever become more real. Moreover, her life and repertoire were not as effectively exploited as they might have been, and within a year she was nearly forgotten. HoriPro had never understood what they had created, and they failed to maximise the interest in Kyoko that briefly arose in Europe and North America. As a musical act, Kyoko died. In the cyberworld, however, she remained a figurehead. Kyoko fans set up homage websites, shrines, not just in Japan, but also in Germany, Spain, Italy, and Hong Kong. Several years later many of these are still being maintained.

Our interest in Kyoko was probably more prurient than HoriPro would have liked. It was better satisfied a few years later by a bustier and altogether more provocative successor to Kyoko: Lara Croft of the *Tomb Raider* games. Lara excited the simmering libidos of the digital fraternity, and soon there were downloadable patches that allowed players of *Tomb Raider* to watch an unauthorised near-naked version of the cyber-gal, running and shooting her way through her adventures. A virtual industry of photo-editing soft porn pushers littered the net with images of Lara naked, sometimes with her 'own' body, sometimes with a real woman's. The demand for Lara's flesh was only satisfied by putting Angelina Jolie, a real actress with real breasts (albeit augmented), in Lara's clothes, and letting her loose on the populace.

Perhaps the unnerving future of the digital *aidoru* can be seen in *Idoru*, by William Gibson, in which an *aidoru*, Toei Rei, adapts interactively to the desires of her fans, so that she constantly fulfils their strongest needs. The book has many nods towards virtuality: vodka-analog (a drink), Whiskey Clone (a bar, perhaps), synthespian (the *aidoru*). In the story, which is set in Tokyo's near future, Rez, a singer, falls in love with, and intends to marry, Rei. She, it transpires, is equally eager to marry him. Others in the business are less sure that the marriage is a good idea, but the concerns are more to do with software engineering than with society. The marriage eventually takes place. Many of the bizarre ideas in the book, such as buildings made of urine, are imaginative extrapolations of Japan today, where urine is turned into bricks for ease of disposal.

We are not there yet, but virtual women (virtual men are less popular and less populous) are hovering into focus everywhere. At the less realistic end of the spectrum are the *anime aidoru* like Parapara and Yui Haga, for whom real people sometimes stand in at public appearances. More real now is Ananova, a sexy virtual newscaster. Aki Ross stars in the full-length movie, *Final Fantasy*, and occupies 87th position in Maxim magazine's top 100 hot girls. The Elite model agency has developed Webbie Tookay, a virtual supermodel who will do anything, wear anything, anywhere, for nothing. She can even handle extreme close-ups.

The phenomenon of virtual women is now attracting serious academic attention. Sociologists are grappling with these people-things, which barely lie within their bailiwick, but obviously challenge them for explanations. And the technology just keeps on getting better. It is now possible to create highly realistic virtual pornography, which will probably have legislators all over the world scrambling to redefine the boundaries of good and bad in imagery. The floodgates have opened.

And there in the new virtual sorority that she founded is a familiar face: Kyoko. She has recently been brought back to life by HoriPro, as opportunely as she was wintered. She now works under contract in San Francisco, as a PR agent for Oz Interactive, a company that creates 3-D web streaming software. It is not as glamorous as the life of an *aidoru*, but I've heard she feels she has grown out of that anyway.

Watch out for plywood children

All over Japan, plywood cut-out children stand at road junctions. They are there to warn drivers to take care. Most of them are painted in a strange uniform, with a blue and yellow hat. In some areas they have been given a little more individuality. One is painted like Elvis; another wears Kendo regalia, including the mask. When I unexpectedly catch sight of these figures from the corner of my eye they give me a start and I relax a little on the accelerator – exactly the reaction they are designed for.

The use of mannequins to guide the driving behaviour of the public is commonplace in Japan. At the site of road works a three-dimensional life-size replica of a road worker often waves a baton with its mechanical arm to slow traffic. On a stretch of road where motorists are inclined to speed a robot cop stands at the roadside. Despite his long hours his uniform is perfect, from helmet to spats. At least one full-size simulacrum of a police car exists. It has flashing lights and real tyres. Craig McLachlan encountered both of these curiosities on the long walk described in his book *Four Pairs of Boots*.

tyger?

'tyger?'

'yes?'

Surprisingly monosyllabic, I think.

'Remember the conversation we had about William
and the rest of the Gibson family?'

'no. when was that?'

'During the winter. Odd of you to forget.'

'tyger's been busy recently.'

Quotidian.

'It came right after our oil discussion, I think.'

'oil discussion? Was somebody squeaking?'

Unusual capitalisation. Is this Tiger masquerading under tyger's password and profile?

'Only if squeaking were a way of hiding words.'

'can't say I remember.'

OK. let's make it really obvious...

'Oil wordplay?'

tyger thinks leo is getting boring.

That's it! tyger would never say that, and she would certainly re‑member our word play with oil company names. I'm now convinced this is Tiger, but there is one more test I've just remembered.

'Off to Moonlight Valley. See you there.'

Leo roars off.

tyger and I have retreated to Moonlight Valley in the past when we have been hassled by other players on Underworld. On Moonlight Val‑ley we have different names. I log in as Kama.

khan waves at kama.

'leo! what took you?'

Damn! She's already here. I didn't expect that. What's going on? Is it tyger, but just acting strangely? Could Tiger know about our Moon‑light Valley identities too?

'Warlike metal prism.'

'eh?'

'Talk implies warmer.'

tyger thinks leo has finally flipped.

'You know where to find me: pier, sawmill,
market. You are puzzled. I'll leave it with you.
Real life is calling. Goddago. Sorry if I am
acting a bit mixed up today.'

I leave it at that. It may be a little rude, but the real tyger will spot that my strange parting phrases have the same letters and the same number of words, and this will alert her. In fact, for her this should be easy, since I flagged the presence of a puzzle and told her where to find *me*. The test though, will be how she responds. The real tyger will reply in kind. She will give better examples. She will reframe the game in a delightfully unexpected way. She will be warm and generous even if she finds it all a little childish – though she never would. To her this kind of play is an affectionate cerebral fondling of one another, a satisfying intimacy.

Akiko's pet

I try several times to contact Akiko, but my calls are unanswered and my messages not returned. At first I think nothing of it but then I recall how punctilious she had been at the start of our relationship. I suspect that something has gone wrong. Perhaps her husband has found out about us.

I call her from a public phone and get through immediately. She sounds tense. She is not pleased to hear from me, I can tell. So, it is true that she has been avoiding me. I decide that I have no time to beat about the bush, so I ask her why.

'It is difficult,' she says.

'Is it your husband?'

'No, not *him*,' she says. I can tell by her emphasis that there is someone else in the picture, and I gather I am not supposed to ask. Suddenly I know I will miss her. I feel bereft, and surprised that I do. I must see her one last time. Even as I am thinking this, I realise I am probably deluding myself. I really want just one more chance to strip her naked again. Her love-making, completely devoid of any personal expectation of pleasure, was always all for me.

'Akiko. I understand. We should meet as friends. Please be at the tea house at 6 PM.' I am telling her, hoping to force her into this.

'It is difficult...' she looks at me pleadingly.

'6 PM. I will be there. See you then.' I hang up and step out into the street. A pile of old bicycles lies beside the phone box. I feel like kicking my way through them.

I wait for her at the tea house, rehearsing lines. I know I am mixed up, because I am not really looking forward to this. I am acutely aware that I have nothing to offer her. Just as I decide that all we should do is have a quick chat and say goodbye, she walks in and I feel something flip over in my stomach.

The conversation is awfully tangential and intermittent at first. Yes, there is another person. No, he is not *gaijin*. No, not Japanese either. He is from Taiwan. When I ask her where they met she grows evasive and uncomfortable. I probe, by voicing hypotheses, watching and listening to her reaction, putting the responsibility on her to set me straight. She falls for the ploy. What she eventually tells me is well outside of anything I expected.

Akiko is in love. It is because of this that she thinks she must not sleep with me any more. It is wrong, even though she wants to. She smiles. She has not yet slept with the new one (as she calls him) but… maybe one day. This sounds odd to me. She continues. They met on the Internet. She has not actually seen him face to face yet, but her feelings are true, she says. It is like nothing before. He does not speak Japanese; they converse in English and basic Mandarin.

Akiko had read about the site called shesay.com in a magazine. It allows women to chose 'pets' from a selection of men and boys who, for reasons of their own, have offered themselves in this role. The power in the relationship resides completely with the woman, who has the ability to reward or punish her pet, even to 'kill' him if he is unsatisfactory. Akiko has been rewarding her pet, whom she refuses to name, with electronic postcards and icon-filled emails. He responds by listening sympathetically to all she has to say.

'Love is much safer with him. No risk,' she points out, quite reasonably. I nod, but I hate the idea of being beaten by an intangible Internet presence. I always knew Akiko took little pleasure in sex, but now I think it means almost nothing to her. I can sense no misgivings about her new relationship. She is actually glowing with happiness now, feeling that she can discuss it openly with me. The more animated she becomes, the sicker I feel.

In order to prop up my self-esteem I ask questions designed to bring out reassuring information. She does not know his real name. Under pressure she tells me he calls himself 'starman.' He is a mechanical engineering student with a part-time job in a bakery, in Taipei. His dream is to go to America. I am feeling better. Does she know what he looks like? Yes, he emailed a photograph. Does she have it with her? Yes, of course. Can I see it? No, it is too private.

It seems starman cannot afford to come to Japan, and he has asked Akiko to pay for his ticket. I slowly shake my head at this, in mute warning to her, but I can see she is already mentally prepared to give him the money, it is probably only the inevitable marital complications that hold her back. He does not have a computer at home, he uses one at university, so they cannot talk at night. Akiko is frustrated by this. She solves the problem by sending him emails, sometimes five or six a night. He says he cannot find time to read them all, she tells me. I raise my eyebrows in a manner intended to indicate that I disapprove of his response but am too polite to blatantly say so.

I am actually starting to feel sorry for her. How can this relationship be fulfilling? When I tell her I feel a little concerned for her happiness, it brings on quite a change. Yes, she admits, she also wonders how things will develop.

While she is reflective like this I realise I have a choice. I can abruptly leave, saying it was good, etc., no hard feelings, etc., goodbye. Or I can sit her through this. A funny little flush of affection comes from nowhere, and I realise that she is so much a child, so lost, so short of resources, so trapped in a marital predicament that she cannot alter and cannot leave, that I have to be on her side. So I tell her to enjoy it while it lasts, be careful, do not make plans, etc. There is, of course, no future for us, either. It is time I put jealousy aside, stepped out of the picture, and made things a little less complicated for her, no matter how reluctant I am to admit that the sex is over.

A last kiss at the door. She hugs tightly to my chest. The tightness lingers as I walk away.

Chance meetings with eccentric academics

A few days later I move into a university guest-house while attending a conference on the campus. The following day I find that several new guests have joined me. One of them is in the sitting room, drinking his way through a bottle of scotch and smoking a pipe. He welcomes me effusively and checks my academic standing in the first couple of seconds of conversation. He is a visiting professor, and keen to speak English, especially when he discovers I am from Australia, because he wants to ask me about the dingo. Now, I happen to be something of an authority on dingoes, relatively speaking, having set eyes on a few during my trips in the outback, so we get on like a house on fire. It turns out that he is adamantly against dingoes for the single reason that they are an introduced species (having been in Australia for only about 10,000 years). This, he feels, is justification for their complete extermination, so that the native marsupials can once again live in peace.

We move on to more general matters. He asks penetrating and well-informed questions about Australian politics, in particular regarding race and immigration. We also cover political allegiances and environmental issues. I have to admit that Australia does not look good under his detailed scrutiny. At about 1 AM he makes me promise to work untiringly to preserve the natural Australian environment. It is, he says, an inspiration to the Japanese, and must not be lost. I retire to bed thinking that tonight's conversation, based, as it was, on the dingo, was one in a million.

A couple of nights later, I am watching television in the sitting room, when another venerable academic opens the door and says 'Chilly, isn't it?' *Aha, a straight translation of 'samui desu ne,'* I think. We start to chat. He says he is very pleased to meet an Australian because he has a few questions about, of all subjects, the Australian dingo. Did I know that it was once imported into Japan in the hope that it would become a popular pet, having the rare distinction, among dogs, of being able to get about its business without feeling the need to bark? No, I knew dingoes don't bark, but I didn't know that the Japanese had tried to solve their canine noise pollution problems this way.

'Did it work?' I ask.

'No,' he laughs, 'because when the dingoes heard other dogs barking, they began to do it too!'

One in five hundred thousand, perhaps.

During the conference I am taken out for dinner by two professors. We sit at the counter of a good *sushi* restaurant, whose owner, having once run a restaurant in Tokyo, has now retired to this small village where he is free to pursue his hobby – running a restaurant. He works at lightning pace, putting the *sushi* together in his cupped palm and placing it in front of us. My two academic friends are forced by my presence to speak English all evening, but they both take this as a challenge to show off and prove to each other that they are cleverer with words, and faster with repartee. Consequently the evening is amusing for me. I sit between them as they attempt to make fun of each other, trying not to laugh too loud at the jokes each makes at the other's expense. So much for Japanese courtesy and formality.

On the way back to the guest-house I ask if we can stop at a convenience store so I can buy some milk. I explain that no matter how adventurous I am at lunch and dinner, breakfast is one meal that I can't vary. Professor Komatsu jokes that if I had to eat Japanese breakfasts I would start losing my identity. When I come back to the car with my carton of milk he asks me if I got my 'identity bottle.'

'Yes, I got my *gaijin*-in-a-bottle,' I reply.

Another curious theory of Professor Komatsu is that in the United States status is defined by money, in Europe it is defined by cosmopolitanism (perhaps the number of languages one speaks), but in Japan it is defined by education. Of course, there are counter-examples to this simplification, but that is not the point. The interesting thing is that in Japan having an education really does carry some weight. In Australia, of course, it can often work against one. I sit in on one of Professor Komatsu's International Studies classes and am introduced as Peters-sensei, from Australia.

'Eeeehhhh,' chorus the class (koalas have given all Australians huge credibility in Japan).

'PhD,' he tells them. I try to look suitably wise and marsupial.

'Eeeehhhh,' they say.

'He's working in artificial intelligence,' says the professor, slowly, and with emphasis.

'Eeeehhhh.'

I am being seen in a light I have never quite enjoyed before. All their wide eyes are fixed on me.

There is a short pause, while we all wonder what to say next.

'Do you know Aibo dog?' one of the braver students asks.

I dare not mention the word 'dingo.'

'Yes, we have some Aibo in my department. Sony gave them to us for research,' I say.

'Eeeehhhh.'

'We have programmed them to play soccer. We were finalists in our first Robocup competition in Stockholm, and won the shoot-out competition. Tokyo and Osaka Universities also competed there.'

'Eeeeehhhh!'

'Then this year we won both competitions, with a record of forty-eight goals for and only one against.'

'Eeeeehhhh!'

'So you could say we are Aibo *yokozuna*!' I exclaim, sacrificing some of my academic gravitas. *Grand Champions* indeed!

They stare at me in frank amazement. What brings such an illustrious (or boastful) being to their humble class? A few manage to overcome their nervousness to ask more questions and we discuss some interesting issues in AI. One student says that the idea of being controlled by machines that are more intelligent than we are is scary. I give my standard response, 'but is it more scary than being controlled by beings who are less intelligent than us? This is the situation we are often in now.' Half of them agree on the grounds that politicians are indeed dull, boring, and therefore probably stupid, the other half think that my disrespectful attitude is difficult to respond to. I pose the question, 'If we really could create machines more intelligent than ourselves, who would you choose to handle the most difficult and complicated problems of the world, the super-intelligent machines, or relatively unintelligent humans?'

'Aaaaaaah.' They nod sagely, seeing the crucial issues at stake. That there may come a time when humans will be obliged to cede control to other entities seems more easily imagined by these students than by others with whom I've discussed the possibility.

A linguistic curiosity pops up during this discussion. In Japanese, the verb 'to be' comes in two forms, *arimasu* for use with inanimate objects, *imasu* for animate things. Curiously, the inanimate form, *arimasu*, is also used for fictional characters. This, according to Roland Barthes, reveals that there is less need to pretend the unreal is real in Japan. Anyway, which form should we use for a robot? Opinions within the group are split down the middle on this, but there is general agreement that when a robot is doing things that make it look like a human or some other animal, the *imasu* (animate) form of the verb should be used. The role a thing performs decides its status.

Arashiyama

On a steamy summer morning when I am to meet Emi she calls to say that she will be late. Instead of waiting in the heat at Hamaotsu station, I nip into the nearby shopping centre, where it is no doubt cooler. I find a little coffee shop and take my seat at the counter. The girl who is serving me is quite striking. She's tall, slim but bosomy, and has rich black hair falling all around her shoulders. Opportunistically, I chat her up. We have exchanged names and telephone numbers when I ask Sayaka if she is at university. 'No.' she replies, 'High school.' Oh. Well, I better leave it at that then, hadn't I? That is the trouble with Japanese females. The girls look like women and the women look like girls. They assume each other's roles too; one cannot be too careful.

Emi calls again to say she is at Hamaotsu station now, so I direct her across the road to the café and she joins me for an iced coffee. Sayaka gives Emi (rather than me, I am surprised to see) a hard look across the counter. When we leave, she waits until Emi is out of the line of sight and then gives me a little wave, which I return ruefully.

On the train to Arashiyama, Emi is amused by a baby girl who dances in the lap of her mother, sitting across the carriage from us. The mother tells us the girl is eleven months old. It is because of this that I am astonished to see her bowing back to Emi every time Emi bows and says *konnichiwa* to her.

At Arashiyama the trees are a lush emerald green. The day is growing horribly humid. A hot suffocating wind blows down the river, and the rickshaw drivers are offering to take us to 'a cool place.' We cross the bridge on foot and duck into the nearest souvenir shop to cool down. Emi gives me the run-down on all the little things that are on sale. Perhaps you consider an ear wax scoop an appropriate souvenir. I don't, but then obviously some people do. I am more interested in the fans. I learn that there are many different kinds. Larger ones are for men, smaller ones for women, those with the same pattern on both sides are for dance. Some fans are simply for display, other tiny ones have some other purpose (I forget). *Kasumi*, which means mist, is a particularly attractive simple style of fan decoration, made of abstract glowing colours.

We look around inside Tenryaku-ji temple, which has a fine garden, best viewed, as it was designed to be, from inside the temple. If you do venture into the garden there are good views across Kyoto from the back. Japan has purpose-built stroll gardens too, but I like the view gardens more. This one is truly beautiful and, judging by the photographs on display, remains so all the year round.

Back in Kyoto we look for an okonomiyaki shop on Kawaramachi-dori. We are fortunate, because the owner of the place we choose takes a shine to Emi and plies us with all sorts of little extras, including squid guts (after politely asking Emi if I can eat them – I can, just), oysters and the smoothest, most delicious *sake* I have ever tasted. As a host, he does a good job, I am sure Emi will go back there, but I often wonder how these little places make money. Even if every seat were occupied all the time the takings cannot be that much, and I am sure the rent here in downtown Kyoto is substantial.

Manga

I buy a *manga*, a Japanese comic. I've been intrigued by them ever since I saw my first one. First, they can be immensely thick, up to 4 cm. The imagery is highly stylised, all faces are either doll-like or monstrous, and the stories can be inordinately violent and sexual. The one I buy has a high level of quite peculiar sex. The women are all portrayed as soft receptacles that men and objects plunge into. The women are initially coy or unreceptive but eventually awaken to have the most explosive drenching orgasms it is possible to draw. Invariably they are left at the end of the story shattered and prostrate, coated with bodily fluids, both their own and those of their mates. *Katakana* script is used for sound effects. See-through drawings show how deeply women are being penetrated, or how wildly the far breast is swinging out of sight behind the near one. Tiny prim areas are blanked out at the centre of vaginas and tips of penises, but they make minimal demands on the imagination. Perspective and scales are skilfully and dramatically varied. The standard of drawing of female bodies is often much higher than that of males bodies. Presumably artists get more practice drawing females.

With this venture into cartoon depravity my curiosity is sparked.

Some time later I locate a shop called Mandarake, deep below Shibuya Beam, which stocks massive numbers of *manga* of all kinds, going back over many years of publication. I find a concentration of men in one part of the shop and pull out a slim comic, sealed, but frankly describing itself as 'sadistic.' Curiosity now ablaze, I buy it. It is similar to the first *manga* I read. More cataclysmic orgasms and contortions, and very little else. Ejaculate practically spurts off every page. The monotony is staggering, and I don't quite get it.

Men openly read these sexually powerful *manga* on public transport – a point often noted by visitors to Japan. I saw a commuter holding up a newspaper on the back of which was a colour, full-page, full frontal nude photograph of a teenage girl. It was only inches from a woman's face. Received thinking in Australia says this endangers and degrades women. If so, there must be evidence of much higher levels of sexual assault and mistreatment of women in Japan, but then women tell me they feel perfectly safe walking alone in dark streets late at night in central Tokyo. I see lone schoolgirls, mini-skirted, insouciantly strolling along at night, quite fearlessly. I am sure our western views on media-borne nudity and sex are not the last word.

Woman-picture

Several times Emi warns me not to copy the way she speaks, for male and female speech in Japan is quite different. When I ask her how I should speak in a given situation, her answer is often, 'You're a man. You can say anything you like.' The truth is somewhat different, but the general idea is correct – men are permitted much more freedom in what they say than are women.

In non-verbal expression, however, the greater latitude seems to belong to women. Whereas men's faces have only two states, dead-pan and riotous laughter, the women's faces are much more complex – more like the surface of a lake, rippled this way and that by the breezes of thought passing over them, and deeper currents below. The delicious crinkling of the brow, the sudden glance to the sky as a new idea breaks the surface, the pursing of the lips, the wide-eyed round-mouthed exaggeration of surprise, closely followed by a giggle of pleasure. Nothing could be more bewitching.

And women exercise greater prosodic range than men.

There are the intense sympathisers: women who keep up a constant stream of interjections while men are speaking: 'mmmm, mm, ahhhh, *soooo-so-so-so*, *hai*, mmmm, aah.' In Japan, men declaim, women assent. These female sounds can be at times so expressive they can lull men back into memories of being in their mother's arms.

There are the female voices so hauntingly beautiful that we are called back again and again to hear them: like Miho, or the woman at the Japanese embassy in London, or the announcer at the Tokyu Hands store in Shibuya, whose announcements always began with a soft, lilting and achingly delicate '*o-kyaku-sama...*'. I was driven to take my minidisc recorder into the store, and tried to capture her voice, but the background noise always spoilt the effect.

There are also those women who speak so slowly and perfectly, deliberately making themselves easily understood for a *gaijin* listener.

And then there are the demure women, who still prefer to be kissed and embraced only in private – even today there are many to be found.

There are the poetic and tantalising literary ladies of Heian times: Fujiwara Michitsuna no Haha, Murasaki Shikibu, Izumi Shikibu, Sugawara no Musume, and Sei Shonagon.

There are the penis-severing vampires and necrophiliacs, like Abe Sada, made famous in Oshima's *In the Realm of the Senses*.

There are the uninhibited exhibitionists, who will demand a kiss in a department store, the tanned *ko-gyaru*, or the otherwise ordinary girls who wear skirts decorated with photographically realistic prints, which make the skirt look see-through, and appear to reveal a pair of thighs and knickers.

There are the married women who manage the house, bring up the children, feed the husband, but also have time to meet their friends every day, for coffee or noodles, or to attend classes in one of the many Japanese cultural traditions. Women who are self-directed, not living vicariously though their husbands' professional doings. Women who seem to have a private life that their husbands can only dream of.

There are the perfect girlfriends (for the undeserving western male) depicted over and over again in the literature; *The Modern Madame Butterfly* by Karen Ma, *The Lady and the Monk* by Pico Iyer, pliant and undemanding women who will do everything and anything for a man, including looking beautiful, cooking and cleaning, enjoying the sex and even providing pocket money.

And there are the lovers who have no inhibitions about showing their bodies, who present themselves as playgrounds for our every fantasy, are enthusiastic about sex, orgasmic to an extreme degree, and as sensually seductive as it is possible to be...

Masks

Geisha wear make-up so elaborate that it completely masks their ordinary appearance. And of course everyone knows *kyogen* and *noh* are performed with masks. But this is not enough to account for the western proclivity to talk about 'the Japanese mask.' Robert Craigie entitled his memoirs *Behind the Japanese Mask: a British Ambassador in Japan, 1937-1942*. Roland Barthes devoted a peculiar chapter, *The Written Face*, to Japanese masks (faces, that is) in *Empire of Signs*. In *A Circle Round the Sun*, Peregrine Hodson talks about foreigners developing a different person living within themselves and thinking different thoughts, hidden behind the mask of their face. He later talks about the key concepts in Japanese culture, *koto-dama*, *sabi*, *wabi*, *shibui*, but as elements in a mask; not revealing, but concealing. Further into the book his original mask idea resurfaces, as it were. Now Hodson feels that his mask is the reality, and that if he were able to remove it there would be nothing behind it, he would 'lose face.' In possibly the worst book about Japan that I have read, *The Art of Being Japanese*, Robert Dunham talks of blank walls and empty rooms behind the vacantly smiling inscrutable faces of simple-minded Japanese people. I only hope he was trying to be funny. The lesson seems to be: don't try to look behind the mask, there is nothing there. Japan is the mask.

When the Japanese write of masks, there is a subtle difference. In *Snow Country*, Kawabata Yasunari has Shimamura seeing the face of his old lover, Komako, as a mask, floating in the dark of a starry night. But this time the mask is a symbol of a relationship that has died inside and exists in appearance only.

Something tells me that many outsiders have been diverted into an obvious dead-end cliché.

Evasion

I notice a few body odours in these wet, humid days. Sometimes it is the women who smell, but to me they have an intriguing animal quality to them that is not at all repellent. I am in good company; even the fastidious Sei Shonagon didn't mind the aroma of sweat.

Though pointing this out is probably unlikely to win me any friends, I am interested that races have distinctive smells of their own. To me, the Japanese have a vegetable smell, African Negroes smell smoky, Australian aborigines smell smoky too, but with a milky overtone. I can never smell Caucasians per se, but I know that Africans say we smell like pigs and Asians say we smell of meat.

I always have a hundred questions for whomever I am with in Japan. I am curious about everything. But I keep running into a phenomenon that begins to get very tiresome. Many Japanese people feel embarrassed to simply say 'I don't know' (they are not alone in this, of course). Or, they are unwilling to tell me what they think. I often find that a question is answered by several questions, and only after cornering the witness do they admit to not knowing, or having a personal view. The circumlocutions might be something like:

'What do you think of this place?'

'Me?'

'Yes, you.'

Silence.

'Well? What do you think of it?'

'This place?'

'Yes. What do you think of it?'

'In what way?'

'Any way. Do you have any feelings about it?'

'It depends.'

'Depends on what?'

'It depends on many things. What do you want to know?'

'I only want to know if you like it, or not, or if you find it interesting, whatever.'

'I find it impossible to answer such a question.'

If the possibility of a potential disagreement arises, suddenly all can become vague, evasive, or contradictory. One's only recourse is to drop the subject and all concomitant interrogatives. Better to go with intuitions than try to force out the testimony to confirm them.

Then there is the inconclusive consideration of alternatives. I have often been quite happy to do any of several things, but my companion first lists the disadvantages of option one. Fine, let's do option two, I say. Then all the objections to that are enumerated. Well, we can do one or two, I am happy with either. Still no decision. I realise that although I am the least informed, I am the only one able to make the decision.

Even Emi has driven me to distraction at times like this. I contrast it with tyger, whose responses are always so *constructive*, one way or another.

Kayo shopping

In time I meet Kayo again, in the Hankyu department store in Kobe. From a distance she is instantly recognisable: tall, elegant, perfectly proportioned, and able somehow to project her body dramatically into whatever space it occupies. I'm always so drawn to her, and the closer I get, the more powerful the attraction. Once I see her I want to touch her, once I touch her I want to taste her. The various smells that linger around her neck drive me to a kind of reckless desire. The note of her hair, her scent, and the smell of Kayo itself, make a heady major chord. No matter what she says, I'm always compelled to move one step closer, to let one thing lead to another...

Kayo is doing some shopping today and wants me to come along as a witness, it appears. We pass aimlessly from one area to another. Each time I think she is going to buy something she makes a polite withdrawal from the counter and moves somewhere else. It is not a purchase-oriented form of shopping, as far as I can tell.

We chat about *mizu shobai*, and I bring up my conversation with Akiko. This elicits barely concealed contempt from Kayo, not for star-man, but for Akiko, which strikes me as very uncharitable. Kayo appears to have a surprisingly strong distaste for relationships that do not match up to the Barbie and Ken ideal. I diplomatically avoid probing her on this, but somewhere at the back of my mind I make a mental note.

Kayo knows a girl, Mikiko, who, she tells me, regularly calls in to a telephone service where she chats or has phone-sex with men. For this

Mikiko is paid a surprisingly good rate. Mikiko's relationships with the men-callers often spill over into the physical realm, too. If they are prepared to pay the fee, Mikiko will be their 'date.' All this is managed by the company that runs the phone numbers. Sex, if required, costs extra. Kayo even takes me out of the store to show me one of the businesses. It is on a busy high street, between a Docomo shop and a Yoshinoya fast food outlet. An open shopfront leads to perhaps ten small white booths, something like an Internet café, but with only a phone in each booth, not a computer. There are no concessions to romance.

No concession to romance for us either. It is one of the paradoxes of Japan that while relationships can so quickly lead to sex, it is often the kiss that is out of the question. I've tried to get close enough to kiss Kayo a couple of times today, but she has turned or dropped her head ever so slightly, and made it impossible to do smoothly.

'I want to kiss you.' I say, eventually, in what is meant to be a serious but light-hearted way.

'Not here,' is the answer.

I and I

A, are, atashidomo, ga, go, jibun, jibun no hou, jiga, jiko, jishin, jita, kochi, kochira, kono hito, kono mono, midomo, mi, mii, mizuka, mizukara, soregashi, touhou, wa, waga, wagami, warawa, ware, warera, washi, washimo, watakushi, watakushidomo, watakushijishin, watashi, watashidomo, and *yo.*

Atachi, atai, atashi, maro, uchi, wachiki, watachi, and *watai.*

Boku, chin, maro, nanji, oi, oidon, oira, ono, onore, ore, sessha, shinpen, shousei, temae, wagahai, waro, wasshi, and *waware.*

Translating the preceding text into English, were it ever required, would be difficult, because all these Japanese terms, all sixty-two of them, refer to the first person. The translation would read something like 'I, I, I, I, I, …'

Either gender can use the terms in the first group. The second group is strictly for female speakers, the third for male.

This collection of pronouns is obviously far more extensive than that of English. Even when we include all archaic and special terms, the list of English cognates is paltry in the extreme: me, myself, I, this one, this person, the royal 'we,' the royal 'us,' the colloquial 'number one,' 'my nabs,' 'yours' and 'yours truly.'

The simplicity of English personal pronouns is potentially one of its relieving features as a foreign language. Yet it is not so for learners from Japan. Komatsu tells me about an interesting difficulty Japanese university students have when trying to translate their thoughts into English. Far from enjoying the simplicity of English first person terms, Japanese students worry about the important social contextual information that they cannot express when forced to simply say *I* or *me*. And Japanese has equally numerous options for the second and third person too. That so many personal pronouns exist in Japanese indicates that social context is much more important to Japanese modes of expression than it is in English counterparts. The additional fact that contemporary students worry about it merely confirms its relevance.

When we refer to ourselves in Japanese we should first decide who we are in relation to the listener, how we feel towards them, and what is our current role – then choose our words accordingly. Though as foreigners we are always taught to use the general-purpose term *watashi*, this usually just marks us as an outside-person, a *gaijin*, and is a sure sign of a beginner.

In English-borne thought, we are automatically more convinced of our own 'true, deep down' identity and individuality, and cannot see the point in confusing things with all the unnecessary alternatives the Japanese have to hand. I am who I am, regardless of context, we kid ourselves. In Japanese one cannot even say things like 'the real me' be-cause to do so would force a choice of words which automatically set us in one social context or another. The meaning of the utterance would be reduced to something like 'how I really am in this situation.'

And oddly, despite the wide range of available first person terms, as one's Japanese advances one more effectively erases self-references from one's speech.

Not naming names

If the discussion of pronouns leads to the thought that identity in Ja-panese culture is a slippery phenomenon, the Japanese attitude to names reinforces it.

In Heian times it was customary to refer to men by their official position rather than their name, except in the presence of the Emperor, when men's names, rather than titles, were used – to avoid appearing to exalt them. Court women were usually referred to by the offices their husbands, fathers, or brothers filled, and concubines were simply named according to the building they lived in.

Sei Shonagon discusses these matters in her magnificent *Pillow Book*. She opines that perhaps she should not be so familiar as to refer to distinguished gentlemen by name, but remarks that were she to use their titles they would be hard to identify in the years that follow, since titles were continuously being passed on to successors. A person occupying one office in one passage of the *Pillow Book*, will later reappear under a quite different title, having in the interim been appointed to a new role. The old title, just to add to the confusion, can now quite easily refer instead to his replacement. Incidentally, Sei Shonagon was not really her name at all. Shonagon means 'minor counsellor' but it is not known which of her male relatives held this office. Sei is an alternative reading of the character *kiyo*, perhaps referring to the Kiyowara family, which has led some scholars to identify her as Kiyowara Nagiko.

Heian attitudes to names were surprisingly casual. Ivan Morris begins the introduction to *As I Crossed a Bridge of Dreams* with the arresting sentence 'One thousand years ago a woman in Japan with no name wrote a book without a title.' The woman he refers to is known today, in English, as Lady Sarashina. The title 'Lady' is a latter-day attempt to give a woman of the Heian court a recognisable minor nobility title, and Sarashina, cryptically, is the name of a district that the author obliquely refers to in one among many of her poems. The word Sarashina does not appear in her book and she may never have travelled there. The arbitrariness with which Lady Sarashina came to be her modern name is consequently quite astonishing. In Heian times she was referred to as Takasue no musume, Takasue's daughter.

Possibly the greatest female author of Heian Japan is nowadays called Lady Murasaki. Her appellation, Murasaki, meaning 'purple,' was derived in her own time from the nickname of one of the fictitious characters in her book *The Tale of Genji*. In Japanese she is called

Murasaki Shikibu. Shikibu is an office her father once held: Minister of Ceremonial. We simply do not know of any better names for her.

At the close of *Diary of Lady Murasaki* there is a description of a ceremony in the grounds of the Imperial Palace. Most of the people are referred to by anonymous titles, but a prized flute is referred to by its own name, Hafutatsu. Hafutatsu was quite a celebrity, also appearing in Sei Shonagon's *Pillow Book* along with a troupe of other musical instruments with names of their own: Gensho, Mokuma, Ide, Ikyo, and Mumyo (all lute-like *biwa*); Kuchime, Shiogama, Futanuki (zither-like *koto*); Suiro, Kosuiro, Uda no Hoshi, and Kugiuchi (flute-like *shakuhachi*).

Even within families, personal names were routinely avoided. Sarashina refers to her husband as 'the man who was the father of my child' and to her father as 'the person who was my parent' not because she was trying to disassociate herself from them (she was particularly close to her father), but simply because direct references to people were disliked. When she says she 'prayed the person on whom I depended would have other people's kind of joy' it means she was praying for her husband.

Names are fluid things in Japan. People give themselves nicknames, and accept them from others, easily. Calligraphers and poets create special names, *haimei* and *gou*, kinds of *nom de plume*, with which to sign their work. *Sumo rikishi* and *kabuki* actors take stage names, *kaina* and *yagou*, respectively. Whole *kabuki* families also take family stage names. In similar fashion, *geisha* take names that refer to their houses and predecessors. In *Bachelor's Japan*, Boye De Mente tells us that the nightclub hostesses of 1960s Tokyo changed their names every time they changed jobs – pretty often, in other words. It is an ancient Buddhist tradition that one is referred to by a different name after death. This is still so important that parents pay temple priests to pre-assign posthumous names, *tsuigou*, to their children. Daishi is a name posthumously conferred on the priest Kukai by the imperial court. Kukai was not his original name either, but the name he took as a priest. His earliest name was Mao or Totomono.

One of the giants of Japanese history, whom I shall perversely identify here (just to make the point) as Hashiba Hideyoshi, but who is better known as Toyotomi Hideyoshi, changed his name on numerous occasions. In *Kyoto: a Contemplative Guide*, Gouverneur Mosher writes:

> In a country where the names of towns, areas, provinces – and even men – are changed often, that Hideyoshi was rarely seen twice under the same name might not seem unusual.

In Hideyoshi's case however, there *was* something unusual about it. Never in Japan has anyone passed through as many social strata as Hideyoshi, so perhaps no one has ever felt quite the same need to repeatedly repackage oneself. Hideyoshi was a spectacularly successful social upstart, and though he proved himself superior to all the political challengers of his time, and dominated all of Japan, the absence of an august cognomen evidently rankled.

Virtual people

Not naming names, I tell Emi about the relationship Akiko formed with starman. Emi has, like Kayo, knowledge of something similar. It is called My Prince Charming.

Users of My Prince Charming can send short text messages from their mobile phones to a virtual boyfriend (girlfriends are also available, on another service called Love by Email). The boyfriend consists of nothing more than a text-processing program which analyses the incoming messages, builds a profile of the user, decides what kind of reaction is appropriate, and sends back a response. Each user may send and receive three messages a day, for a monthly fee of 350 yen.

The personality of the program is designed to react negatively if the received emails are interpreted as moving the relationship along too fast, or not fast enough. There are unwritten rules to the courtship, and the better these are observed, the more readily the program will divulge information. The trick is appropriateness, a trait highly valued by the Japanese. If the contents of one's messages are appropriate to the length of the relationship, the time of day, the season, and what each party knows about the other, then one's lover will become receptive, revealing, and intimate. The object of the relationship is to learn all fifty-two secrets of the lover.

Emi's registration was paid for by a work colleague who had been in constant dialogue with his email (barmaid) lover for some weeks.

Emi chose a racing car driver personality for her lover, and sent him several messages, but lost interest after a few days. She then received a sequence of cajoling, then angry, and eventually insulting messages from her jilted racer – and then nothing. I imagine him looping endlessly around a virtual racetrack until another girl summons him into existence.

Meanwhile Emi's work colleague had talked of little else. He began to act as if he had a real girlfriend, earnestly asking Emi for tips on what to say, and how to handle her. Emi tells me she gave him hours of serious advice. She thought it covered several good lessons for a man to learn, and was a worthwhile investment of her time.

Tanuki – immortal, live, dead and inanimate

Tanuki are native Japanese animals mistakenly called badgers, or raccoon dogs. They live in burrows in the woods, and play a large part in Japanese mythology.

To see a dead *tanuki* means that snow is on the way. One evening I see a dead one at the side of the road. Its body has already been hollowed out by scavengers, but its leathery black paws and luxuriously thick pelt are still intact. Poor thing. I wonder if it had been foraging for a litter of pups. Better not to think about it.

Tanuki statues are everywhere. They always appear to be sitting on sacks, but these are huge testicles. Even the ones made to look like women are so endowed. It is possible to buy family sets of *tanuki*, and the whole family has big balls. I have never had a satisfactory answer to why this is so.

The wonderful thing about *tanuki* is that they are magic. They can make people forget who they are. As if Japanese identities were not already fragile enough. Japanese people are curiously cautious about being near the habitat of *tanuki* at night. Night-time is when ghosts and magic are afoot, in lonely places, away from the security of company.

The other mischievous beast of the Japanese night is *kitsune*, the fox. Whereas *tanuki* can make us forget who we are, *kitsune* can get inside us and make other people see us as something different. Again, it is a fantastic assault on identity, rather than being eaten or chased, that haunts the Japanese. We choose our nightmares to threaten where we are most vulnerable.

Typically, men have divided women into two groups: the *tanuki*, who are short of calf, round of face, and perhaps of peasant stock; and *kitsune*, who are long and thin, in limb, face, and finger, and perhaps of courtly heritage. Emi and Kayo are *kitsune*, without doubt, so too Miho. Akiko is a classic *tanuki*. Satomi something in between, the height of a *kitsune*, but a touch of the *tanuki* about those hard-working thighs.

Another link in the chain of relationship

After hearing about Shesay.com, My Prince Charming, and Lover by Email I feel I have to discuss this virtual relationship phenomenon with my social commentator friend, Komatsu – it is right up his street. He takes in what I say, treating it as both seriously funny and peculiarly thought-provoking. He feels rewarded by my interest in these matters, he says, and issues a most intriguing invitation. Next time I am in Tokyo, he will take me to a virtual home. He explains a little of it on the phone, enough to whet my appetite for what sounds like another curious Japanese exploration of the unreal.

Within a month Komatsu and I are travelling upward in a lift in a building in Shinjuku. When the doors open several floors above street level we find ourselves in a traditional Japanese lane: cobbled pavement, bamboo fences, the eaves of the buildings almost hanging over them – all this under a typical suspended panel ceiling found in any modern office. We walk a few steps down the lane and push open a small creaky gate. Both of us duck to pass through into a tiny garden, complete with carp pond, mossy rocks, *tanuki* statue and wooden buckets of water. Komatsu calls out *tadaima*! and he is instantly answered by a female voice inside the house.

'*O-kaeri nasai*!'

A middle-aged woman in a heavy pink *kimono* bustles out and kneels down on the veranda. From the *seiza* position she places both hands on the wooden boards and bows so deeply her forehead touches them. When she straightens she beams at both of us and briskly ushers us inside. She calls Komatsu *oto-san*, which means father, and is often used by older women to address their husbands. Another woman, much younger, is called to look after me. She is an ordinary-looking girl, but the prospect of her ministering to my needs is undeniably exciting. Komatsu explains who I am, and tells the women we want to stay together. They are all nods and smiles and agreements. We are led through a couple of paper screens to a warm and peaceful room. Komatsu already has his slippers and a drink. Mine arrive a little later because they have to ask me what I want. As Komatsu and I settle into armchairs in front of a television, Komatsu's lady shuffles around behind him and starts to massage his shoulders, which he rolls every now and then. She asks him about his day.

Komatsu, between theatrical yelps and guffaws, explains to me that this is the Virtual Home Service. It is provided for men who do not get a sympathetic enough reception when they come home from work. Here they get the ideal wife. He asks me what I would like my wife to do, and for a while my imagination runs riot. How far do the services of these virtual wives go? I play it safe and say I will just have what he's having. My wife is in position and working on my shoulders and neck right away. Komatsu jokes that I must have a very conservative view of him to so confidently follow him into the unknown.

My wife asks me how things went at work. I can't take it seriously and don't want to offend. I play along, but fear I am dull company for her. I am happy to accept the massage and space out, staring blankly into the television.

Komatsu tells me that there are less expensive alternatives to Virtual Home Service. Men can buy life-size wife dolls that are programmed to make the appropriate soothing 'welcome home' noises, and to deliver a constant supply of encouraging and sympathetic conversational interjections when their 'husband' talks. I want to see one, but he doesn't know where they can be found.

The wives move to our feet, lifting and gently massaging each one in their laps. My wife checks with me that her head is not in the way of the television – surely the ultimate act of consideration. With my heel nestled at the apex of my wife's thighs I reflect, once again, on how adeptly Japan conjures up new experiences.

Behaviour versus personality

The most admired behaviour in Japan is whatever is determined by the current role, and for any particular person that can be parent, offspring, superior, underling, benefactor, supplicant, and so on, depending on the prevailing situation. In Australia the most admired behaviour is that of one's true self, and it should not vary excessively, regardless of the situation one finds oneself in. If it does, one is simply regarded as a fake.

Self and hyperself

The self: something that can only be realised by throwing it away? I cannot explain why, but I feel more like myself here. *By losing myself I find myself* – ugh! the phrase makes me shiver. It has a kind of truth, but it is against all logic. In Japan I cannot express myself properly, either verbally, because of language limitations, or behaviourally, because of a self-imposed censorship. I cannot pursue my supposedly self-actualising roles, in which I normally make myself appear competent, such as at work, or in the university. But none of this really matters.

The transmutation of the self in Japan is well documented by *gaijin*. In *Love Upon the Chopping Board*, Claire Maree describes her time spent in Saitama as an experiment in self. She was free to explore new ways to act, without the resistance to change of the people she knew. On her return to Perth she missed the new person she had become in Japan, and somehow felt imprisoned in her self. David Mura, a third generation American Japanese, a *sansei*, describes in *Turning Japanese* how he visited Japan and underwent the same hyper-real transformation of self.

Gaijin are not the only ones who can simultaneously appear both less and more real. Even Emperor Hirohito, an identity if ever there was one, was really just a distant mythical figure to all but a tiny few, so different and unworldly that most people could not even imagine him, and had no idea what he was talking about when he announced to the nation, on 15 August 1945, that Japan had surrendered. For some, that was the day that the Emperor became human, for others, it confirmed his unreality.

Kabuki, Takarazuka, bunraku

A Japanese word for actor, *hai*, is written with a *kanji* that combines the radicals for person and negative (or un-). The visual impression is that of an un-person. Curiously compounding this inhumanity is the fact that the counters for actors and people were once different. Japanese is one of a handful of languages that enumerates objects according to what they are. There are different counters for people, sticks of thin things, animals, cupfuls, sheets of flat things, storeys, large furniture 'devices' such as televisions or pianos, suits of clothing, shoes or socks, slices of food, birds and rabbits, and anything else. For example, the name of the Tokyo suburb of Roppongi, meaning 'six trees,' is written with three characters. The first is six, the third is tree, and the middle (the *-pon* of Roppongi) is the counter. A transliteration would be something like 'six sticks of tree.' For people, the counter has always been *-nin*, but for actors it was once *-hiki*, the same as used for animals.

The use of *-hiki* was more a case of social class distinction than a nod to the illusion of actors' characters. Acting was considered a base profession. Curbs were placed on *kabuki* in order to minimise its lasciviousness. One of these was the Tokugawa ruling that no women could take part, so all the parts, whether male or female, are now played by men. There was a brief experiment that took place in the 19th century, in which real women were given the female roles. It did not work. Audiences could not accept the change, and concluded that women could no longer play the female roles properly, it had to be men. Ian Buruma offers the explanation, in *A Japanese Mirror*, that no woman could represent the synthesised ideal, only a man, who has no particular female identity, can do this. In Peter Greenaway's *Eight and a Half Women* a Japanese woman wants to become a female impersonator, a male *kabuki* player of women, an *onnagata*. It is only then, she feels, after all the careful training, that she can become truly feminine.

To counterbalance this sexual asymmetry is the famous Takarazuka theatre, near Osaka. Here, all the men's parts are played by women, who speak gruffly, strut, fight with swords, and look so gorgeous that their female leads swoon in their arms. The predominantly female audience swoons too. Akiko was a fan of Takarazuka and, when I asked her why she liked seeing women pretending to be men, she told me that Takarazuka men were just like real men, but much 'nicer.'

Any first-time visitor to *kabuki* cannot help but notice that black-clad stage hands often appear onstage during the action. They will sometimes follow the actors to straighten their clothing, or to position their slippers. More often, they will be positioning props and cleaning up. These men are called *kuroko*, and as far as the reality of the story is concerned, they don't exist. Following from this, as far as the reality of the audience is concerned, they similarly do not exist.

A similar situation holds in *bunraku*, Japanese puppet theatre. Unlike western Punch and Judy shows, or Balinese shadow-puppet theatre, the *bunraku* puppeteers are in full view, surrounding and often outnumbering the puppets. In *bunraku* then, the all-too-visible real people are the non-entities, and the puppets are the real protagonists. Non-entities do not need to be hidden.

In *kabuki* there is even unreality within the unreality of the play. Alex Kerr writes of the *danmari* sequences in his book, *Lost Japan*. The word means silence, but what *danmari* sequences lack is not sound, as there is music, but something more profound. The entire cast appears on a darkened stage as if sleepwalking. Actors appear not to see each other, they wander without direction, they even collide, then continue as if nothing happened. Dramatic links are provided by objects that may be dropped accidentally by one character, and absent-mindedly picked up by another. The effect is ghostly, disturbing and hypnotic at the same time.

Capgras syndrome

Like many people of my generation, I read the books of Carlos Castaneda. I found them strangely seductive, but of all the remarkable events that took place in these books, the most disturbing, and one which still occasionally returns to my thoughts, involved a suspicion that a familiar person had, in fact, been replaced by a replica. The replica was perfect, and yet it was someone different. This is a paradox, but not an unrealistic one. People really do have such suspicions in real life, not just in books. It is called Capgras syndrome. Why is this suspicion so disturbing? There could be many reasons, just one of which is that if a person is not who they purport to be, then nothing we know about them is valid. We cannot predict, with the least bit of certainty, anything about them. In the next hour, or minute, they could do anything.

Can Turing pass his test?

During the 1940s, Alan Turing was the first person to think seriously about the question of what separates real and artificial people. His final proposal for a test amounted to nothing more than reliance on other people's opinions (normally considered the least worthy of bases for science). In the decades that have elapsed, legions of artificial intelligence researchers have been unable to make significant enhancements to this questionable test of humanity.

Late one night I watch a TV drama about Turing, entitled *Breaking the Code*. I particularly like the title, since this is what Turing did in both his official and (insufficiently) private life. In his official role he worked at Bletchley Park and figured large in the Allied efforts to keep up with German code enhancements during World War II. In his private life he rationalised that since his homosexuality *per se* did no harm to anybody, there was little point in hiding it.

What is interesting is that I begin to feel that I am really watching Turing. And yet the Turing I watch is an actor interpreting a role in a TV dramatisation, based on a stage play of the same name, which is based on Alan Hodges biography of Turing, *Alan Turing: the Enigma*, which is based on *post hoc* reports and documentation. Turing the reality is buried deep within Turing the idea.

How odd then, to be able to walk into the laboratory a few hours later and nod 'good morning' to Donald Michie, who, over sixty years ago, was a colleague and lunch-time chess opponent of Alan Turing at Bletchley Park. And how much odder to see Donald's name, and point it out to him, in a scene with Turing in the book I am reading, Neal Stephenson's novel, *Cryptonomicon*.

Primal sweat milker, Master Mike will rap

```
'lo leo, my logogriphic griffin'
'Hi gerty.'
```

'which leads one to say robins go airmail, olé!'

Aha, let's have a closer look at this...

'liar airing bosom, ambrosial origin'

Leo nods appreciatively.

'Very tasty!'

'having established my identity, let me now
present my credentials... i'm mr will's parakeet:
william's pet, kramer'

I have to work for a while.

'Well, I'm Artemis Park, prim Malawi Kestrel.'

'oh leo, a wonderful flight of fancy! i'm raw,
skeletal, prim'

This came so fast she must have had it prepared.

'Let's walk a primal rim.'

'... tramp warlike miles, sire limp, mater walk'

A little slower this time, but faster than I am.

'Let's impair warm elk.'

'i will spark ammeter: imperial welt-marks'

'Let's milk a raw prime, permit male raw silk.'

'ooh la la, leo! wanna see my versoid?'

'Nothing would please me more, young gerty.'

'pat will immerse ark,
trample irma wilkes.
reptile marks wilma,
we stalk mr imperial'

Leo applauds long and loud.

'It's terribly dark, tyger, not to say densely
populated.'

'actually, it's by miriam kelp-walters; rather
alliterative too, unsurprisingly'

'You certainly went to town on names, didn't you?'

'well, i thought that was the idea, and they do
permit an extra degree of anagrammatical
flexibility, i must confess'

'It was a wonderful return of service.'

'master like warm lip?'

Leo kisses tyger.

tyger purrs and wants more...

'kill swim parameter'

'OK!'

'imperil market laws'

'Brilliant, but enough!'

'aw, shucks... and i was just about to get serious'

Leo raises an enquiring eyebrow.

'leo, thank you for forgiving my truly unforgivable behaviour vis-à-vis the non-boarding of aeroplane and the deplorably bad treatment of my dearest feline friend. i don't quite know how to show you how grateful i am to have your forgiveness'

'You don't have to.'

'i just got so scared on the day that i couldn't stop shaking. i even made myself ill'

'Poor little kitten. Lost your Whiskas?'

tyger nods.

Leo hugs his tyger affectionately.

'leo, i really want to make it up to you. can we try again?'

Drifting Clouds

The valley

I COME TO LIVE IN A VILLAGE that sits in a sloping crook where a flat valley floor skirts a curving wooded hillside. Behind the village the forest rises steeply; before it hundreds of level rice fields stretch north and south. The single road that leads into the village curves up from the main road for about half a kilometre through the rice fields. Down at the turn-off, set away from all the houses, a post office and a tavern sit beside a space for the buses from Himeji to turn around. The turn-off area is called Araki, meaning 'rough tree,' so I choose to call the village by the same name. Its real name is Marron Town – an awkward mingling of French and English, commemorating the chestnut trees that were destroyed to make way for it.

The Sugo River meanders through the valley. From every branch of the valley flows a little tributary, and so the river fattens quickly on its journey south. It sways from one side of the valley to the other, and the main road crosses it many times. When I first arrived on the bus from Himeji, moving up the valley along this road, I looked down at the river from every narrow bridge. At each crossing the river was smaller and more rocky.

The name of the surrounding district, covering the Sugo Valley and two more to the east, is Yumesaki, 'dream-approach.'

It is now mid-October, the rice has just been harvested for the first time this year, and the fields are brown and sere. In July, on a reconnaissance trip, I had seen tadpoles and a turtle swimming among the rice plants, but now dry rice stalk stumps stand stiffly in hardening mud. The trees that cover the hillsides are still deep luscious summer greens, and the air remains hot and heavy. Sweating so hard that I can feel drops running down my sides, I drag a suitcase up the road from the bus stop to the house I am to live in, and wonder how quickly the news of my arrival will spread.

The mud nests that swallows built on the walls of the house are deserted now. In July, both nests housed families of fledglings who were just learning to fly. Then, they flapped around in energetic loops and circles. Under the eaves I can see the grease marks left by their feathers as they passed in and out of their nests. I wonder where they fly now, if they fly at all.

Weeds have grown back all around the house, and the fence has sagged even lower. I ought to tend to both. Neighbours will complain.

Persimmon trees here outnumber the drinks machines. The fruit, now so delicately coloured it makes peaches look coarse, hangs un-picked all over the valley, beside the roads and in the gardens. Despite this, persimmons are on sale in the shops, even here, at about 100 yen apiece.

At this time of year the insects screech and trill all day, and in the evening small bats come out to catch them. The smoke from fires in the rice fields, where farmers are enriching the soil with ash, rises slowly and hangs overhead, or drifts silently down the valley on the soft wind. Hawks are nearly always wheeling on the thermal up-draughts, over the hillsides. In the river, tall storks and cranes, some grey, some white, some white and grey, stalk around the weed beds and reed islands, in search of fish. They lean forward, staring intently, and then with a dart and a jerk, a small bewildered fish is transferred from stream to stomach. Turtles claw their way unsteadily onto rocks in mid-stream while crows wash themselves in the shallows – some-thing I've never seen before.

Not long after arriving, as I stroll along the road, I hear a soft rustle in the grass verge and turn to see a snake slither out into the rice field. We both stop. The snake is about four feet long, brown, and nearly two fingers thick. I stamp on the ground to induce more movement. The snake slides silently deeper into the rice stalks and disappears. A couple of days later I see another snake, dead on the road, near the house.

Frequent as these animal encounters are, the village is far from rus-tic. Nearly every house has a small car parked beside it. The relative remoteness makes cars a necessity. There are about one hundred houses, all small, most of them new. It looks like a housing estate, detached from some larger town and left here to fend for itself. Boys practise softball in the nearby playing fields, and in the morning the children all ride their bikes to school.

Rubbish, *gomi*, is collected according to a strict schedule, and I presume there are penalties for anyone who flouts the rules. The rubbish must be deposited at the *gomi* station on Tuesdays and Fridays. All bags must be of the correct type, and one's name must appear on the bag. There are precise rules about what kinds of rubbish can be thrown away: particular days for particular rubbish. At first I am in an agony of anxiety about getting something wrong and perhaps suffering the humiliation of having my *gomi* rejected and unceremoniously thrown back at my door. So I squash it all flat and take it in my backpack to Himeji station, where I suffer the lesser indignity of being seen jamming it into one of the bins in the smoking corner. Emi tells me this is not so unusual. Japanese men, finding themselves responsible for this household chore for the first time, and being equally afraid of getting it wrong, have often resorted to exactly the same solution.

Many houses in the village have a dog, some two. At night the barking and howling spreads in rabid chain-reaction through the lanes, and can be incessant. Most of the dogs are chained or caged – another example of man's ability to interfere in the nasty, brutish short lives of animals, and make them even worse. The few cats I see in the streets are excessively wary, a sign that they have learnt through experience that most humans are better steered clear of. Or perhaps they have seen the fate of the dogs and decided it is better not to be loved so much.

At 5 PM, a gentle tune begins to play over the public address system. The network of speakers covers not just the village, but the entire valley. A motherly voice urges all good children to go home now. I do not know its effectiveness with children, but it never fails to set the dogs howling.

In other towns the public address system is even more intrusive. In some places, Kurayoshi in Tottori prefecture, for example, it is a local law that all houses must have a speaker installed in the kitchen, so that the authorities can speak directly to the populace at any time of the day, whether they like it or not. I wonder if the councillors were inspired by Orwell.

Small business is the order of the day in Araki. Apart from those engaged in fieldwork, many families run little rural businesses either from or beside their houses. There are carpenters, builders, mechanics, and – almost everywhere – barbers. This valley must promote hair growth, as the barbers have the numbers over all other businesses. Except perhaps for *sake* shops; yes, *sake* shops are the most numerous. One of the barbers, perhaps under the strain of excessive competition, appears to have diversified into electronics retailing. The wall of his salon is stacked floor to ceiling with stereo systems. The village also has a Lawson Station convenience store, two petrol stations, two supermarkets, and a handful of restaurants, two of them excellent. Further afield, dotted up and down the valley are other little shops and businesses.

Most flat land in Japan is either built upon or used for agriculture. When I ride the bus into Himeji, the nearest big town, there is not so much a shift from rural to urban, as a shift in land share. Buildings become denser, and the fields thin out. The rice fields never completely disappear, they can be found even in the heart of Japanese cities, overshadowed by banks and electronics stores, and perhaps suffocated by petrol fumes, but surviving nonetheless.

I go for a walk this evening. A group of children chasing each other in the street all stop, turn towards me, say *konbanwa*, and solemnly bow. The moment has a rare kind of cinematic beauty. Often children shout 'hallo' at me. I don't mind. I parrot hello back to please them, and then say *konnichiwa*, eliciting the automatic response: *konnichiwa* and a bow of the head. Why should I be offended at being treated as a thing when they so readily react like things themselves?

The dogs are out, barking at each other, and walking their humans, who stoop impassively now and then to fold the dogs' turds into newspaper or plastic bags. Two lads pitch a baseball. It smacks hard into their mitts. The lane I explore fades to a track that winds through a wood and a cool bamboo grove, and opens up into another village. I've climbed over a low pass into the next valley. I walk on through this valley. People here are just as friendly. They bow from their cars and gardens. I find flood control dams in many unexpected places at the edges of each village. There are fish ponds too. Continuing to bear left around the peak behind the house, I expect to see familiar landmarks soon. According to the sketchy and probably unreliable map I carry, I should be able to loop around and re-enter my village from the other end.

Distant hamlets are dotted randomly among the rice fields. The rice stalks hang drying in long racks set out in the fields. In all directions lie small hills, dark with forest, steep, and rising straight up from the rice fields, like Norwegian mountains rising out of fjords. Many small fires smoulder in the fields and the smell of smoke is never far away.

I come to where I expect my village to be, but it isn't. Undaunted by this surprise, I press onward, trusting that the problem is due to poor scaling of the map rather than my sense of direction. I come to a fork where one road rises high into hills on the left, and the other leads ahead into a valley. Logic says that I should go left, but not that I should go up. I choose left anyway. The climb into the hills is so long and winding that I several times consider giving up and retracing my steps the long way back. At a pass I look down into a new valley. It has a main road that may or may not be the one I know, but if so, I am now unsure which side of it I am. I plod on, despite the worsening light. I soon see a sight that raises my hopes: a tree that stands much higher than its neighbours, like a lollipop stuck on top of a hill. It is so prominent, I am sure I've seen it before, improbable as this may seem. And soon I confirm my location. I've travelled exactly as planned, the journey was just longer than the map suggested. Walking back through the fields to the house, I hear, for the first time in all my months in Japan, the word *sayonara*. Two women who had been talking in the smoky dusk say this to each other as they turn their bikes in different directions.

It isn't long before the second rice growth has painted the fields a fresh green again. Here and there on the hillsides a few leaves transform. Autumn colours, scarlet, ochre, yellow, are spreading one tree at a time. The persimmon trees have lost all their leaves, and their now bare, now luridly flaming, fruit resemble drops of paint on the autumn landscape. Evenings are cooler and shorter. At times a vesperal mist slumps in the valley like a fallen cloud. I've been cold at night. Winter is coming as surely as ever.

Some days are still clear and sunny, and it can be hot at times, but deep in the gullies, under the bamboo, the cold always lingers. Walking beside the groves I feel it grab at me suddenly, then fade away again.

Friends are a little offended that I have chosen to live alone here, rather than be with them. They say it is selfish. This dumbfounds me. My time in Japan has until now always been over-complicated, cross-hatched by travel arrangements, expensive and dictated by other people's schedules. This is the first time I've been able to take things slowly, without thoughts of wasted days and dollars. Opportunities can rarely be shared, we must take them alone, which requires nerve, and which is why so many go unanswered. My opportunity was to borrow an empty house for a few months. I can't imagine the foolishness of not taking this opportunity, when work and home and other pressures have all released me at the right time.

The dogs keep breaking into awful riotous song, like deranged choristers. It drives me insane too. My first two edicts, should I ever become Shogun, would be to ban the keeping of dogs and put all cables out of sight – just like Huis Ten Bosch.

News of my arrival does spread fast. I become known as *o-gaijin-san*, which roughly translates as 'honourable Mister Foreigner.' I like the sound of this. People know there is a foreigner in the valley, but I don't want to confirm any preconceptions they have, which might allow me to be too easily pigeon-holed. I try to blend in. It is hard to gauge the reaction of the people to my presence. As I pass a group of young guys outside a shop I catch my foot against the ground and stumble. Some of them laugh derisively. Passing a primary school, one of the children stands at the fence and shouts what sounds like '*Dare? Dare?*' at me. 'Who? Who?' As I walk on he shouts louder and more demandingly. Another shouts '*Amerika-jin!*' Many people bow and smile, and some pretend I am not there. Passing a high school I hear '*Mite! O-gaijin-san!*' One of the girls cuts across the playground to intercept me at the fence. 'Where are you living?' she asks coquettishly, and 'Where are you from, America?' I answer her questions patiently and when I've finished she returns to her friends to report back. A woman parts the curtains to stare at me as I walk past her house. I bow slightly and mouth *konnichiwa* to her, but she doesn't react at all.

I feel my every move is watched and discussed. This is not because I am unusual. It surely happens to everyone here. Like most Japanese communities, the village is one large recursive panopticon. Trying not to fulfil too many uncharitable expectations, I behave politely, decorously, and, most important of all, conventionally.

I often carry a simple *kanji* dictionary and painstakingly decode signs. This can be inside the bus, or waiting at the bus stop. I know the meaning of most of the signs inside the bus now. They say commonplace things like 'in the event of sudden stops, please hold on tight,' and 'do not stand in the way of the door.' I don't know what else I was expecting.

I never use English unless my Japanese and gestures have first proven unproductive. It usually transpires that English will be unproductive too, though not always. At the dry cleaners, I struggle with dictionary and phrase book to find the word for bed-sheet. It turns out to be *beddo-shiito*, but I only discovered this after making a silly mistake. When I look up 'sheet' in my phrase book I skip a line without knowing it, and consequently ask the woman at the dry cleaners how much it would cost to clean *hitsuji*, a sheep.

The gentlest of rains fell this evening. And immediately the air was full of tiny hovering insect apparitions – milky blurs dancing among the even tinier raindrops. It can be so quiet here when it rains. The falling mist hums on the leaves. On another damp afternoon I walk past one of the ponds and hear the curious soft smacking sound of carp sucking insects down from the surface.

In the first few weeks the days grow noticeably shorter. This is partly because of the approaching solstice, but also because the sun disappears below the hills early in the afternoon, and a false twilight ensues. Each day, I have time for breakfast, a couple of hours of work or reading, lunch, a walk, and then the day is almost over.

I gather a bit of geomorphologic insight into my surroundings at an exhibition in Himeji. On the floor is a large composite satellite image showing the mountain contours for the central third of Japan. The scale is 100,000 to one, but after careful study I am able to identify my valley and even the little hillock that creates the curve for Araki to nestle in. From here I am able to trace where my walks have taken me, and where the Sugo River meets the sea west of Himeji. Japan seen like this – as if I am two-hundred kilometres high – looks much like a fractured spine whose flesh has begun to fall away. The central mountains stand out like broken vertebrae but the land softens towards the coast until it reaches a uniform absolute flatness at sea level. This confirms my thoughts, based on the flatness in the bottom of the Sugo Valley, and what my GPS unit tells me, that the valley floor is close to sea level.

Emi calls from afar

An unfamiliar chiming echoes around the house. At first I wonder what it is, then, realising it is my phone, hunt desperately for it. Suddenly a phone call seems a precious thing, not to be missed.

'*Emi desu.*'

'Oh, Emi! How nice to hear from you!'

'Maaku, are you happy in your valley?'

'Yes, I'm happy in my valley. How are you?'

'You must have found a nice girl there, *ne*?'

'No, there are only schoolgirls here, Emi,' I answer automatically, before the import of Emi's question dawns on me.

'But it is so long since you called me, Maaku. I thought maybe you forget Emi.'

'I'm sorry.'

I am, and there is no alternative but to apologise. I don't like to do anything to upset her. I have no excuses, no reasons. It is as if I have deliberately forgotten how good she can be to talk to. I know it would sound weak to Emi, but I came here to get away, somehow, and frequent telephone calls would have disturbed my solitary sojourn. Now, belatedly, I realise I must compromise.

'You don't forget about me?'

'Of course not. *Koibito desu, ne*?'

'*So desu.*'

'*Shimpai shinaide, ne*?' Don't worry.

'*Hai.*'

Slowly, haltingly, the conversation gets off the ground. I give Emi a run-down on what I've discovered here since we last spoke. She begins to laugh a little; I begin to relax. I really wonder at my not having called her earlier, she is such a soothing presence on the phone.

'And I'm sorry I didn't call, Emi. It was bad of me.'

'Is OK, Maaku. Nice to talk to you again.'

'And you, Emi. Do you have to go now?' I sense she is wrapping things up.

'*Hai,*' she answers, then pauses – or rather, she pronounces the word so slowly that it turns into a thought unspoken. Almost under her breath she adds 'Maaku…,' and in a whisper, what sounds like '*suki yo.*' She hangs up.

Suki is the Japanese verb 'to like,' but said in a conversation like this, with *yo* for emphasis, by a woman to a man, and particularly with the shy tenor of Emi's tiny tense voice, it means only one thing: I love you.

I find myself hoping this is what she said, but to call back now and seek confirmation would only embarrass her. She's put my head in a bit of a spin and it is some seconds before I remember to take a breath.

Set up

Belatedly, I set about installing the game from MagA on my computer. An awful lot of personal information is requested in the process, such as my name, location, those too of my mail and address files. I also enter my phone number and web site URL. I permit access to local files and directories. I describe myself, and others, in response to dozens of impertinent questions. I have options for linking my profile to photographs, so my appearance can be more accurately rendered. I wonder if this is all going to be worth it. Meanwhile, I make notes on a pad beside the keyboard: excessively demanding set up procedure? major privacy issues? system integrity?

Walks

I go walking again this evening, in the hour before sunset. Although the sun is still in the sky, it is hidden behind the hills to the west, and the darkening valley is already chilly. The cold doesn't seem to affect an old man sitting on the concrete floor of his shed, patiently snipping away at his bonsai tree. I watch a column of hawks circling in the up-draught on the hillside. They are silhouetted against a backdrop of pink and grey clouds, sparse brushstrokes in the sky. The high keening of the hawks has a surprising light quality to it.

An old woman is startled to see me walking past her house. I ask if it is all right to walk this way.

'Eh?' she squawks.

I repeat my question and she gives the go-ahead.

Somewhere near the house a cat has whined pitifully for hours. I have tried to find it, at first thinking it had fallen into a drain, or got itself stuck on a roof, but it always eludes me. It may be caged, I've seen others so imprisoned. At the other end of town a wild pig is kept in an iron cage outside a shop. I sat beside the cage and tried to find out who owned it, but no one would tell me. These things distress me. Today I discover more animal misery – a few dozen cattle stalled in a tiny barn. Some lie in their own shit. I know they are not there just for the night or for milking, they are there forever. There is nowhere else in this valley to keep them. I wish, again, we could just leave animals alone.

The autumn seems to have arrived quite suddenly. The hillsides are parti-coloured, like an old greatcoat stained every colour from chocolate to lime, custard to plum. There are no maple trees in the valley, so I miss their vivid scarlets and vermilions.

The old people work in the hardening fields, even this late in the year, until it is dark. The tough old *obaasan*, some so bent they can only look at me by standing sideways and twisting their necks, work the plants and soil with their hands. With bonnet and basket, they move slowly from one row to another. Some have wheelbarrows instead of baskets, some have tiny trucks. Beside the rice there are fields of soy, whose beans dangle like pendant testicles among the leafy foliage. Just now most of the soy plants are being cut and turned upside-down to dry more thoroughly. Huge *daikon* radishes, so eager to be big, literally push themselves out of the ground. Cabbages are planted in alternating white and purple rows, right beside the road, particularly at junctions. I wonder if there is a reason for this. Large plants that look like wild rhubarb, onions, tall lettuce, and small plants like strawberry that have not yet borne fruit proliferate. The second growth of rice is well advanced now.

Today is one of those memorably beautiful autumn days. The sun is strong and warm, and the clear air is so still it is only after several minutes of watching a tree that I see a leaf move. The valley is utterly peaceful. I visit a small temple I spotted from the road the other day. It is deserted, so I just wander around the graves, deciphering the names and dates. Only the recent ones are legible. The older ones have crumbled, or given themselves over to moss, as will the new ones, eventually. At home after my walk I make some coffee and sit in the sunshine at the wooden table outside the front of the house, working at my computer. The poor plaintive cat, aching to be patrolling the fields, but caged in the garden down the road – I now know – wails ceaselessly.

Some time recently many of the persimmons were picked. They hang, skinned and drying now, on strings outside the houses and sheds around the village. The fruit shrivels so small it almost disappears beneath its calyx, the hard leafy part that fans out from the stem. I wonder how they'll taste. I expect they will appear on menus in the coming weeks, so perhaps I'll find out.

All of my evenings are spent at home. I read, watch television, and sometimes study Japanese by *kanji* card, book, minidisc, or CD-ROM. I pick up a bit more Japanese from the TV, but only slowly. If I want to understand what is happening I have to use the 'bilingual' soundtrack, when it is available.

I found a cutler on the road into Himeji, and bought an expensive knife from him. It has the wavy marks of lamination along its blade, like a samurai sword. It is dangerously sharp – I've cut myself already. I bought the knife because I plan to eat only fresh foods while I live here, and expect to be chopping vegetables every day.

My meals are almost unvarying. Fresh salad, initially the familiar: carrots, lettuce, tomato, rocket, cucumber, eggs, gradually adding local touches: *daikon*, ginger, *shiitake*, *nori*, *tofu*, lotus root, bean sprouts, bamboo shoots, and fresh but unidentified herbs. I take pleasure in chopping and slicing all these things before throwing them into the bowl. Occasionally the baked potato man comes by in his little van. He sings in a mournful voice 'Ishi yaki imo, yaki imo' (actually it is a recording). I buy a red sweet potato from him, wrapped in newspaper, and eat it immediately, with a spoon. Down at the junction with the main road most evenings is the *takoyaki* man. He sells cooked octopus, as yet untried. For dessert, and for lunch, I eat apples, oranges, persimmons, bananas. Breakfast is simply coffee and toast.

The diet does me good. I lose weight around the middle, and rediscover my abdominal muscles, tightened from all the walking in the hillsides. My hunger is satisfied without feeling bloated and immobilised after dinner, and I enjoy thinking of new things to do with my limited range of ingredients – but it is not enough. I crave occasional variety. I discover what a lovely combination *tofu* and potato crisps make. I buy a bottle of *umeshu* and drink it all in four days. I find Swiss rolls on knockdown special at the supermarket, and give in to the temptation. Today I bought some chocolate – but of the strong dark bitter kind, my least favourite, so I won't eat it all at once. My more constructive response to the need for variety is to buy a range of different salad dressings and some *aji no moto* (literally, 'origin of taste') monosodium glutamate for flavouring.

Another day of hot sun and still peacefulness. I wander west into one of the branches of the valley. My first impressions of the valley had been of a long and irregular rille. In reality it has many side-valleys, some of which open into complex systems of their own. Some valleys end in a steep ravine, but others have roads that lift up over low passes into valleys beyond. Far from being one-dimensional, the valley is actually part of a network of connections in all directions.

Today the number of insects and grubs I've been seeing every day finally surprises me. Evidently, insecticide is used sparingly or not at all hereabouts. I find a glorious orange moth on the road. Its camouflage is perfect for autumn, but not for life on tarmac. I try to move it to a safer place, but it is having none of that. In one of the streams I see a shoal of fish, one of which is also startling orange. I wonder if he is a natural variation or an outcast from someone's goldfish collection.

Scattered around the valley I find *kura*, old family storehouses with crumbling earthen walls, all approaching terminal decrepitude. Many of the buildings have thatched roofs which have been boxed in by corrugated iron. Beside the older buildings are markers erected by the local council. The markers explain some of the history of the buildings, but little is done to preserve them. Many small shrines and temples can be found in odd places around the valley. They are among the oldest buildings still standing here. Some shrines are little more than roofed cabinets, on raised platforms out amongst the fields, or hard against the hillside, in the shade of the trees and bamboo. They are all in use, as far as I can tell, even the run-down ones.

On all my rambles, I have an invisible companion. She is a participant in all my internal dialogues, the audience for all my exclamations and observations. Having her ear helps me verbalise all my impressions. She stands and applauds as I balance on a rock or leap a stream – the same way she applauded my climb on a wall in a ninja village. Not having her is devaluing something for me.

I see a *torii* set across a track leading into the forest, and turn to investigate. About half a kilometre into the trees the climb gets much steeper and, there, in a clearing, I find the Nihyaku-amaru (two hundred too much) shrine. An impressively large fertility symbol stands to its left. The shrine building has the traditional 'folded fingers' Shinto roof structure, but just to the side of it is a small pavilion housing a Buddha, and hiding the shrine is a Buddhist-style fore-structure. A strange mixture of religions. And science, too. An enthusiast has attached botanical labels to almost all the plants in the vicinity. From these I learn that I am in a grove of *sugi, hinoki* and *mominoki* – cedar, cypress and fir. It is eerily quiet. Another small wooden building has sliding screens across the front. Through a gap I can see that this building is empty except for a few items such as bowls and mats. As I tentatively touch the screen to slide it further open a violent gust of wind buffets the clearing, leaves shower down on everything, as if the spirit of the place had just been disturbed. When my heart stops thumping I step back from the building and walk away.

Back at the village I watch the children stop to pet the caged dogs in the garden down the street. Nearby the poor trapped cat pleads loudly with them for… something. They pay it no attention. The same children show remarkable compassion towards insects they find on the road. Why don't they pity the cat?

Perhaps the best walk of all is one that heads south down the valley to a little village called Katanade. It was here that I saw a small wooden signpost pointing to Mount Shosha, which is where Engyo-ji, a sprawling thousand-year-old Buddhist temple complex, is situated. At first I laugh because the sign appears to be pointing exactly the wrong way, but then it gets me thinking. *Perhaps the sign is correct, and perhaps there is a path curving over the hills*, I think. So I walk in the direction of the sign and stop to ask an old man I find working in his shed. 'Yes,' he says, 'go into the trees, follow the path up, left, and up again.'

I return a few days later and start the climb. I have eggs and apples and chocolate in my backpack, and cold tea to drink. After verifying directions with a woman at the roadside, I set off into the woods. I come upon many stream crossings – small bridges or jumbled stepping stones. The trees are tall but attenuated. I think the area has been logged at least once. I climb for nearly two kilometres, and though the day is cold, I grow hot. As the gradient levels off I hear voices and see part of the temple – a tiled roof – through the trees to the left. The trees are suddenly much larger, evidently having been spared by the loggers because of their proximity to the temple. For a while I wander slowly around the temple's paths and courtyards. It is difficult to get an idea how large this complex is, as buildings are scattered over a wide area, hidden among trees. I work my way east through the complex. I have developed a craving for the hot thick and spicy *amazake* they sell in the shop near the great Maniken building at the heart of the complex. I am also anxious to catch the last cable car down from the mountain, not relishing the idea of climbing down in the dark. Japan is a new experience in so many ways: architectural, religious, cultural, even recreational – it is not often that we can go hiking from where we live and stumble into a huge and ancient mountain-top religious centre.

The Maniken building resembles Kiyomizu-dera in being built out over a large terrace high on a steep hillside. The roofs and rafters are covered in name cards, plastered there by pilgrims. This temple is on the great thirty-three-temple pilgrimage that runs through western Japan, from coast to coast. With the sun streaming in through the clouds of incense smoke, the rattles of bells and change being given at the *mamori* counters, the place is full of atmosphere. A large crowd of pilgrims is making plenty of noise and bustle. The priests are busy scribing and stamping their pilgrimage logbooks, and the Buddha that sits to the left of the temple is being rubbed for all he is worth. People are using hair dryers to dry the fresh calligraphy in their logbooks. Outside the sky is now bright and the sunlight filtered through the autumn leaves has warmed the wooden floors underfoot.

From the temple I descend to the south-east, facing Himeji city, and catch the last cable car of the day. By the time I reach the bottom of the valley it is cold and dark and all that remain to be seen of the temple are two small lights high on the mountain.

Later I return and try an alternative start to the climb up the mountain. It soon joins up with the first route, and not long after that I am at the temple complex again. I criss-cross the complex, discovering that a few of the more remote buildings are near-derelict. Nearby is a marker, at the very summit of Mount Shosha, 371 metres, a good thousand feet above the altitude of the house.

I believe there are two small buildings further to the north. I strike out in their general direction, trying one path after another, discarding those options that appear to turn in the wrong direction or head down into the valleys below. Soon I find one building, and then a little further on, the other too. They are some way distant from the main buildings and are accessible by only a winding path, rough in places, so it is no surprise they are deserted. Both are practically ruins, though some desultory restoration work seems to be in progress. Below one is a small spring (actually it is a stream that disappears underground higher up the slope, and then pops up again).

It is raining now and getting late, so I decide to go home. Perhaps rashly, I rely on my sense of direction and choose a new path that heads north towards the house. If my hunch pays off, this will save me having to make the detour west to Katanade. The path follows the ridge, below thin foliage. Most leaves are now underfoot, sometimes making the way difficult. At a few places vast fields of ferns extend up and down the gullies, a brilliant emerald against the black earth and the pale grey of the clouds. With every turn and dip, the path looks more promising, so, though the valleys below me have now filled with cloud, I proceed confidently.

Lower down the hillside I see familiar buildings through the clouds. I see my local supermarket and know I am only fifteen minutes from the house. I arrive home cold, tired, but elated at having found this direct and delightful path to Engyo-ji. After a hot shower and a change of clothing I receive a call from Emi, wanting to chat and hear about my day. Another great day completed.

A few days later I climb this new-found path, reaching Engyo-ji in only forty minutes. My hiking has steadily improved with my time here. I feel balanced and powerful as I surge up the hillside without breaking pace. In the sunshine the path looks completely different. Before, unable to raise my head because of the rain, I had overlooked quite a few of the wayside Buddhas that stand among the trees, watching over all travellers. The clouds also hid the spectacular view north, past Mount Seppiko to the high ranges in the centre of Japan, now dramatically lit by a bright winter sun in perfectly clear air. Another surprise is the sudden draft of hot air blowing up from the sunny sides of the ridge. At Engyo-ji I scout around for other paths, but fail to find anything promising, and so return the way I came, home early this time.

First contact

My induction into the life of the village begins with a meeting in the road. I had been exploring the other side of the valley when I noticed a woman had stopped her car and was waiting for me to draw level. She asked if I was lost, in English, and I assured her I wasn't. Later, on another road, she stopped me again, introduced herself as Kato Harumi and invited me to her house for tea, mentioning enticingly that her twenty-five year old daughter Naomi would be there.

Tea at the Katos' becomes an almost daily ritual, as does helping out at the after-school English classes Harumi holds for village children. By taking part I lay a network of obligations on parents who are grateful that their children, here in the semi-remote Sugo Valley, can experience English conversation with a native speaker. I am invited to watch the *karate* class at which two of the children are black belts. I am given a present of a green *furoshiki* by a shy small girl whose parents are so glad that she can talk with me. Many of the children arrive with little cakes and snacks for me. They shyly give them to Harumi, who passes them to me. It is quite touching. And thus, I begin to develop a village presence as someone who has a purpose and a contribution to make, rather than a distant Sasquatchian figure caught now and then lumbering through the woods.

Harumi also arranges for me to spend a day practising calligraphy with a *sensei* friend of hers. It is a children's class, and my large presence causes much disruption. Few of the children can concentrate with me kneeling beside them at the undersized bench. One little girl comes over and stares at my face.

'He has beautiful blue eyes, *sensei*,' she says, in Japanese.

'He's very big, isn't he?' observes one of the little boys.

They watch closely as I struggle to get a few *kanji* onto the paper.

'Skilful!'

'Beautiful, *na*?'

'They are very nice children,' I say to the *sensei*.

'*Eh*? He speaks Japanese!'

'Leave him alone!' the *sensei* commands. 'Get back to work, *na*?'

At first I wonder what this *na* means, but I suppose it must be a local variant of *ne*, the Japanese equivalent of 'eh?'

The calligraphy is hard at first, and I have to stop at lunch time because my hand and arm are aching. But I enjoy this morning more than I could have expected. In the proper surroundings, and with an informative teacher, calligraphy is something I could easily get hooked on.

Harumi invites me to lunches with the ladies of her English conversation groups, and also links me up with one of the local universities. My local social life bursts into action and soon becomes so complex that I have to keep track of my appointments in a diary.

My ability to look after myself is questioned. Harumi feeds me *oden* and noodles at her house and gives me eggs and yoghurt to supplement the apparently poor nutrition of my coffee and toast breakfasts. Because of her frequent invitations, I am exercising less and eating more cakes and biscuits. I expect my weight to start climbing back up again but it appears to be holding steady.

Knowing someone in the village brings all kinds of useful information. One of the shops in Himeji has a good selection of English books, I am told. A calligraphy teacher lives just a few minutes from my house; if I am interested an introduction can be arranged. Sunpia, a strange modern building I saw in the hills on one of my earliest walks, turns out to be a spa and general entertainment centre.

All kinds of unsuspected activities are going on in the dark village evenings, like *ikebana* flower arranging, the *karate* school I mentioned, and *soroban* classes.

Harumi is studying the *soroban*, the Japanese abacus, for fun. I meet her teacher, Miki-sensei, and am invited along to her lessons too. I pick up the basics of the *soroban* quite readily. Like most Japanese pursuits, *soroban* study is governed by a scale of grades and levels, ten *kyu* and nine *dan*.

The students rattle the beads around so fast that I cannot follow them. They are able to operate the *soroban* with their eyes closed. They even practise moving the beads in an imaginary mental image *soroban* (the 'soroban image in the head,' Miki-sensei calls it) and, astoundingly, get the right answers. Their real *soroban* are packed away in their carrying cases for this exercise, and Miki-sensei reads out a long list of numbers in a staccato monotone. The sound of fingers rapidly tapping bare desktops issues from all parts of the room. Watching the fingers move over their imaginary *soroban* is an eerie experience. It is a glimmering of just one more of our surprising mental capacities. If we can really do such complex arithmetic with imaginary *soroban*, what is the role of the real *soroban*?

Miki-sensei is pleased with my interest in *soroban* and gives me a huge one. I swallow a guilty lump in my throat – I know I will never repay her with the serious study she hopes for.

Being in the game

The game has some remarkable features. Like other games, it populates itself with names stolen from my email files. It also adapts its weather to mine, providing I play while logged on, and have supplied my location to the game web site. My name, and other barely audible messages will be whispered to me at random times if I am playing late at night. An AI component builds up a model of me and my interests from the files on my hard disk. If I give permission for this feature to operate, every single document in my computer will eventually be scrutinised and analysed. What I said in my emails and, in particular, how I responded to other mails will help form the user model. Given permission, the game will send text messages to my mobile phone, ostensibly from characters both real and fictitious.

Computer games are a new art form *in utero*. Like an embryo, they have the beginnings of form, but not yet any sensibility. Until now. This game is a significant departure from the competition.

Sumo initiations

Most afternoons in mid-November I find time to watch the Kyushu *sumo* tournament on television. *Sumo* grows on you. What starts as something of a morbid curiosity begins to acquire all the magnetism of any sport taken seriously, with the addition of an exotic and deeply historical aspect.

I'd developed a more than passing interest in *sumo* in July, when I realised that the Nagoya tournament, or *basho*, would be on while I was in town. Everything I had read or been told about *sumo* led me to believe that tickets were booked for months in advance and that getting in on the off-chance was virtually impossible. I'd even been discouraged from heading out towards the gymnasium to see if tickets were on sale. It was a waste of time, I was told.

I went anyway. Tickets for the day were on sale at about 2,500 yen, and even though this was the final Saturday of the tournament, and it was late in the afternoon, seats were still available near the back. The gymnasium was decorated outside with colourful banners indicating the names of the *rikishi*, wrestlers, competing. Inside the perimeter of the main hall was filled with stalls selling food, drinks, souvenirs and clothing. Many of the children in the audience had soft cuddly toys modelled on their favourite *rikishi*. Among the set of available toys is one with a noticeably darker skin than the others. I wonder if this is meant to be Musashimaru, an enormous lugubrious hulk. I buy a couple of beers to cool myself down, and settle into my seat high in the stands.

The activities of *sumo* are thoroughly traditional. All the officials wear archaic Japanese clothing, and the proceedings are conducted with the utmost formality. *Sumo* is a ritual. Above the ring is suspended a large Shinto roof structure, beautifully decorated with the aesthetic sense that accompanies *sumo*, despite the grossness of much of the flesh on view.

What goes on before me is a mystery. During the preparations for one of the bouts, the entire audience laughs. I'd been watching intently, but obviously missed something. I mentioned this to Emi later that evening, and this is how she explained it. There are rules about everything in *sumo*, and the *rikishi* use these boundaries to psychologically disadvantage their opponent. By transgressing, or appearing to be about to transgress, a rule, they can annoy an opponent and so gain an advantage. The art is to transgress the rule so minutely that disqualification or censure would be deemed an over-reaction. Knowing that they have succeeded in doing this, the *rikishi* can occasionally allow a cheeky smile to flitter across their swollen features. The crowd sees this and is amused.

Emi tells me this is 'charming and adorable' behaviour. This is a surprise. I ask if she finds *rikishi* attractive.

'They usually marry the daughters of *yakuza*,' she replies in typically oblique fashion.

The *yokozuna*, the highest ranking *rikishi*, of which there are only three at present, compete last. Earlier in the day the lower ranks competed. Just before the appearance of the *yokozuna*, the second-highest rank, *ozeki*, have their bouts. My late arrival gives me time to see the twenty or so best *rikishi* of the tournament.

The first of the *yokozuna* to compete is Takanohana, the only Japanese. He is my favourite among the three. He is the least physically repellent, and has an outward calm and frank confidence that is monolithic. He has won twenty *jusho*, championships, which puts him at third place in the all-time list.

Next up is dark-complexioned Musashimaru, already mentioned. He also has the bearing and dominance of a *yokozuna*, but his face is so heavily featured that he can hardly be admired for anything other than his remarkable success.

Finally, an even bigger Hawaiian behemoth, Akebono, comes to the *dohyo*. His body is so strangely proportioned that he resembles a huge insect. He stands a head higher than most of his opponents, who themselves are this much taller than ordinary people. He dwarfs giants. His belly is the largest in *sumo*, and this is saying something. His arms and legs are disproportionately long, and relatively thin, adding to the insect-like impression he creates. His head, with a top-knot that refuses to grow properly, is thrust far forward from the line of his spine, resting at the summit of a large, quivering slope of pocked breasts and pendulous gut, propped up by his *mawashi* belt. His back is so fat that it has no shape, or rather, it has become two great bulges of flesh, reminding me always of a beetle's back. He looks awful, in both senses of the word. His great weight has distorted his face into something truly ugly, and he appears to be suffering the unhealthy consequences of what he has done to himself. His stare, brought to bear on his opponents, and punctuated by a conspicuous clenching and unclenching of his jaw, is full of malevolence and disdain.

Akebono defeats nearly everyone he meets, usually by simply stepping forward once and pushing at them with his long arms. One step, arms outstretched, and Akebono does not leave much room for an opponent to fight in. They find themselves outside the ring. Akebono gives them a final stare, questioning the temerity they had to face him in the first place, and returns to his corner.

So far in the tournament, both Akebono and Musashimaru have won all thirteen of their bouts.

Then Akinoshima beats Akebono, and Musashimaru is also beaten, for the first time in the tournament. When lower-ranked *rikishi* beat *yokozuna* like this, the crowd go bananas, and hurl their cushions towards the ring as a gesture of great excitement and appreciation. The cushions form a great whirling purple vortex as they all fly into the centre, landing on *rikishi* and judges, in the salt, on the ring, and on other spectators. It is such an exuberant spectacle that I laugh out loud. It is a splendid finish to the day, and leaves tomorrow, the decider, perfectly set up.

That was July, and Akebono finished as winner, beating Musashi-maru in the last bout of the tournament. In this, the November tournament, the great talking point is the young Kotomitsuki, a *rikishi* rising so rapidly through professional *sumo* that his hair has not yet had time to grow long enough for a proper top-knot. His performance during the initial bouts is excellent, giving him a ten-win, one-loss record. Then he faces Musashimaru, the great *yokozuna*. Kotomitsuki is noticeably edgy, making false starts twice at the beginning of the bout, and apologising excessively to Musashimaru, whose serious dark expression never changes. The bout, once it begins, is a clash of the titans, great effort on both sides, fortune swinging first one way then the other, before Kotomitsuki finally wins by hurling Musashimaru ingloriously onto his great belly in the middle of the ring. Purple cushions rain down.

The next day Kotomitsuki is matched with another *yokozuna*: Takanohana, his greatest hero. He says that he couldn't sleep the previous night because he was so elated after beating Musashimaru. Also, he has often dreamt of one day facing Takanohana, and is excited that it is to be the last bout of the day. He never thought that this experience would come so soon. It is another great fight, which either could have won, but which eventually goes to Takanohana.

On the final day everyone has fallen away from the lead except for the mammoth Akebono and the rising star Kotomitsuki. Several of Kotomitsuki's wins have been brilliant. On the fourteenth day he used a move that had not been seen at the top level of *sumo* since 1974. Akebono leads the contest with thirteen wins to one loss. Kotomitsuki has twelve wins and two losses. Akebono must lose to give Kotomitsuki a chance of taking the *jusho*. Akebono faces the other huge Hawaiian *yokozuna*, Musashimaru, whose bulk rivals his, while Kotomitsuki has a lesser but still formidable opponent in the *ozeki* Musoyama.

Showing no sign of nerves, Kotomitsuki grabs the *mawashi* of Musoyama and simply bounces his huge opponent around the *dohyo* until Musoyama is forced to step outside. Kotomitsuki, now with thirteen wins to two losses, ties wins with Akebono who, watching malevolently from the *hanamichi*, hangs his head, knowing that the *jusho* that was almost in his grasp is now one more difficult bout away. He must defeat Musashimaru, or be forced to take on Kotomi-tsuki in a decider bout. Akebono and Kotomitsuki have never met – Kotomitsuki has risen so quickly to these levels of competition.

Kotomitsuki, who has an Utamaro face, with eyes that are no more than thin curved lines, and a smoothness of cheek that suggests a deep calm, has already been awarded all three special *sansho* prizes – for fighting spirit, technique, and outstanding performance. He is the first to have done this since Takanohana, his hero, did the same thing eight years ago. Back then, Takanohana went on to take the *jusho* too.

Akebono and Musashimaru face each other across the *dohyo* while two other bouts take place. Musashimaru sits with arms folded, seem-ingly at peace. Akebono sweats, and clenches his teeth, his cheeks bul-ging rhythmically. They have been fairly evenly matched, Akebono winning twenty-one of their thirty-seven meetings.

The *dohyo* is hardly big enough for the two of them. Akebono sets Musashimaru going backwards almost immediately. They lock up at the edge of the ring, arms around each other, but Akebono's greater height, weight, and positional advantage leave only one possible ending. Imper-ceptibly, in the slowest of slow motion, Musashimaru is forced past the point of balance and steps out of the ring. Akebono takes his eleventh *jusho* and Kotomitsuki's fairy tale ending is not to be.

Despite his formidable appearance, Akebono is reputed to be as genial as a favourite uncle, and so no grudge can be held against him for stealing Kotomitsuki's dream. Although he is currently at the top of his sport, he has been plagued by injury, and had to battle harder than most as an outsider; his success has not come easily, and his fu-ture is not assured. And Kotomitsuki, surely, will have his day.

Japanese heroes

I find it slightly disturbing that of the three figures most influential in shaping mediaeval Japanese history, Oda Nobunaga, Toyotomi Hide-yoshi, and Ieyasu Tokugawa, the first and most brutal is by far the most popular. My Japanese friends, mostly women who are not a blood-thirsty lot, are all quite unanimous in preferring Nobunaga. He is said to have inflicted the most horrible tortures on the children of his enemies, as a deterrent to anyone who might think of opposing him, but perhaps also because he enjoyed it. There is a much-told story that if these men wanted to hear a bird sing but the bird refused to, Hideyoshi would himself sing instead, Tokugawa would simply wait, but Nobunaga would kill it. People recount this parable with obvious relish. Why should such a character be popular?

There are a couple of explanations. Of the three leaders, Nobunaga was the most inclined to learn from the west, and had he not been assassinated and succeeded by the two other more conservative men, Japan would perhaps have become the world's greatest power. At the time of these three great figures, Japan almost certainly had the greatest military strength in the world, but was unable to impose it. As it was, the west eventually took Japan by surprise, caught napping in an introverted Tokugawan stupor. So, the idea of a great leader thwarted before he could lead his people to their greatest glory is obviously appealing at one level.

Second, though Tokugawa was the ultimate strategist, a military and political genius who achieved total power over Japan, he did so through methods that are often considered too indirect, treacherous, devious and cold – almost cheating. Japanese heroes are pure and imprudent, not calculating. So Nobunaga, open and single-minded in his pursuit of power, the theory goes, was not as tainted as Tokugawa by the impurity of deception. Nobunaga died for his purposes, Tokugawa profited from his. There is something of the ancient *samurai* snobbery about this analysis.

Tokugawa does not even come second. Hideyoshi wins approval for clawing his way from lowly origins to total power. Relentlessly making one's best effort is also much admired in Japan.

Forward to the end of the 20th century and it appears that Speed, a young female four-piece that was literally everywhere last year, is soon to be no more. Hitoe, the oldest member of the band, is almost nineteen, so it is really no wonder they feel they must be coming to the end of the road. Nearing maturity a sign of the inexorable approach of an *aidoru*'s preordained use-by date? The band are already touting their 'final album.' It is entitled ironically, or perhaps imploringly, 'Carry On my way' (capitalisation correctly preserved). Is this a synthesis of the two Sids, James and Vicious, God rest their souls?

Second Christmas

In early December the temperatures plummet. Frost appears in the mornings, and I have trouble keeping warm. Any heat in the house just rises uselessly to the rafters. I wake one night shivering and covered in goose pimples. I spread all my clothing on top of the *kake-buton* and hope this is good enough. During daytime I wear my coat inside the house. The sun really only warms the rooms from about three o'clock, but not long after this it drops below the hills to the west. I move mats to those parts of the cold wooden floor where I stand most, otherwise I lose too much heat through my socks. On my daily walks I now march along at top speed to create as much heat as possible. I would enjoy snow, but I worry that if it gets any colder I will not be able to cope properly. On television this afternoon they were discussing the official starting date of the snow season, as if it really matters. A few days ago the evening overcast was pink and heavy, threatening snow, which had been forecast but never came. I am told that there was a small snowfall early one morning, but the snow on the ground had melted away before I got up.

The second growth of rice is blanched, already looking like straw. Breath curls around people's faces as they speak, and a meandering bank of fog hangs over the river like a ghost of its former self. The colour seems to have drained out of everything, but it is not depressing. Japan manages to look gorgeous in rain, snow, sunshine, and mist. I don't know why; perhaps it is the aesthetic appreciation of the local people that causes us to see their landscape with their eyes.

By mid-December most of the trees have lost their leaves and rocky outcrops on the hills can be seen through a skein of branches at the skyline. The cold bites harder. Watching the daily progress of the rice outside my window I suspect that the plants are going to lose their race against winter. The frost has already brought their growth to a standstill, and they are still tiny. I start to accept the idea that there was never intended to be a second harvest, and that all the little grains budding so optimistically at the top of their shoots are hopelessly doomed. On Christmas Eve someone dumps a pile of old planks and bales of twigs into a rice-field – a sure sign that everything is going to be burnt off. I find this surprisingly sad.

The night of Christmas is severely cold. I spend the whole night shivering. Despite the freeze, I am assured this winter is milder than usual. On one of my walks I see a child's sledge leaning against the side of a house, so I know we can expect snow deep enough to play in. The second snowfall of the winter occurs on Christmas Day, in a biting cold north wind. Again the snow is not heavy enough to settle, but it at least gives me a pretext for claiming a white Christmas.

On Christmas evening I notice that the price of Christmas cakes has been cut by half, so I buy one. It looks like a Christmas cake from the outside: blocky, and covered in thick white icing. It also has a little Santa Claus on top, in cute Japanese pink rather than hearty European red. But the similarity does not extend to the content. The cake is a fluffy creamy sponge, a pure confection – soft in the heart.

On Boxing Day I wander towards the northern part of the valley, simply because so many of my recent walks have taken me south. No one is about. The fields are dead, and a soft fog of smoke and mist drifts over them, equally aimless. It is a hard cold day, so I try to corral my own body heat by limiting my movements. This just makes me feel more stiff and less inclined to move and so, as I come to a raised levy, beside the river, I pause.

I move only my eyes to take in the scene, once so fertile, now so desolate in appearance. A few cars move sluggishly along the road. Some small black birds are squabbling in the distance. I see them jumping at each other but apparently not making any sound. A feeling like hunger impinges on my awareness. It blends with today's deep sense of isolation out here in the open. I wish Emi were beside me. Without taking my hand from my pocket I short-dial her number. In the profound silence I can hear her phone ringing at the other end.

When she answers I tell her how much I miss her. She reciprocates. We sympathise with each other's predicament, but take a comfortably fatalistic view of it all: *shou ga nai* – it can't be helped. I tell her how I have started to organise my notes about Japan because I think there is something special about the way the Japanese people treat the concept of reality.

'We say "Life is a dream",' says Emi.

Exactly, I think.

Dreamtime

Dreams are important in Japan. They are important in Buddhism, for their transience and insubstantiality reveal the fleeting illusory nature of existence. In Zeami's *noh* play about *The Tale of Genji* he expresses the idea that the novel was inspired by the Buddhist goddess Kannon to show that life is as empty as a dream. But dreams also have a strong secular tradition in Japan. Lady Sarashina's *As I Crossed a Bridge of Dreams* is cited by Ivan Morris as the first of many Japanese works in which dreams play a central part. In her latter life Lady Sarashina took her dreams seriously, and felt they contained warnings and guidance, being messages from another realm. Morris, writing in the 1960s, was a little Freudian in his discussion of Lady Sarashina's dreams. They were invariably concerned with themes of romance or salvation, and in that respect are not so different from those of modern dreamers.

Prefiguring Emi's words, Lady Sarashina writes 'I live forever in a dream world.' It is evident in almost everything Lady Sarashina wrote that the physical reality of life was not for her, and that dreams were a refuge. When her husband dies she writes that she 'lost him like a dream.' This ambiguous phrase indicates either a degree of indifference or a quite shattering loss, as of having one's dreams destroyed. Towards the final pages of her book, as she becomes progressively more reflective and regretful, dreams are mentioned every few lines, and things dreamt and things real are difficult to keep apart. Her dreaminess, sad dissolution, sense of unfulfilment, and gathering loneliness are certainly part of what has made this book such a favourite in Japan.

Yume, which is 'dream' in Japanese, often appears in single-character calligraphy, and is one of the most often used words in Japanese poetry. In Japan the very word *dream* has all-round positive connotations, as does *new* in most cultures. Whereas companies in the west at best try to focus all their force in a concise hard-hitting vision statement like Nike's 'Crush Adidas,' in Japan the statements are often of the vaguest and most general form, involving such concepts as improving the quality of life, or helping people realise their dreams.

Dream is a word beloved of Japan's huge advertising industry, but its currency goes well beyond the commercial. In *Looking for the Lost*,

Alan Booth devotes a whole chapter, well worth reading, to dreams in sundry Japanese manifestations. By applying the word to ordinary things, like machines and fountains, the things (dream machines, dream fountains, etc.) automatically become better.

If these artefacts can all be given a 'dream' form, then perhaps life can be made more like a dream, for those who, unlike Shimamura in Kawabata Yasunari's *Snow Country*, do not already live in a dream. But I wonder if there really is anyone in Japan not already living in a kind of dream. In *South of the Border, West of the Sun*, by Murakami Haruki, the narrator says 'For me the boundary dividing the real world and the world of dreams has always been vague.'

And the coming of the west to Japan serves only to intensify its oneiric quality. In *The Lady and the Monk*, Pico Iyer describes the exotic foreign themes chosen for ordinary bread shops and cafés. Décor and terminology borrowed from all over the world create dream-like sets in which Japanese people perform their parts with effortless surrealism. He describes television as a kind of communal dream training. Children's imaginations are captured (in the sense of taken prisoner rather than stimulated) by the mass media, and their naming of pets and toys is usually after well-known TV characters. Towards the end of the book, and his relationship with Sachiko, Iyer tries and fails to find common ground with her on the subject of dreams. For her, dreams are a part of life, and hanging on to them is not an indictment of one's life, but an enrichment of it. Iyer wants Sachiko and her friends to be more realistic. He can't see that they would find this simply perverse. Iyer has to hang on to the barrier between dreams and real life as hard as Sachiko wants to hang on to her dreams.

'There was indeed something dreamlike about walking along this quiet, almost deserted street lined with massive Western-style buildings' wrote Tanizaki Junichiro in *Seven Japanese Tales*. As Iyer pointed out, the borrowing from other places has added to Japan's feelings of counterfeit and surrealism. In places, this has been taken to an extreme. Dreamland, within sight of the ancient keyhole tombs of Nara, is such a place. Fake Swiss Alps have been constructed for the enjoyment of those who cannot or do not wish to visit Europe, and are not satisfied with two-dimensional representations thereof.

If thoughts and dreams are the mind, and the mind is the soul, then, to the extent that our thoughts and dreams wander, we really do leave our bodies at night and roam over the landscape.

Dreaming Emi into reality

Seeing Emi, once so simple, has become rather difficult. For her, so much time is devoted to work and study. She tells me that she has been castigated by her evening class *sensei* for falling behind with her reading. Though she doesn't say so, it is my once constant demands on her time that created this problem, and now she needs to be more studious or face being kicked off the course. For my part, I cannot justify the expense of staying in a hotel in her area just to be able to see her for a couple of hours after work each day. Her mother is adamant that no man will sleep with Emi under her roof, not knowing that this has taken place several times already – and Emi refuses to stay with me in the business hotels around her town. On top of all that, I now have obligations of my own, which make it harder to get away. We've often talked about how much closer we've grown to each other, and neither of us wants the relationship to end, but for now it is the phone that couples us. I manage to catch her sometimes in the evening, when her phone is on, and we chat and discuss ideas for future trips, perhaps even to Australia, one day. She can be deeply relaxing to talk to, listening intently, sympathetic and encouraging about everything. We never need much to talk about to make the call worthwhile. On the phone, she is always beautiful.

I have a dream about her, which I feel compelled to share.

'*Moshi moshi.*'

'Hi Emi. It's Mark.'

'Maaku, *genki*?'

'Yes, I'm *genki*. How about you?'

'I *genki* too,' she says, brightly. 'Nice surprise.'

'Emi, I had a funny dream about you, do you want to hear it?'

'A dream? About Emi?'

'Yes. You were living here, with me.'

'In Himeji?'

'Yes, and we were in bed together—'

She giggles.

'—when suddenly you said you had to go outside. So I followed you, *hadaka*, out into the street.'

'Naked, in the street?'

'Yes.'

'And you too? You were naked too?'

'Ah, I don't know about that. I suppose so, yes.'

'Funny dream, Maaku!'

'Yep. So, you walked down to the bus stop and went into the tavern...'

'*Hadaka*?'

'Yes, yes, still naked. And you and I made love there, in front of all the people.'

'Maaku! This is a funny dream, *ne*?'

'Well, actually, I quite liked it. Maybe we should try that one day?'

'What happened next?'

'Well, that was the end of it, I think. I can't remember any more, but I've been thinking about you all day.'

'I've been thinking about you too.'

'Have you?'

'Always.'

'Maybe we should plan a little trip some time soon. I miss seeing you.'

'Yes, Maaku, that would be nice, for both of us, *ne*?'

Which led, by simple steps, to my last time with Emi, a short trip north into Tottori prefecture.

Game plan

I am completely dumbfounded to find Emi is in the game. Her avatar bears a fairly close resemblance, and though she is always sleepwalking I can communicate with her. Her responses are not yet highly personalised, but she does speak both English and Japanese – an amazing bit of game technology. She occasionally teleports to another location, which is a little baffling.

Then Harumi appears too, but this avatar looks nothing like its... what?...mistress? It passes notes to me, always in English. In time, many other people I know make their appearance, with varying degrees of verity. Miho, Satomi, Akiko, Komatsu all turn up. Colleagues from Australia are also there, Graham Mann among them. I amuse myself by adjusting their profiles to make them look more real. Only Emi's refuses to accept my changes.

Many other characters in the game are able to perform a large repertoire of outlandish tricks, such as morphing into other characters, calling me on my telephone, and sending me email. They discuss real events that are only just breaking on the TV news. Some characters have TVs and radios in the game itself. Some have houses, even large mansions, cars, planes and submarines. Clearly, there are great depths to this game.

One day, a character called Greenfeld walks up to me and asks if I'd like to hear what he thinks of the book I've been working on. To my amazement, not only does he know the real book, but he has some sound and interesting observations to make. Busily I try to keep notes while he is talking.

My admiration for the designers increases every time I log in. More tomorrow...

Degeneracy

Any shift in rulers' interests from matters of power to matters of art is usually described as a form of degeneracy. This may be a reflection of the historians' values rather than an objective analysis of whatever happened and what its effects were. In the case of the Japanese imperial family, a truer view may be that it was the emperors' social elevation and promotion of arts that gave the aesthetics of Heian Japan their unique delicacy and refinement. It is known that the appetite of the Heian court for art and highly accomplished craft work drew to Kyoto a large community of artists and craftsmen among whom quality of work was the only serious criterion. And this, in turn, has probably been instrumental in shaping the aesthetics of modern Japan. Today there is still a marked concentration of skilled craftsmen in the Kyoto area and Kyoto is synonymous with many fine crafts.

The shift in imperial interest gave the world, not tragic decay, but something new. So there was also a power shift. So what?

Dinner with the teacher, tea with the monk

Luther, a garrulous and argumentative friend from Germany, joins me for a few days at the house – keen to get the full Japan experience in five days before flying back to Frankfurt.

Luther is as tall as me, thin, untidily blonde and rosy-cheeked, with that great dynamism that infuses people from the heart of Europe. He carries with him a sense that he is right about things. Somehow this creeps onto his face and is visible even at a distance. He can argue a point down to the death, with little regard for its importance. I like him because we can talk long and illuminatingly about many subjects. He is a polymath, well read in a scattering of languages, yet knows nothing of Japanese.

We have been invited for dinner by Harumi. We walk to her house this evening. I've briefed Luther on what to do and say. He thinks there is a lot to remember.

At the *genkan* we are greeted by the whole family and shown to the places of honour in front of the *tokonoma*. They struggle with his name. It sounds like they're calling him 'loser.' '*ru-za-a*' I suggest, and they try to imitate, '*ruzaa-san*,' but after one try they never use it again.

I ask Luther where our gift of sweet biscuits is and he tells me he left it in the *genkan*. I ask him to get it and give it to Harumi right now.

'I didn't know when we should do that,' he says.

'It's OK.'

The family make a huge fuss about the biscuits, big smiles on everyone's face, and much exclamation about the unparalleled excellence of our gift. Luther describes it correctly as a small gift.

Over dinner the conversation goes reasonably well. The family knows enough English not to be totally lost, and Naomi can help her father with translation of anything she thinks important enough. We talk about the coming New Year celebrations.

'Do you send many New Year cards?' Naomi asks Luther.

'No, I don't. Everyone writing a hundred cards every year and signing them like a production line, sending them to people they can hardly remember. It is all a big waste of time to me. Too artificial.'

'You are too honest,' says Naomi, and Luther takes it as a compliment.

Talk switches to what we each do and have in our respective countries. Luther does most of the talking since they have already heard from me. He describes his house on a hillside overlooking a river, and tells them how remarkably advanced his new daughter is for her age. They smile and say complimentary things.

It dawns on Luther that he has been doing all the talking, so he deliberately asks whether Naomi's younger brother, who is sitting beside her, is doing well at school.

'No,' says Naomi.

To Luther this is a shock, like a slap in the face. He reels for a moment, wondering how to respond. Naomi knows enough to realise that under western protocol another answer was required.

'Actually, he is doing fine,' she adds.

Luther is even more confused now, but inside I chuckle. Naomi's first response was the Japanese one, in which everything connected to her but not her interlocutor is lowly. Rather than say anything that could be interpreted as boastful, she talked down her brother's school performance, regardless of his presence. The second response came because she is westernised enough to know that Luther will interpret the first response literally, and attribute a coldness and disregard to it that she doesn't intend. She may also be playing a little game of her own.

Later in the conversation, Naomi refers to Luther's 'mansion.'

'It's not a mansion,' he says, 'just a nice house.'

'But when you said it was a "nice house" I thought it must be a *very* nice house,' replies Naomi, with a touch of playfulness.

'No, it is just a nice house.'

'In Japan, when we talk about our own home we say "our shabby house." If we said we live in a nice house it would mean a very special house,' she tells him. She is on to him, and has begun the careful crafting of a Japan-sensitive *gaijin*. 'A husband will refer to his wife as "my stupid wife." It is the Japanese way.'

Luther nods. He realises that complex Japanese etiquette, which he has feared, has come to the party.

'In the same way, when you present gifts, you say "please accept this worthless little thing."' I say, showing which side I am on.

'Yes, the same,' says Naomi.

Nevertheless, Luther habitually talks about himself. He tells them what he's done, what he thinks, what he is going to do. I hear Naomi tell him 'You are teaching me many things,' which he takes at face value. He warms to his subject, and tells them he doesn't think etiquette is important, it is what is really meant that is important. People should just be themselves. He doesn't have time to figure out what people might think. He prefers to talk straight. This is all designed to help them see him the right way, to help them understand how it is. From the noises they make you might think they were convinced.

After dinner our biscuits are brought out and everyone exclaims at how delicious they are. When we have nearly finished the biscuits the real desserts are brought out – several elaborate confections of fruit, pastry, cream, caramel, cheesecake, icing, sauces and chocolate. Our biscuits look decidedly mundane by comparison. I praise the desserts, Luther does too.

On the way home I talk to Luther about the idea of the 'real Japan.'

'I think I've seen the real Japan tonight,' he says.

Yes, it was dinner of *sashimi*, *tempura*, *oden* and *sake*, kneeling on the *tatami*, in a room of *shoji* screens and precise decoration. It was a Japanese family talking among themselves in Japanese, happy to let their guard down a little and just get on with things. It was something many visitors to Japan do not get to see, especially during a trip as short as Luther's. But I want to tell him about all the undercurrents I detected, all the double meanings and skilful handling of guests that had been going on.

He feels chuffed that he taught them so many things about our way of looking at life. He tells me so.

'I think they really enjoyed having us. Naomi told me several times that I taught her a lot,' he says.

'Yeah. It is not quite as straightforward as that though,' I say.

'Oh yeah?'

'Yeah. That is really just a Japanese way of saying your ideas and mine on this subject are quite different.'

'Oh.'

A few seconds later he says, with a chuckle, 'she told me I was too honest.'

'Naomi knows about the things you were talking about. Obviously she sees things differently. It *is* important that you send all your New Year cards, *even though* everyone knows it is a chore. No one would ever admit that. She was being polite. In Japan, appearances *are* important. If you remember 'appearances are important' and act accordingly you will be much closer to the real Japan – if such a thing really exists.'

He is crestfallen.

'What you say makes me doubt they even liked us now.'

'Oh no. They enjoyed the evening. There's no doubt about that.'

'How do you know?'

'It's not what they say, but how they act. You can tell if people are comfortable or not. If they are comfortable, they enjoyed themselves.'

He is not confident in using abstract intuitions about comfort and tension levels to judge how things are going. He would like to be with people who say things like 'Gee, this is a great evening!' and mean it, but he knows that even back home, they often don't.

Next day we stop at the Okamoto temple. I want to let Luther meet the family – and they have been looking forward to seeing one of my friends.

After the introductions – his name causing problems again – we shuffle in under the *kotatsu* for tea. We chat for half an hour, and then it is time to leave. Maya pulls out two painted *uchiwa* fans to give to us. She looks at them and sees that one is clearly prettier than the other, and is thrown into indecision. Who should she favour with the pretty one? Luther, who is more of a guest than I am, or me, since I am a much closer friend of hers, and Luther has only been here a few minutes. After a second's hesitation she solves the problem by giving them both to me and, giggling mischievously, says I can decide who gets which. I know exactly what to do. I turn to Luther and ask him to choose.

'I'll take that one,' he announces triumphantly, and quickly grabs the pretty one out of my hand. He had been sure I would give him the other. I am deeply irked by what he has done, but my reaction is nothing compared to that of the Okamoto family. They all suddenly stare at Luther in disbelief, as if he's just shouted a few obscenities at us.

Luther is pleased and oblivious. I feel ruffled, as if the finely tuned harmony of the day has been broken. Of course, I would have liked the more graceful fan, but these days that doesn't matter as much as getting along harmoniously. He should have offered to let me choose, then I could have insisted that, no, no, he should choose. *Then* it would have been OK for him to grudgingly admit that he did privately covet the pretty one, and it would become a treasured reminder of a fine afternoon with pleasant company. Who could have argued with that? Now the fan is back in Frankfurt he admits he doesn't know what to do with it, so what was the point of all the brutal honesty anyway?

The problem is I'm turning Japanese, and he isn't. Over the few days of his visit I develop a nagging irritation with Luther because he does not pick up on my subtle suggestions. I know if I tell him it is his turn to do something, like carrying the backpack, he will do it, but I feel it is undignified for both of us to have to be so direct about it. If he listened to the gentle signals he could pretend that he had thought of it himself, and I could have given him credit for this. We could have been comforted by how smoothly, how naturally, how intuitively, how instinctively, we were getting along.

Beauty cult

If there is one thing I appreciate more than anything else about Japan it is the constant physical reminders that beauty can be achieved in all things. Japan has as many venerable crafts as it does fine arts, but the pursuit of aesthetic perfection goes beyond even these practices. I have seen brushes, sweets, wooden bridges, road works, schoolbooks, even pieces of toast, all prepared with as much care, almost reverence, as we reserve for the finest of our arts. This strikes a resonant note for me, for I've never known when to stop, always fiddling with things in the pursuit of perfection, usually only cut short by exhaustion or exasperation. Meticulousness is sometimes perceived as prissiness or, in the *mot de la mode*, anally retentive. But, given the choice, I'd always prefer to be anally retentive than incontinent.

Any society that respects its craftsmen ultimately becomes spiritually rich. And Japan certainly respects its makers of paper, basket weavers, potters and carpenters, more than most. Ian Buruma points out that in Japanese media it is rare to find a ridiculous artisan, the figure of fun is usually a *sarariman*. A Japanese master of any form, whether it be calligraphy or flower arranging, will always be referred to as *sensei*, even by those who are not part of the same profession. This respect for someone who simply does something *well*, and for no other reason, strikes me as terribly civilised.

Japanese art is often remarked upon for its minimalism. I wonder if there might be three reasons why Japanese *objets d'art* are often so simple: beauty, symbolism, and purity. First, if beauty can be achieved in all things, it need not be achieved through assemblage, a single simple object can serve the function of providing aesthetic inspiration just as well as a collection of objects. Second, if symbolism is important, the object is more powerful when it is an abstraction and less like that which it symbolises. Third, purity is more directly achieved through subtraction than through the complex.

The game expands

Geographically, the game has some curious qualities. People who are near in real life also appear to be close in the game. However, the landscape bears no similarity to real places. Harumi, who lives only a couple of kilometres away, on the other side of the Sugo River, resides in the game in a tree house some way up a large tree in a wood just visible from my 'home,' which I have made into a thatched Japanese house, whose roof beams extend beyond the body of the building, like a Shinto shrine. I have been able to make this house from scratch, and it has already had several admirers, a few of whom have copied elements in their own buildings.

I discover some special buildings in the game. There are libraries, with extensive multi-media collections; night clubs; observatories; and sports arenas, where football, *sumo*, even *jai alai* are being played. Large crowds are sometimes assembled in these places. There are a few company premises where machines and other nameless things, which appear to be nothing more than abstract procedures, are being created.

Emi and I have a close relationship within the game – when she is there. Of course, I have found, by talking to her on the phone, that she is seeing much of what I am seeing. I often get so involved in our scenarios that it is as if she is with me. We haven't figured out how to take our clothes off, yet, and our short encounters often leave me with a heightened sense of sexual frustration.

Just for fun, I file my book draft in one of the libraries. A few hours later I notice that it is available from all libraries, scattered across the landscape.

Tottori ryokan to jinja

Knowing that opportunities to spend time with Emi are now rare, I try to get as much of her as I can. If I could, I would spend all day naked with her in the *o-furo*, and all night naked with her on the *futon*. We cannot bathe together at our *ryokan* in the mountains behind Tottori, the curses of western morals have made this pleasure a rarity even in remote parts of Japan. To compensate for this I make the most of her unconcern about being naked. She lies on top of the *futon* and I look at every inch of her. I turn her hands over and over, scanning first the backs, then the palms. Her long white fingers seem too delicate to be of any use. I trace the blue veins up her arms, from wrists to roughened armpits. My fingers tickle her.

'You shave everywhere, Emi?'

She nods imperceptibly, her lips as still and pushed out as those of a bronze Buddha.

'I love your body.'

I sniff the skin of her arm. It is heavy with soap, or floral scent, even after the *o-furo*, or maybe because of it. I move up to her face and push the untamed hair away from her eyes, softly massaging around her hairline; at the temples, and behind her neck. I kiss her mouth occasionally while I am doing this. Her eyes are closed, but I push one open, to her surprise. I look at the iris. What looks black is actually a collection of all colours from deepest brown to tiny creamy lines linking together like a fishing net. Her lashes and eyebrows are thin, but very black. Her skin is so translucent that I can see where the lashes go for a couple of millimetres below the surface.

I run my fingers over her lips, realising I have never touched them like this before. They are spongy and stuck together. I push up the top one and Emi chokes on a laugh and asks me what I am going to do now.

'Show me your tongue.'

She sticks it out a few times for me. I try to catch it with my teeth, but let it get away each time.

Next I nose and kiss one of her nipples until it is taut and pointed. It is knobbly and rough close up, like a desert mesa, but just playing with it is stirring me in my guts and in my loins. She's made a big crease in her neck by bending to look at me. I look back at her, with the nipple in my teeth.

Then I count her little ribs with my fingers for as long as she will let me; *one two three, lost it, one two three...*

Like this, I try to memorise every part of her. Every fingernail, every hair, every smell. I want to *know* her now, for all times in the future. I'm building a pile of memories that I know the wind will blow away. I'm happy and sad, both aroused and content.

'I wish men and women could still bathe together these days,' I say.

'Mmmmm. That would be so nice, *ne*?'

I nod slowly.

'There is a place...' she begins, then stops.

'Yes?'

'It is *roten-buro*, beside the river, where a man and woman can bathe together.'

Now this is good news.

'Can we go there? Is it far?'

'Not far. Are you brave enough? It is *roten-buro*.'

Roten-buro are open-air baths, and most certainly I am brave enough to try this. We put on our *yukata* and *geta* and clop-clop down to the bridge. Just below it is a series of pools, cut into the rocky flats beside the river. We have been past this spot many times, but I have never looked down at the river bank. There are no lights down there, so it is dark, but as our eyes adjust I see racks for hanging *yukata*, and steam rising off the hot water, which pours from a broad pipe, splashing into the uppermost pool. Several heads are visible in the water, and all appear to be male. I ask Emi if she is really willing to do this, and she astonishes me by acting quite excited at the prospect.

We leave our *yukata* at the racks and, naked, approach the pools. First we try the top pool, since it is deserted. It is too hot to even dip a toe into, so we join half a dozen men in the next pool down, which is just bearable. The men all look away courteously as Emi slips, white and ghostlike, into the water. She turns her back to them, hunches forward to hide her breasts, and faces me. I lean back and enjoy the unexpectedness of the moment, and the delicious feeling of privilege. Above, up on the bank, the windows of a restaurant allow the diners to look down at us while they crunch their *tempura*.

After I've adjusted to the temperature of the water I tell Emi I want to try the hot pool again, so we move over. We can now sit in the water despite the great heat. I am delighted that Emi's nonchalance about being naked extends to this, a public roadside pool. In the dark we can relax and touch hands under the water. Beside us the river rushes over rocks and gravel and drowns out most of the noises of the town. Occasionally cars pass over the bridge. Some stars are visible, but the town lights hide all but the brightest.

Soon, the heat becomes too much for me, though Emi is still comfortable. We decide to leave, and Emi shows the first sign of nervousness.

'I have to walk past all those guys,' she says.

We slowly lift ourselves out of the water, dripping and steaming, and walk carefully, because the rock is so slippery, past the other pool to the *yukata* rack. At the last minute, Emi slips and lands on her bottom, then continues to slide further down the slope for a few feet. I pick my way down to her and help her up. She is unhurt, but burning with embarrassment. We make it back to the *ryokan* without further trouble. There we have a shower to clean our feet – and Emi's bottom.

It is about 1 AM by the time we settle down on the *futon* again. We play with each other for a couple more hours. She massages my back endlessly, until I fall asleep, wake, fall asleep again. We spend the night entwined together against the cold.

In the morning Emi dresses me in *wafuku*, Japanese clothing. My feet are buttoned into black *tabi*, the short split-toe socks of Japanese dress. I draw two long *kimono* around me, the inner one a plain purple, the outer one a patterned dark blue, and hold them while Emi wraps a thin gold *obi* around my middle. She pulls and jerks me off balance as she ties the knot. Next, I step into the *hakama*, a complex pleated skirt in chocolate brown and grey stripes. She lifts it up around my hips and ties it front and back. Over this I pull a loose black *haori* jacket, which I tie at the front with a *himo*, an ornamental knotted cord. And, because it is so cold, I pull a thick black quilted *kimono* overcoat over the top. All of this is preparation for a traditional visit to the shrine.

Emi has single-handedly wrapped herself in a series of *kimono*, the outermost of which has a pastel pink and baby blue background supporting a complex and colourful embroidered pattern that winds around the bottom and diagonally across the back. Her *obi* is a stylish white and gold affair with a huge butterfly-shaped knot at the back. I rarely see her with her hair up like this; she looks fragile and beautiful. She is wearing much less than me, but appears not to feel the low temperatures.

At the *genkan* I slot my feet into *zori* sandals. These ones have funny clear plastic toe caps to keep the snow off my *tabi*. My feet soon go numb in the snow, and the cold air is blowing into my sleeves and up my *kimono*, chilling me in parts, as we pick our way across from *ryokan* to shrine. We join a procession of a few hundred people all making their annual visit to the shrine today. We totter perilously up dozens of snow-covered stone steps. At the top we are permitted a couple of seconds before the shrine before we have to move aside and let others take their turn. Wooden tables to the right are covered in little pottery tea cups, so we take the opportunity to drink the hot tea. I find the cold and the uncertain footing of my *zori* on the ice too distracting to make much sense of the proceedings, but I do notice that instead of feeling self-conscious, I actually feel like something of a celebrity. Three or four people have complimented me on my *kimono*, and they sound genuinely pleased to see a foreigner taking pains to learn their way of doing things. Emi too. She says she is delighted to show me some of her culture. Of course, this is just the sort of thing she *would* say, but it is true.

We return to the *ryokan* and our room. Removing the traditional clothing of a Japanese woman has always been a little fantasy of mine, and I enjoy these much-anticipated moments, as does Emi. But then it's a strange mood that takes over. We seem not to know what to do any more. In fits and starts we talk about things we might do in the future. All that is really certain is that tomorrow she will drop me off in Himeji, we will hug, kiss, and wave goodbye, and she will continue on to Otsu, and a new year will be upon us.

Perils of isolation

Reading between the lines of Japanese history one sees a world so insular it has little in the way of national or cultural self-awareness. There was apparently no word for Shinto in Japan until Buddhism arrived and the need to differentiate arose. This indicates the absence of any external viewpoint from which Japan could examine itself. I wonder whether this precondition ingrained deep habits of thought which continue to avoid the practice of looking for one's self.

At a national level there may have been something of an over-correction. A genre of books, known as *nihon jinron* (meaning 'Japanese people theory') is a perennial best-seller in Japan. The Japanese appear to love reading about what makes them different or even unique. Many of these books have little to commend them in the way of scientific rigour, but that doesn't seem to matter. They appear to fill a psychological, rather than intellectual, need. Indeed, one would have thought that the simple, rational, question of Japanese uniqueness was answered long ago.

What is truth anyway?

One of the ubiquitous problems of artificial intelligence is building a true representation of the world, or finding ways to survive without it.

In classical artificial intelligence, this representation is conceived of as a set of known true facts about the world. Thus, if for example a door is open and a robot's memory has a statement of the form 'door_state=open', then the robot, both functionally and theoretically, 'knows' the truth. This is the correspondence theory of truth, and much AI relies heavily on it.

However, maintaining this correspondence proves to be extraordinarily difficult; so difficult, in fact, that many researchers have given up and are convinced that the whole enterprise is misdirected, and that there must be a better way of dealing with the world. Think of the problem like this: how can the robot ever verify its representations, without anything *except* representations to depend on? The answer is it cannot, and nor can we.

Our concept of truth is an elusive one, to say the least. We are more convinced of the truth of a thought if it is reinforced by experience. Let us assume we leave the house convinced that the iron has been switched off, but after a while a doubt arises and we have to check that the iron really is off. For most of us a single check is enough, but for certain individuals (whom we classify as suffering from obsessive compulsive disorders) one check, or even a dozen, is not enough. Why is it that one brain reaches certainty after one check but another doesn't? Why does the idea that the iron is on overwhelm the evidence that it is off in one brain but not another? The situation is the same, so it must be the brains that differ. But if brains are subject to such variation, how is any brain able to know whether it is able to tell the truth or merely think that it is? In fact, the sensation of certainty, which most of us identify with some notion of external truth, is actually created by (or simply is) activity in an area of the temporal lobes. Stimulate this area and the experimental subject will be deluded that whatever happens to be passing though their mind at the time is certain, suppress this area and they will suddenly and in great panic doubt the most obvious facts. If this particular area of the temporal lobes is inactive in my brain, then I will rarely feel certain that the iron is off, regardless of the facts of the matter. Similar temporal lobe disconnects are possible with our sense of the familiar. A sense of familiarity when no real familiarity exists produces *déjà vu*. A sense of unfamiliarity in familiar situations produces *jamais vu*.

Underlying much of our adherence to the notion of truth is the moral argument that truth is good, and lies are bad. But we also know that there are occasions encountered every day when the truth would cause offence or unhappiness and a lie is much gentler and more considerate. When challenged over these 'little white lies' people often deny that they really are untruths, with vague references to 'higher truths,' and more important things.

Imagine how different our social processes might be if we attached no real importance to truth, if we recognised the weakness of the foundations truth habitually rests on, if harmony were more important than being right, or if we knew that this was all a dream and that anything could happen.

Emi once telephoned me while I was *en route* between Miyazaki and Kumamoto, though she thought I was in Kyoto. When I told her where I was she asked me what kind of lies I was trying to make her believe. She really did not believe me, but her tone of voice was teasing rather than accusatory.

Exactly the same tone was used by the Empress, who, as reported in an episode in Sei Shonagon's *Pillow Book*, knows that the Chancellor is deceiving her about the clearing of the cherry blossoms. In his notes, Ivan Morris remarks that lies were considered more amusing than sinful in Heian times.

In *No Longer Human*, Dazai Osamu writes:

> I am convinced that human life is filled with many pure, happy, serene examples of insincerity, truly splendid of their kind – of people deceiving one another without (strangely enough) any wounds being inflicted, of people who seem unaware even that they are deceiving one another.

Kayo KO

It is, for once, with a sense of authority that I travel to meet Kayo in Kobe. The train arrives around lunch time and she meets me on the concourse a few minutes later, having just got out of bed. I have decided that I cannot keep dancing around the point any more because our relationship is just not developing organically. I have to tell her that I desire her, or prove it, or do something to put an end to the terrible strait-jacket of sexual tension I wear whenever I am with her. It is, to be quite honest, more trial than pleasure.

First I talk of her coming to stay at my house, soon, or any time in the future, whenever she can get a night off work. I talk of the wonders of the Sugo Valley, its high temples, its secret restaurants. She prevaricates, makes no commitments, lets me do all the work of the conversation, until I have repeated myself too often, and the subject has to be dropped, unresolved.

Plan two. Under the old pretext of looking for a shop I lead her to a quiet area in the back-lanes of Kobe and, holding her hands, tell her:

- She is the most beautiful woman I have ever seen
- Her beauty is driving me mad with desire
- I cannot hold out any longer
- I must make love to her today
- We must do this now, in a nearby love hotel.

I paraphrase, of course.

Her look is one of great compassion, painful regret even, but not excitement. She offers many reasonable reasons why my proposed course of action is untoward. I counter with what I hope is a heartfelt passion, but it is all a matter of foregone conclusion. No dice.

As a possible antidote to the bitter truth I have just been dealt, Kayo starts talking about what she likes about me. It seems to boil down to my strangeness, something unusual about me that made her curious.

'Surely it is more than that,' I protest.

'Yes,' she agrees. 'You look like Kevin Costner, and your clothes are always cool.' This, to her, is a perfectly reasonable answer.

My third sally is the harshest of all. I say I can't keep seeing her if my desire for her has no release – we can't just be friends.

'*Zannen da*,' she whispers. 'That's too bad.'

And so ends my fruitless relationship with one of the world's great beauties. Of course, I know that from the start I was besotted and that, for my part, there was little to the attraction other than the unthinking, irresistible, constant cellular urge for sex – an urge triggered by every look, touch, motion and aroma of her.

Storage

Ideas, fragments of prose, email, short accounts of my travels – I shovel them all into the library. I am assembling a bit of a collection, and have been looking for ways to recruit both a researcher and a curator. So far I've not seen how to do this, but many people say that such things can be done.

Barriers good and bad

Moving back and forth across Honshu and the other islands, I passed through miles of uninspiring country. Though Japanese people profess to love nature, they have done some awful things to it. Not a single river I see has not been tamed in places by hideous concrete banks. The sky over the towns and cities can only be perceived by squinting through a dreadful web of cables, power and telegraph poles strung overhead. It is truly ugly. A sickly photochemical pall also hangs over the cities, even historic Kyoto. The absence of trees and the unplanned and mundane nature of most of the architecture challenge people to endure as long as they can before retreating to the country for rest and recuperation. How do the Japanese cope? Are they able to set up hermetic mental barriers, non-permeable membranes, to separate the *kirei* from the *kitanai*, to quarantine the clean and pretty from the filth?

It probably indicates something amiss deep in my psyche that I often wonder what cleaning really means. We cannot actually destroy dirt, we can only move it around. We clean things by putting the dirt out of sight, off-site, behind a barrier of one kind or another. Which, incidentally, makes ideas of holism suddenly seem laughably naïve and meaningless. We tell ourselves the house is cleaner if all the rubbish and dust is contained – in the bin or in the vacuum cleaner. So does Japan, where cleanliness simply *is* godliness, shed any light on this paradoxical subject?

One of the most interesting differences between the Japanese and western way of seeing things is in the attitudes to barriers, or discontinuities.

Many of Japan's most beautiful sights are hard up against her greatest monstrosities. Scores of Kyoto's historic buildings are pressed on all sides by modern concrete, a theme park looms up beside the giant burial mounds of Nara. Most visitors find this at least disappointing, if not disturbing or downright tragic. The Japanese, on the other hand, can erect a temporary blind spot against the eyesores. At first, whenever I encountered this I felt it was symptomatic of a greater mental discipline, a purity of thought. The spatial barrier that surrounded the beautiful didn't really exist for me, and I wished it did. My inability to feel happy when I was in sight of the concrete hillsides that are now common in natural Japanese settings seemed mean-spirited and churlish.

So much for spatial barriers, what about temporal ones? Here the situations appear reversed. When westerners learn that the building before them is not the original, not even the original replica in many cases, they suffer an attack of disappointment (again). The discontinuity is an issue, and we feel that because of it, we lose something. The Japanese viewer doesn't attach great importance to temporal discontinuity. They do not see it as a cut in the link to the past.

So, westerners are bothered that the spatial boundaries between the beautiful and the ugly are not hermetic, the ugliness seeps through. They are also bothered by the temporal boundaries for the opposite reason, the historicity doesn't seep through. Conversely, the Japanese think the spatial boundaries are strong and the temporal ones are weak.

Why are westerners insensitive to spatial barriers, yet disapproving of temporal ones? And why are Japanese people insensitive to temporal barriers, yet approving of spatial ones? I think the explanation is that westerners indiscriminately equate barriers with bad. In almost any discussion conducted in English, the expressed desire to break down barriers, between classes, sexes, ages, organisations, etc., goes unquestioned but, for the Japanese, barriers are simply recognised as essential.

Buruma goes as far to say that the Japanese want barriers and circumscription because they are 'terrified of the amorphous.' I do not know if I would go that far, but I think his argument leads in the right direction. Perhaps the barriers, those that run around our family, our friends, our neighbourhood, our company, and our recreational societies, are the only things that shore up a sense of identity in the absence of an illusion of individual self. Perhaps Japan couldn't be Japan without its barriers.

Purity is something dear to the Japanese heart. Purity requires refinement, a removal of the impurities and a placing of them *somewhere else* – preferably on the other side of a boundary they cannot recross. Hence the Japanese affinity for barriers and boundaries, demarcations and morals driven more by local customs than universal decree. In fact, such boundaries are so important that even if they do not exist physically, they are put up in the imagination.

Japanese gardens are often deliberately walled off from the natural world they are meant to symbolise. If not, they could not be thought to stand for something more than they are. Both symbolism and purity would be lost. The tea ceremony, designed to empty the mind in order to allow pure contemplation, works by shutting out the outside world and keeping it at bay throughout the proceedings.

Japan was treated almost as a work of art itself, cut off from the west for hundreds of years in order to retain its purity. And these days is it cut off from the nasty brutish world of mosquitoes and tornadoes by layers of technological intervention that serve the same function as the garden walls of yore? Actually it is worse. Technology now *is* reality. Technology has reached the point where, as Karl Taro Greenfeld says in *Speed Tribes*, it has become the comforter, protector, entertainer, and employer of Japan. The solution to everything.

No exchange rate

I grow conscious of the great effort it takes to understand another culture, but feel certain it can be done. Even our enemies are explicable when we see things their way, but this entails having their values too, which is the hard part. It is the values that are at the crux of things. People cannot destroy what they find beautiful, but they cannot agree on what is beautiful.

In *An Artist of the Floating World*, Ishiguro talks of the difficulty of appreciating the beauty of a world without some idea of its validity, and thereby reveals himself to be a kind of Englishman. Validity is not material to Japanese aesthetics.

Another kind of Englishman, Iyer, realises that endless reproduction of the beautiful, in Japanese sensibilities, does not devalue the beauty, it can even multiply it. In Japan, rarity bestows little cachet. After all, if a treasure is lost, it can always be recreated.

More than that. The idea of something lost, *monoganashii*, or of something doomed, *aware*, is felt to be intrinsically beautiful, reminding us of the infinite sadness of knowing that every cherished thing, every new born thing, will one day die. Such fatalism is nothing short of disastrous when applied to the totality of nature in the form of the environment, but it is nevertheless the way of things in Japan. When applied to oneself, fatalism can have both an emotional profundity and a talismanic reassurance. Death is inevitable *and* sweet.

These are just some of the values that one needs to hold, or recognise, to understand Japan.

Large-scale assembly

One evening the mist grows thick, like a pea-souper, and chases everyone inside. I do everything to keep warm, including baking and eating a large sweet potato. Still the cold is uncomfortable, so I dress as warmly as I can and head off for a brisk walk, down silent streets that are now intimately familiar, hoping to raise my body temperature and thereby escape the fear of freezing.

I recall my first evening high in the European Alps. I had climbed to a deserted and dilapidated climbing hut, and settled in for the night. I tried to eat, but the exhaustion and thin air took away my appetite. The cold was relentless, so I lay in my sleeping bag, fully clothed. This didn't work, so I searched my rucksack for spare clothing and put that on too. Finally, I pulled the empty rucksack up around the foot of my sleeping bag, for whatever extra heat conservation it would provide. I slept fitfully for a couple of hours, half-consciously trying to ignore the cold. At about midnight I suddenly woke, shivering convulsively and driven to distraction by the cold, and afraid, knowing there was nothing more I could do to mitigate it, and actually fearing for my survival. When dawn came and the sun broke clear and bright against the peaks around me, I headed straight back down to the valley below.

As I walk between the dark rice fields, with the breath curling over my shoulder, and the mist swirling around my feet, I try to assemble my thoughts about Japan. Our naturalistic fantasy says that nature is good and that anything that we do not like or cannot accept must be a dysfunction or perversion of nature and, therefore, ought to be corrected. This attitude, like the belief in a benevolent god, must swiftly perish in the face of continuous and calamitous natural disasters, as have been visited upon Japan. In fact the view of nature that is more likely to develop is a finely tuned and situational appreciation of it, a wise recognition of its essential moral neutrality, its caprice, and an automatic acceptance of the need to constrain it.

As we have seen, the replacement of things natural with their virtual substitutes is a common and long-standing practice in Japan. It is a phenomenon not limited to Japan, of course, but it is here that it finds its most extreme forms of expression. And even though the process is gathering pace all over the world, Japan remains in the vanguard, and this may be why we find it such a fascinating place – it shows us where we are going.

In all cases of substitution, there is something good that must be re-created, say a view of Mount Fuji, but there is something bad about it too, say the fact that Mount Fuji just happens to be too far from where we are – so we make a new version, which has the positive characteristics of Mount Fuji, but none of the drawbacks. There are three parts to this.

The ideal original, which is truly an ideal, in that it has only ever existed in our imaginations or dreams.

The actual original, which has disadvantages that we sometimes cannot ignore or hide behind a barrier.

The virtual substitute, which has only the ideal qualities, and is the dream made real.

This triangle underlies both the old and new Japan, linking them tightly, and remaining hidden to most eyes, even Japanese eyes. We may catch glimpses of the triangle here and there and think we are seeing Japanese imitation, or the need for continuous improvement in arts and business.

The crafted substitute becomes the hyper-reality because the experience of it is closer to our memory – rose-tinted and therefore emotionally reinforced – of the original. By contrast, experience of the original will be dirtied and confused by all those aspects we didn't remember or want to see. And the more we experience the substitute and not the original, the more real the substitute becomes and the more the original is forgotten. And then it is probably time for something else to be created in place of the substitute, and so it goes on.

Is there a danger that the fantasy and reality become confused when our experiences are no longer grounded? Probably.

Is the substitute an outcome of the process of improvement? Yes, because sometimes the original is made redundant.

Is the substitute meant to hide reality? No, because the reality can always be ignored.

Is the substitute just an invention? No, because the original always exists in some way.

Is the substitute digital or physical? It can be either.

Is the substitute a machine to replace a life? Sometimes, look at the robots.

Is the substitute an ideal? It is meant to be, look at Kyoko Date, but it sometimes fails.

Is the substitute a compromise? Sometimes, look at the virtual pony tours, or My Prince Charming.

Does the substitute duplicate something already existing? No, duplication is not possible for ideals.

Does the substitute reconstitute something lost? Yes, such as a hymen or Nagoya Castle.

Does the substitute refer to, acknowledge, or allude to something else? Yes, look at view gardens, or Huis Ten Bosch.

Does the substitute still use the original, but make it more acceptable, or easier to get along with? Yes, look at user interfaces.

Is the substitute a representation that doesn't attempt to reconstruct the original? Yes, what else are *ukiyo-e*?

Does the substitute buffer us from raw experience? Yes, look at the photography mania of Japanese fathers and young girls.

Does the substitute pretend to be itself? Perhaps this is true of Kyoto, but is it the Kyoto of the mind that is doing this?

Is the substitute a perfect replica of something that was once in its place? Often. Look at the hundreds of castles and reconstructed buildings throughout Japan.

Is the substitute a remnant of former glory? In the case of Kyoto itself, yes – a few relict oases in a desert of concrete.

Is the substitute something that is kept new so that it cannot metamorphose into something else? Yes, Ise-jingu springs to mind.

Is the substitute made non-existent by context? Yes, look at *kabuki* stage-hands and *bunraku* puppeteers.

Is the substitute able to conquer the feeling that 'something is miss-ing'? Often, and increasingly so, but not always.

What is the ultimate destiny of the substitute? To become the reality.

In Praise of Shadows

Unself-awareness, self-unawareness

IT IS DISCONCERTING TO DISCOVER that not only have what I once thought were my own original ideas already been published by someone else, but that there was a time when I knew they weren't mine. Since the time of first acquaintance, those ideas must have settled so comfortably into my head that now they just feel like they belong there. Or, they simply got lost and turned up one day on my doorstep, and were adopted, and became indistinguishable from my natural mental offspring. How can I know if any of my ideas are really my own? I can only know when they aren't. At first appraisal this doesn't seem at all fair.

At one stage in the preparation of this book I decided to name each chapter after a Japanese book title in English translation. Thus each chapter would refer indirectly (via two steps) to another piece of writing. The idea was to instantiate the 'chain of derivates' idea that I felt resonated so strongly in many things Japanese. I think it was Dazai Osamu's *No Longer Human* that started this idea off. It was such a good pointer to the notion of virtualisation encroaching on the personal. For this chapter I chose Tanizaki Junichiro's *In Praise of Shadows*. Then I noticed chapter two of Alex Kerr's *Lost Japan* is subtitled *In Praise of Shadows*. Kerr makes the connection to Tanizaki's book because his chapter describes his house in Shikoku, of which darkness was at first the dominant feature. As Kerr renovated the house, and removed its clutter and partitions, something brighter was born. Tanizaki's book had discussed the process of Japanese art arising from the darkness in which people live. In both connections there is a theme of lightening, leavening, disencumberment.

But we can also travel in the other direction. From art to darkness.

Self-mythologising

Often, these days, I have a mounting feeling of imminent enlighten-ment, which abruptly shatters to a frustrating nothingness, like a word lost from the tip of the tongue. And many of my once cherished ideas now appear naïve and meaningless to me.

What is it that ever gives us our high faith in individual identity and creativity in the west? Is it, perhaps, the great pile of novel ideas each of us has coined, which are ours alone, and not those of other people? If so, then where are they? Where is the creativity in the deluge of shib-boleths we pour at each other every day? Is it in the torrents of media cliché that people everywhere seem preoccupied with? Is it our con-stant self-reinforcement, which becomes so pathological that other people, our reluctant audiences, now just automatically discount any-thing good we say about ourselves? Is it the simple social unacceptabil-ity of being dull that convinces us that we couldn't possibly be?

Ego *is* a dirty word in Japan. When interviewed, Japanese sports heroes often mumble and discount themselves in an endearing way. Being smooth and socially cool, having no sign of nerves, is not per-ceived positively. Promoting one's own talents is seen as terribly reg-rettable. It is as if it is only proper to be accidentally discovered, if at all, and that any craving of recognition would be a stain on one's char-acter. Consequently, every lane in Japan seems to hide extraordinary skills in arts and crafts that hardly ever get noticed.

Haiku interlude

When Roland Barthes deigned to describe *haiku*, he did it by pointing to all the European literary notions that *haiku* was not. He defined it by what it wasn't, told it where it couldn't go, and in so doing artifi-cially trapped it in a tiny space. He did not consider that the *haiku* form is as much about writing, *physically*, with a brush, and seeing, *physically*, marks on the paper, as it is about reading or hearing. *Haiku* is one of the dramatic arts.

Shodo beginnings

And I was to find out that *shodo* is, too. *Shodo* is the Japanese name for brush calligraphy, the most exalted of all art forms in the east. *Shodo*

is closely translated as 'the way of writing.' As in all such construc-
tions, *shodo, judo, kendo, aikido, bushido,* and so on, the practical and
semantic emphasis is on *do,* meaning 'road' or 'way.' The important
thing is not so much what we do, but *the way* we go about it. In these
practices, a novice is expected to be disciplined, committed, and serious in pursuit of the right frame of mind. The components of *do* are a
symbol for 'head' framed by a symbol for 'advancing.' The same character may be better known to some in its Chinese reading, *tao.*

The importance of calligraphy in Japan, China and neighbouring
countries is hard to convey, but perhaps the closest parallel is the importance, now passing, of having the right accent in English society. To
have good handwriting in the east still suggests the characteristics of
education, intelligence, refinement – in short, what the English once
called breeding. Even today, in the age of computers and roller-ball
pens, all Japanese schoolchildren are taught *shodo* for several years.

Of course, the position of *gaijin,* who generally cannot even read
kanji, on such a social index goes without saying. So it was with modest aspirations that I started to learn about *shodo.*

I'd been closely examining *kanji* written in all styles, and I'd concluded that *shodo* must always be done with the right hand. There are
two reasons for this: all strokes flow in directions that allow the right
hand to pull, not push, the brush, and the finely shaped ends of calligraphic brush strokes reveal that the tip of the brush is usually pointed towards the top left. To angle a brush this way is natural with the
right hand, awkward with the left. This discovery is disappointing because, being left-handed, I had been looking forward to writing right
to left, leaving behind the smudges and weirdly cocked wrist of cack-
handed writing. I resign myself to writing English with my left hand
and Japanese with my right. The worst of both worlds.

The paraphernalia of serious *shodo* are initially a little daunting, but
there are alternatives for the casual. During my first few days in Japan
I had discovered inexpensive pen-like brushes on sale in stationery
stores. Called *fude-pen,* their ink is held in a fat squeezable cartridge.
The ink is fed into the centre of the bristles by occasional gentle finger
pressure. I tried for a while to get good results with this kind of brush,
experimenting with two or three kinds, but the springiness of the

hairs always spoilt my efforts. Then I found another modern innovation: pens with a long flexible felt tip that can be bent like a brush by pressing hard on the paper. In fact, it may be that *shodo* was the original purpose of the felt-tip pen, invented in 1962 by Miura Masao and Horie Yukio, and now so ubiquitous. Specialist *shodo* felt-tip pens allow better control than the *fude-pen*, but the effects are even worse. After trying a few of these, I finally decided to adopt the traditional methods. And that's where the real problems begin, for it is not obvious how to make a start in the ancient art of *shodo*, and the beautiful effects of the masters at first seem impossible to emulate.

What books should I read? With the exception of the *shodo* chapter in John David Morley's sexually charged *Pictures from the Water Trade*, and Todd Shimoda's *The Fourth Treasure*, most of the literature about *shodo* is blandly tutorial in flavour. It talks about how to hold the brush, how to sit, and identifies the tools of the trade. What it does not tell us is what we need to do with the tools to achieve a particular effect.

What equipment should I buy? All the local supermarkets and general stores sell *shodo* paper, brushes and ink of the cheapest varieties, the sort of materials that mothers must occasionally replace for their junior-school children.

Like many Japanese children do, I make my start with a child's portable *shodo* kit. Inside are a *shitajiki*, a piece of felt that supports the paper as I write; *sumi*, a small engraved inkstick; *suzuri*, a simple inkstone; *fude*, a large brush for writing; *kofude*, a small brush for signature; *bunshin*, a paperweight; a plastic water dropper; *boku-eki*, a small bottle of liquid ink and a tray, *bon*, for holding these things. I supplement this collection with some more brushes; a small stick of high quality ink; *fudeoki*, a brush rest; *suiteki*, a water bottle; *fude-maki*, a stylish woven bamboo brush roll; and three grades of *hanshi*, transparent Japanese paper. The design of each item is simple and plain. I intend to use this child's kit as a basis, and over time replace each of the items with something more graceful. This will give a focus to my growing love of Japanese objects. With the goal of assembling a lovely set of *shodo* tools, I can satisfy my acquisitive desires and also collect useful memorabilia for the places I visit.

Shodo is obviously an activity for aesthetes, and this is reflected in the materials that are available for the true follower of the way. Price really has no ceiling, so it can be ruinous to ask for the best. And there is always something more wonderful to wish for. I particularly wanted to have an elegant *suzuri*, inkstone. I looked in many shops in several towns. The prices seemed excessive. In Tokyo I saw a *suzuri* for two million yen – more expensive than a car. I surmised it could only be antique at that price. I had ideas about supplementing the small *suzuri* in my portable kit with a large one, one that would enable me to use my largest brushes, but I soon realised that the combination of large size and high quality was beyond the range of my pocket, or at least my idea of fair price. I settled for quality, knowing that if later I still need a large one I can get it in China for a fraction of the cost. The *suzuri* I finally bought for 5,400 yen, in the arcades of Himeji, was a *san go sun tennen*, which means it measures 90 by 150 mm, and is in the natural *tennen* style. It is a tapered and slightly squared-off oval, with a silky smooth well, and roughly carved exterior. The inkstick glides easily over the surface of the well, unlike the grinding effect of my cheap *suzuri*.

I've assembled a few more things since then. I bought the best *shuniku*, red ink paste, I could find, not because it was the best, but just because it looked so fine, starkly orange in a little ebony pot, held in a wooden box, wrapped in *washi* paper, and then boxed in cardboard and enclosed in plastic. When the shop assistant sold this to me she felt it was necessary to further wrap it in brown paper. I also have a large *inkan*, carved in the shape of a dragon, and engraved by a Chinese calligrapher and engraver, Mr Shi of Xiamen. I bought a delicate *washi* paper box at Kurodaya in Asakusa, just big enough to hold a few hundred sheets of *hanshi*. A selection of other little items has also been added: a *washi* folder for carrying calligraphy, bamboo grips for holding inksticks as they wear down to awkwardly small sizes, a plastic tube to hold two wet brushes, a thicker *shitajiki*, another with markings on it to help with character placement, a small irregularly shaped *inkan*, a chisel for carving it, a large plain *bunshin* of luminous rosewood, a special cloth for mopping up spilt ink or for supporting an inkstone, caps to prevent wet brushes from drying out, and a book of styles for about a thousand *kanji* characters. Is this all now? No, I still want a rosewood brush rest to replace the little cast metal dragon that I am currently using, and there will certainly be other things that take my fancy.

Even though excessive cleaning is a form of wear, I keep all my things pristine. One thousand years ago, Sei Shonagon would have noted this with satisfaction. She was particularly offended by the sight of a dirty inkstone, and read much of a person's character into how they treated their *shodo no dogu*, their calligraphy tackle.

I practise *shodo* during my morning solitudes. Making ink is far from dull. The books on *shodo* take a typically oriental view of this process, claiming that while gently rubbing the ink stick against the inkstone, the artist can clear his mind of all distractions, and settle on what poem or proverb he wishes to write. This is not entirely baloney. I often feel deeply relaxed and virtuous after some minutes of empty-minded ink-making.

My biggest troubles start when I actually try to write something. I am always fiddling with irritating technical problems that prevent me from even getting close to the aesthetic issues I want to deal with. When the brush is overloaded the ink spreads out in a wide rough stain as soon as the tip touches the paper. Other times there is so little ink that the brush mark peters out and the stroke scratches to an invisible end. Somewhere in between there must be an optimum, but I can't find it, because sometimes I experience both problems in a single stroke.

So much for the ink, but I have difficulty with the paper too. Some paper is deeply absorbent – so it draws ink out of the brush, making both spreading and dryness more likely. Smoother paper helps to avoid these problems, but crinkles badly when the ink dries. This can cause the paper to lift in ripples as I am still trying to write on it – with ugly effects. So I am currently undecided about paper preferences. The paper I liked most a few weeks ago now seems too hard and prone to crinkling, and I today prefer a softer variety that cost four times as much.

Somewhere in the confluence of ink density, ink loading, brush size, brush stiffness, paper type, and writing speed I know there is a combination that will create a certain desired effect. What troubles me, as a complete beginner, is that even if I get all of these factors right, I may unknowingly be trying for the wrong effect at the time.

Paper and ink are two of the crucial three items in *shodo*. The third is the brush, or *fude*. Brushes come in many varieties, including those made from human baby hair. Bristles are usually bound together by glue when brushes are new and, as I am soon to learn, the kind of *shodo* one can do depends on how much glue is washed out of the bristles. For fine *shodo* it is usually better for beginners to leave the upper two-thirds of the bristles stiff.

After a few weeks of unrewarding experimentation I sense I am losing my way with *shodo*. I need advice on some technical problems, and I need to watch someone who knows what they are doing. So, I ask around, making it clear that I am serious about *shodo*, and need a good teacher. Soon, I have been put in touch with Segawa-sensei, through her daughter, Kazuyo, who does volunteer work at the tourist information desk at Himeji station. Segawa-sensei meets me at the station to show me which bus to catch, and at which stop to get off to reach her house. She is a genial-looking woman in her mid-fifties, energetic, and carefully dressed. On the bus we communicate in Japanese, but it is difficult for me to answer her questions about my abilities.

At her house, in the district of Abokou, she leads me up a steep set of stairs to a warm sunny room overlooking a small back yard. The walls of the room are hung with mounted works of calligraphy. A large bookcase is packed full of books on *shodo* and other arts. The only item of furniture is a low table, covered in old brushes and ink pots. I show her my *shodo*, and all my materials. My brushes are too hard, she says immediately, I must wash the glue out of them. My *shodo* reflects my personality, she informs me, plain and honest.

She asks if she may correct my work. This is done by taking a brush laden with red ink and painting on top of any strokes that are wrong. If one of my *kanji* is well drawn, she circles it in red. If it is really good, it gets a red spiral. An exceptionally good *kanji* receives a flower. I'm as pleased with the flowers as I was with gold stars at junior school.

I want to discuss all my various tools, and how to use them, but she instead directs me to start making ink. After fifteen minutes of soft grinding she asks me to write something, so I begin. I write a few large *kanji*, then some smaller ones, I show her the strokes I find most difficult, I practise strokes, I write some more complex *kanji*. I try a few different compositions. This goes on for an hour, without comment from her. I began to wonder what we are doing – am I so awful that she is bereft of advice, dumbstruck? Then she breaks her silence.

'May I make a suggestion?'

I nearly collapse with relief.

She lifts my elbow away from the side of my body, and straightens the brush so that it is vertical. Both these adjustments make things more awkward for me, but I give her the benefit of the doubt and persevere. I've since learnt that the vertical brush grip helps the calligrapher execute changes in stroke direction without splaying the brush. It is good for beginners to develop this grip early in their career. The high elbow position can be tiring, and at first reduces my control over the hand – but it looks the part, and in time it allows much greater freedom of movement of the arm, which is essential for the longest strokes.

Segawa-sensei now says I should decide on a phrase to draw on a card or good paper, for mounting. I like this goal-oriented approach. I put together some seasonal phrases in my head. 'Winter, empty trees, empty heart' is one of them. Later, on the way home I will buy a *shikishi*, a hard display card edged with gold paper, for my first attempt at a piece of decorative *shodo*.

We have coffee. Segawa-sensei shows me photographs from her trips to China and Australia. I keep repositioning my legs when they hurt or grow numb. We are joined later by Kazuyo, who says she can't sit comfortably on the floor like her mother and I, and perches on the window-sill. She is clearly more westernised than her mother.

Segawa-sensei explains that students usually do their work at home, and bring it regularly to her for correcting. She runs classes twice a week, and suggests I come to both. If I like, I can come a little earlier on the day and do some *shodo* there with her, before the rest of the class arrives. It sounds encouraging.

Watching Segawa-sensei draw lively fluid strokes, I am inspired. She crafts beautiful balanced *kanji* with great discipline but complete ease. I am surprised, given the enormous gulf between her abilities and mine, that she gave so much consideration to the work I brought.

Finally, after nearly three hours, she says that's all for today. I ask what I should pay her, and hear 3,000 yen being discussed between her and Kazuyo. This sounds expensive for today, and it is too much for me to spend twice a week. Then when Kazuyo translates I discover that the price is a flat monthly rate – which effectively covers eight visits. Very reasonable, I say.

I take a GPS reading in Segawa-sensei's garden so that I can always find my way back to the house through the haphazard maze of unlit streets that make up south-east Himeji. Then I ride back to the station with Kazuyo.

The next day I practise the *kanji* Segawa-sensei asked me to write. I use a completely softened brush and load it with ink just as she did. Remarkably, the ink does not spread. There are two factors in this: the ink holds little water, so it is viscous; by removing the glue from the brush there is more room for ink to be held higher in the bristles. Although fully laden, the brush is not *over*-laden with ink. The difference is crucial. If any sort of a drop forms at the tip of the brush, I can expect the ink to spread on the paper.

The density of the ink, I now find, is less problematic. Dense inks give a strong solid effect, watery ones give a lighter feel and subtly show the difference between slow and fast parts of the brushwork.

Over the next couple of days I self-consciously make up a phrase to write. It evolves into 'Winter breath, the sky listens.' Because both subject and object precede verbs in Japanese this can also be read as 'Winter breath, listen to the sky.' It can also mean 'Winter son, an empty spirit listens.' It can be read as an intensive rhyme too:

Tou-ki iki

Kuu-ki ki

By practising this again and again, I develop the right mix of thick and thin brush strokes so that all *kanji* occupy roughly equal areas. I return to Segawa-sensei's house to receive her verdict, on both the calligraphy and the phrase itself.

After some difficulty identifying the house in the near-total darkness of Abokou, I climb the stairs to the *shodo* room and show her my homework. This consists of thirty-seven sheets of *hanshi* – everything I have done since we last met. While she goes through all this two other students arrive, Nobuko-san and Harumi-san. They are both middle-aged ladies, naturally friendly and encouraging. All three women heap praise on my work – quite inappropriately, I am certain. I gather that I have brought too much, and that from now on I should probably only bring the most successful efforts. What pleases me is that as each sheet is drawn out for inspection and correction I sometimes know which parts Segawa-sensei is going to correct before she does so. My poem is not commented on. I don't even know if the women bother to try to make sense of it.

Segawa-sensei then goes through the work of Nobuko-san and Harumi-san. They are tackling far more ambitious projects than I am. All of the women refer constantly to a monthly periodical. It contains reproductions of fine *shodo* submitted by other calligraphers. In the October edition I see an example of Segawa-sensei's work. The two students show Segawa-sensei which piece of work they would like to attempt and she copies these out for them at the right scale. Her copies are astoundingly accurate. I've never seen anything like it. Nobuko-san and Harumi-san take her *tehon*, models, home with them, leaving early.

Segawa-sensei asks me to do some exercises she has prepared – one of which comes from the magazine. I start on this, wondering when to leave before I overstay my welcome. I marvel at how well her paper handles the ink. The ink just falls into it, like a wave disappearing into sand. Though she has told me that I should be using cheap paper for exercises, it is not really good for finished effects. The high sheen of cheap paper holds the ink on the surface in shallow puddles which dry to a coarse sheen. Her paper, on the other hand, drinks the ink in before my eyes, and dries to an absolute matte black. She meanwhile plays with a design that she would like me to put on a *shikishi*, display card. It is a celebration of the New Year. We refine it both in terms of *kanji* choice and style. *Shodo* has several styles, all of which come naturally to Segawa-sensei. She obviously favours the more fluid styles such as *sousho*, and I suspect she would like to have me use them, but I want to build a solid technical foundation on the basics first, and that means concentrating on *kaisho*, the regular block style often used for printed *kanji*.

Nobuko-san had brought *o-miyage*, a souvenir cake, from Okayama. Segawa-sensei suggests that we stop work, have some tea and eat the *o-miyage*. Over tea we try to communicate as best we can. We do not have much common technical language to work with, so it sometimes gets difficult. Two or three times Segawa-sensei phones Kazuyo for help. It is an enjoyable and instructive evening, but it is getting close to the time of my last bus and I must leave.

During the conversation we talked about brushes and I asked what she would recommend for me. The answer was something of a surprise. She told me all my brushes were acceptable for children, but not adults, and that I should take them to a temple and burn them in a ceremony called *fude kuyo*. She suggests I buy a lambs-wool brush for at least 3,000 yen. I had been under the impression 1,500 yen was a high price. No, she tells me, she has paid 40,000 yen several times. This is the equivalent of $800. The next day, when I tell Maya (at the temple) about this, she is not surprised. Though still a student, she normally pays 8-10,000 yen for her brushes.

On the day after I spoke to Maya I go to the imposing and aloof *shodo* shop near the castle – one that Segawa-sensei had recommended. This, it appears, is the place for serious calligraphers in Himeji. The shopkeeper recognises me as Segawa-sensei's *gaijin* student as soon as I step through the door, and he rushes to waylay me before I can walk any further into his shop. He shows me the two brushes he has selected for me (she had asked him to give me the 30% discount enjoyed by all her other students). I choose the slightly longer of the two brushes because of its delicate handle. It is a piece of polished bamboo, mottled with darker brown ovals, and with a knot near the top. The glassy white hairs of the brush will wash out to a fine softness.

I take a brief look around the shop. It is dark inside, and harks back to the early part of the 20th century, with most items enclosed in wooden cases. The shopkeeper stands in a small enclosure near the back of the shop. Along one wall are dozens of unlabelled drawers, where the papers and *shikishi* are stored. On the other side of the shop is a good collection of *shodo* literature. Some individual volumes cost up to 20,000 yen, and there are at least two massive multi-volume encyclopaedias of *shodo*. Space is limited. It is not a shop for browsing. One is expected to tell the shopkeeper exactly what one wants.

On a previous trip to Kyoto I found a traditional *shodo* shop in the Teramachi area. It was so small that I couldn't enter, there already being one customer inside. He was sitting on a small stool talking to the owner, who knelt on raised *tatami* in the other half of the shop. A small selection of brushes and inks were visible in cabinets, all within arm's reach, and there was no room for anything else. I contented myself with peering through the window for a couple of minutes.

Despite my lessons, I grow increasingly frustrated with *shodo*. I really had hoped for more improvement than this, given my hours of daily practice. My brush strokes are now developing ragged ends because I am trying to minimise the number of times I refresh the ink in the brush. The result of this is that the hairs of the brush are often slightly bent or spread from the previous brush stroke, which makes the next a little harder to do neatly. And when I focus on my brush strokes I lose control of the overall composition.

My lessons create a situation that exacerbates this general frustration. Segawa-sensei often springs surprises on me. Yesterday she asked me to write on the *shikishi* I bought the other day. I wasn't ready to do this, I hadn't practised the design; in fact, I had not even seen the design she wanted me to use. She asked me to grind the ink, but gave me an inkstone so deeply encrusted with old ink that little lumps of it found their way onto the *shikishi*. The tiny *kanji* that she has written out for me to use in my signatures are so cursive that I can only guess at them, which is a trial and error process that creates more failures than successes. All of these problems are endured while kneeling *seiza*-fashion on a wooden floor on which only a piece of cloth has been spread. It is sometimes so cold that I cannot keep my hands still. The other students and Segawa-sensei are happily unaware of the ink drops that find their way onto everything, but I constantly fret about getting ink on my clothes or other items I'm trying to keep clean.

After ruining all three of my *shikishi* with awful *shodo* (to the point where not even the excessively complimentary Miyuki-san and Kumiko-san, two other students, can find anything good to say) I feel deflated and thwarted. I buy four new *shikishi* on the way home and plan to do them in private, when I am more prepared for it. I even have a new saying planned. I saw it at Engyo-ji temple the other day, and I think the Okamoto family would like it. It is the four characters 'nature empty, raise person' – which I take to mean that ridding oneself of material preoccupations is the way to achieve elevation to heaven.

The bottled ink I use today has, like all the bottled inks, a curiously dry smell. The paper, by contrast, can sometimes smell moist. The ink was once made from soot, mixed together with animal glues and moulded into hard blocks. I do not know if the modern methods are the same.

I experiment with different approaches to all the things that cause problems. I trace Segawa-sensei's models with pencil and then try to fill in the tracings with simple clear brush strokes just like hers. This shows me that even when I have an exact model of what I should do, I cannot get the brush and ink to obey me. I am not confident that I can do better than this. I wonder at times whether I should give up *shodo*, as it is pushing me to the point where I want to throw or break things. The satisfaction and relaxation that I used to feel is almost forgotten.

My tracing of characters leads to a mildly embarrassing incident. At the following lesson, Miyuki-san and Kumiko-san exclaim at the perfection of my composition on one particular sheet of hanshi. Miyuki-san picks up the paper to show it to Segawa-sensei, who is also quite obviously impressed. Segawa-sensei explains to the others that I am a graphic designer, so such good composition (they use the word *baransu* – that is, 'balance') is to be expected. Looking at it myself, I have to admit *yes, that is a surprisingly well composed page – maybe I am getting better*, and therefore accept the compliments of the women rather than denying that there is anything worthy in my work, which would be the proper form. But after a few of my self-satisfied *domo arigato*'s, Miyuki-san suddenly notices a portion of the pencil tracing on the page.

'*Enpitsu!*' she exclaims, and points an incriminating finger. I suddenly realise, as does everyone else, that the compositional balance for which I have just taken all the credit, actually belongs to Segawa-sensei. We are all a little embarrassed, and I weakly explain that it was *jikken*, an experiment, and quickly point out the other two sheets where I did the same thing, before anyone else notices them.

I enjoy the lightness of *hiragana shodo*. I like the goal of achieving fluidity in one's writing – and *hiragana shodo* is such a manageable pursuit, requiring the tiniest amount of ink and only one small brush. My right hand really improves, but its movements are not as smooth as those of my left. The tiny curls and wispy lines of *hiragana* demand perfect control, and I don't yet have this. Frustration sets in again, but by forcing myself to practise, and taking every stroke seriously, I get the minimal improvement I need to sustain motivation.

Segawa-sensei keeps suggesting I sign and stamp my work. It is partly this, and partly my need to have something else to keep my hands busy that prompts me to start engraving an *inkan* for myself.

I scratch the characters in reverse on the face of the *inkan* and discover that the chisel cuts the stone readily, with little need for force. Within an hour or so I have the rough strokes sketched in, and then spend the next four hours refining the contours as carefully as I can. My eyesight is not really good enough for this sort of work, and my hands start to cramp but, after a series of trial stamps on paper, I home in on the finished design. It has a few irreparable mistakes in it, but they are only small scratches and I am pleased with the overall effect.

Next door to Segawa-sensei lives her sister, who is a potter. One cold evening we visit the pottery. I am given two little pots to decorate with *shodo*. In one I write *hana*, the character for flower, and in another I write *tsuki*, the character for moon. I sign both pots with my *katakana* signature, *maaku*. A week later the pots are waiting for me on my desk when I arrive for *shodo* practice. The red pigment has metamorphosed the flat grey glaze into a rusty metallic. I am delighted with the effect and proceed to show everyone. This one episode, on its own, makes me glad I went to the trouble of seeking out a *shodo* teacher.

As I become more practised in *shodo*, something changes. It is no longer *the thing* that is important, but *the act*. When I practise *shodo* now it is the temporal arts, rather than the spatial, that come to mind. In particular, I think often of dance and music, whose rhythms and hierarchical structures are so isomorphic with the building up of characters with brush strokes.

What we have between us

In *Japanese: the Spoken Language in Japanese Life*, Mizutani Osamu tells of an informal translation test he gave to two students, one American, the other Japanese. The American was asked to translate *itta-to iimashita* (he said he went). He produced dozens of English forms; 'he said that he went,' 'he told me that he went,' 'he said that he had gone,' and so on. The Japanese student was asked to translate the English sentence 'he said he went' into Japanese in as many ways as he could. He also produced a long list of alternatives: *itta-to itta, itta-to iimashita, irasshatta-to itta.*

While neither student produced a sentence that the other could not have translated, each was guided in their choices by personal and cultural predispositions, the familiarity of language forms, and a sense of what the sentence is really all about. Mizutani observes that the English forms produced by the American student were concerned with slightly different interpretations of the past facts of the matter, whereas the Japanese forms the other student produced were concerned with various possible social relationships surrounding the present speech act. This, Mizutani thought, reflects the different preoccupations of the languages; English is rich in forms concerned with facts, Japanese is rich in forms concerned with social relationships.

Talking up

We make our own words, but they add up to make us. So what happens if we use the wrong words? Before I met Harumi, I was spending days at a time in complete silence, but my internal dialogue was as continuous as ever. Now I am speaking to people every day, I constantly feel I am failing to express myself properly, and this is somehow leading me in a direction I do not want to go. My words are chosen to be understood, not to be true. People are just understanding the words, not me. That's how it feels. I'm certain no good will come of it.

Being sociable is destroying my focus. Ideas are constantly slipping through my fingers and it is all the fault of language. I've been too careless in its use. I make a New Year's resolution to watch what I say from now on. My old motto 'avoid cliché, avoid compromise' comes to mind. Why did I ever forget it? Yes, I must think more about my words.

Absorption

I have noted, as have others from time to time, that visiting a foreign country renders one both an infant and a lover. An infant because of a deep dependency on others, and an inability to converse about or understand anything not directly linked to one's needs. A lover because suddenly life is lived in Technicolor, emotions are intensified and the flaws of the beloved are so easily overlooked. Perhaps this is the real appeal of travel, the realisation of our most fundamental fantasies: being in love and being taken care of.

Curiously, I come to realise that this explains much of what is peculiar to Japan. It is as if the Japanese are visitors in their own land. There are drives to be childish and child-like, and there are dreams aplenty in which the dreamer desires something truly, deeply, pathetically. It is the freedom of a child and the devotion of a lover.

For women, the childishness is in the adolescent or kindergarten-style clothing, the decoration of everything with cutesy cartoon characters, the high piping voices, the stumbling pigeon-toed walk, the coy giggling and the meekness. For men, it is the immaturity of their voyeuristic sexuality, the schoolboy jokes and rowdiness when it is time to let their hair down, the easy submission to paternalism of any stripe.

The pretence of being in love – with dreams, with hobbies, with foreign musicians, film actors, writers, or anyone of note who is unattainable – is so commonplace. Having something to love with abandon and selflessness is always so important. And it puts one's self in its place, off to the side.

Iroha

Legend has it that Kobo Daishi sought to translate from Sanskrit to Japanese four lines of the Nirvana-sutra – the essence of Buddhist doctrine. The stanza in the original Sutra (rendered in English) is as follows:

All earthly things pass away;
This is the law of all existence.
Going beyond this law of extinction,
We are in the bliss of Nirvana alone.

The outstanding achievement of Kobo Daishi's putative translation is that it uses each of the forty-seven basic Japanese syllables exactly once. It is therefore a minimal *kana* pangram.

I don't believe for a minute that Kobo Daishi was actually responsible for this linguistic acrobatics. There is a tendency to attribute far too many accomplishments to this single historical figure, and there is considerable scholarly doubt that the *hiragana* writing system as we know it existed in his day.

Regardless of its provenance, Kobo Daishi's *iroha*, as the translation is called, goes as follows:

i-ro ha ni-ho-he-to chi-ri-nu-ru wo

wa-ka yo ta-re so tsu-ne na-ra-mu

u-wi no o-ku-ya-ma ke-fu ko-e-te

a-sa-ki yu-me mi-shi we-hi mo se-su

Students of Japanese may object that *n* is missing and that *wi* and *we* are not part of the modern syllabary. This is true. Written Japanese has changed. Meiji era reforms led to the introduction of *n* and made *wi* and *we* obsolete, replacing them with *i* and *e* respectively.

The original *iroha* – with *wi* and *we* – is now used chiefly as a mnemonic for children and as a sequence for locating elements in an arrangement, much as the letters A, B, C… are often used to identify, for example, rows of theatre seats.

To be understood today, it is better to write the *iroha* as:

iro wa nioedo chirinuru o

waga yo tare zo tsune naran

ui no okuyama kyou koete

asaki yume miji ei mo sezu

English re-translations of the *iroha* are found everywhere. Individually, these translations all leave something to be desired. Nevertheless, I think a reasonable understanding of the mood and intent of the *iroha* can best be distilled by sampling several English versions together. A selection follows:

Brightly coloured though the blossoms be, all are doomed to scatter,
So in this world of ours, who will last forever?
Today, having crossed the mountain recesses of Samskrita,
I shall be free of floating dreams,
Nor shall I be fuddled (by the pleasures of this world).

Ivan Morris

Though gay in hue, the blossoms flutter down also,
Who then in this world of ours may continue forever?
Crossing today the uttermost limits of phenomenal existence,
I shall no more see fleeting dreams,
Neither be any longer intoxicated.

Basil Hall Chamberlain

Colours are fragrant, but they fade away.
In this world of ours none lasts forever.
Today cross the high mountain of life's illusions,
And there will be no more shallow dreaming,
No more drunkenness.

Andrew Nathaniel Nelson

Leaves and blossoms in all their brilliance fall,
Who among us will tarry in this world?
We shall cross the deepest mountains of this Samsava, the world of illusion, and dream no more shallow dreams, nor yield to drunkenness.

Peregrine Hodson

Flowers, although fragrant, will be left behind.
Who in this world will remain immortal?
Today, we pass the high mountain of illusions,
There will be no more empty dreaming,
And no more drunkenness.

Oliver Statler

The blooms are fragrant, but alas! They fall.
Who in this world can remain forever?
Crossing this day the mountains of transient existence,
We see no more shallow dreams nor get drunk on them.

Trevor Leggett

And finally:

> All is transitory in this fleeting world.
> Let me escape from its illusions and vanities.

Oliver Statler

Escape? How?

Now that is the question. I was living in Garmoyle Road, in Liverpool, a street where John Lennon once lived, when I heard he had been killed. My friend Paul shouted the news through my bedroom door. At first, my feelings about this were not strong, but as the day progressed I was affected by other people's reactions. The call-in radio shows could talk of nothing else. Dozens of people were asserting that Lennon could never die, even though this is precisely what he had just done.

Lennon's music played all day. In the afternoon I walked along Mathew Street, home of the Cavern Club, and already wreaths and letters were piling up on the pavement. Several photographs of Lennon had been stuck to the brickwork. I could hear people talking about him everywhere I went. Liverpool was in a state of shock.

The real dimensions of what had happened dawned on me late in the day. I began to feel the great sadness of the waste. I thought again about the assertions of Lennon's immortality, and they finally began to make sense. I never met Lennon. I knew him only through his music, his books, the Beatles films, what I read in magazines and newspapers, and what I had seen on television. It wasn't Lennon the person that I had ever touched, only representations of him. And now, with him dead, the representations were more numerous and conspicuous than ever. The only Lennon I ever knew *was* still there, even more so.

In *The Tale of Murasaki*, Liza Dalby has the young Murasaki watching the smoke rising from her mother's cremation. Murasaki stays to the very end, and as the smoke thins she tries to hold on to the last faint wisps of it with her eyes...

Fiction parent, fact child

About one thousand years ago, an introspective Heian-kyo woman began to turn her fantasies and imagination, and perhaps also observations and hearsay, into a series of stories. She showed them to friends and relatives, and soon the stories entered wider circulation, establishing a name for the author. Literally. She became known as Murasaki Shikibu. We do not know whether she had a name more 'real' than this. In English, we refer to her as Lady Murasaki, and to her collection of stories as the world's first novel: *The Tale of Genji*.

The Genji stories drew the attention of the Heian court, and Murasaki was eventually summoned by the regent Michinaga to act as tutor to his daughter Shoshi, first wife of the Emperor Ichijo. While serving as a lady in the court, Murasaki wrote about its events. These writings also survive, and are now known as *The Diary of Lady Murasaki*. They provide detailed information about courtly happenings, but only the lightest of sketches of Murasaki's private life. In recent times a fictionalised version of her life, drawn from the diary, her poetry, her *Genji* and other sources, has been published by Liza Dalby, under the title of *The Tale of Murasaki*, a sub-theme of which just happens to be literary descendancy.

Liza Dalby is notable for being the only westerner ever to have become a *geisha*, which she did as part of her doctoral research. She published a book about these experiences, entitled *Geisha*. Nowadays, however, what people think they know about the life of *geisha* comes from the much more widely read, but fictional, *Memoirs of a Geisha* by Arthur Golden. Though Golden declares that many elements of the story are taken from the life of the *geisha*, Iwasaki Mineko, she herself denies several of them.

Thus is fiction linked to fact, fact to fiction to fact, and back to fiction.

God to Milton to Huxley to Gerster

I am reading, and enjoying, *Legless in Ginza*, a travelogue by fellow Australian academic Robin Gerster. The title's allusion to Aldous Huxley's *Eyeless in Gaza*, which is itself an allusion to John Milton's *Samson Agonistes*, which retells the story of Samson in the Old Testament Book of Judges 13:24-16:30, echoes the representational recursion of Japan that so fascinates me.

I toy briefly with the idea of employing a character called Isla St. Gazer (which is what I thought I heard when my more cultivated school friends were discussing Huxley) in order to knit further the pattern.

Cored

One of my favourite desserts as a child was baked apples, smothered in custard, and stuffed with sultanas and brown sugar. My mother had a special tool for cutting out the apple cores. She called it a corer. I remember thinking that it should be called an 'uncorer' since it took cores away rather than put them in. To be cored, I realised later, could mean either having a core, or not having a core. All of which is made more confusing in Japan, where cores often aren't, and in not being, often are. In the words of Roland Barthes, the centre is rejected, the notion evaporates and, despite the unintended irony of his overblown passage on empty containers in *Empire of Signs*, emptiness is crucial. Meals have no main course, Tokyo has no city centre. Alex Kerr aired the same idea in *Lost Japan*: an elaborate preparation leads to nothing, the final secret of an ancient art, once revealed, is nothing but prosaic pragmatism. This meeting of the Buddhist void, he claims, is what makes Japanese art so unlike that of any other culture, so plain, minimal, indirect; creating through the negative, as it were.

Buddhism revels in the idea of there being – precisely where one most thinks there should be, *must* be, something absolutely crucial, pivotal, essential and central – nothing. It is the entirely bearable darkness of not-being. A Japanese word for nothing, *mu*, is one of those words that automatically has good connotations. A fine Hyogo *sake* has been named *mu*. It is often found in product names. *Mu* is a popular *kanji* with calligraphers. The message is that *mu* (nothing) is good. Daruma says 'I looked for it, and I couldn't find it' Not because it wasn't there, but because he was looking. I read this in *A Circle Round the Sun*, by Peregrine Hodson, and am interested to follow the story of Hodson's escape to the Japanese countryside, intending to write a book, first person, about himself and Japan. The rural surroundings he describes are so familiar to me that, having similarly retired to rural Yumesaki-cho, I half expect to look across the road and see him in the house opposite. He came to the country to write, but self-consciously realises that he is installing himself in a scroll painting, an image of Japan, the steep hillsides and the dense forests enclosing him and settling him down. Here, he says, he found what he was looking for, but it was not what he had hoped for. His ideal has been shattered. He went the long way round, but he got there, he got to the heart, *kokoro*. 'Japan' is not ideal, but it can seem that way because it is just not there. Or as everyone likes to describe the idea of Zen, 'the moment we go to capture it, it disappears.' It is the emptiness of Mahayana Buddhism that is ultimately acknowledged as having been there all the time, and realising that it is all we really need: nothing. All in nothing.

This theme... true in so many ways. For example, Ian Buruma, in the gorgeous *A Japanese Mirror*, talks about the difficulty of finding the locus of power within Japanese organisations. It is like the empty chamber at the heart of a Shinto shrine, the selflessness of *satori*, the crater at the hypocentre. Yet it is here that the power really does reside, in the emptiness. The Buddhist pilgrimage of Shikoku, circular and Mecca-less, shows there is nowhere to get to, there is only somewhere to go. The shrine at Ise, as close to a Mecca as one can find in Japan: hidden from sight, left entirely to the imagination, like the sacred mirror that resides there, or doesn't, as the case may be. Shinto and Buddhism share this essential vacancy, and it may be why they cohabit so well, forever in orbit around one another, their common centre of gravity floating in the empty space between them. *Satori* cannot exist without the arduous apprenticeship. The truth of Buddhism is practice, not dogma. The truth of Shinto is ritual. The procedural wins over the declarative – how behaviouralist!

The famous emptiness of classical Japanese interiors creates echoes of the void. The Japanese value of appropriateness practically *dictates* that most household belongings be kept out of sight until they are appropriate to the time, occasion and those present. To take the other alternative – of assigning occasions to single-purpose locations, as is normal in European houses – necessitated too may rooms too infrequently used, and this is in conflict with the other Japanese virtue of economy.

Empty book

Japanese literature poses a puzzle for many western readers, because so often nothing happens, or what happens does not constitute a story. This is often because the authors are intent on painting a picture, with mood and colour, a frame, a surface, a texture to feel, rather than drawing on the dramatic traditions of Europe in which the steps of a plot lead the reader to a moral dénouement. When we seek the core, central theme, plot, or structure of Japanese stories we often come up empty-handed. These stories cannot be easily condensed into another form without losing their essence.

Seen through the Japanese prism, even history assumes a theme of inconclusive dismal dissolution rather than a march of time. In *Kyoto: a Contemplative Guide*, Gouverneur Mosher writes:

> When one looks back over Kyoto's history, the heroes he sees are not benefactors, reformers, or liberators. They are hermits, exiled emperors, martyrs, and other tragic individuals or famil-ies whose relatively short periods of prosperity always pre-ceded some ghastly inevitable doom.

We miss the crescendo and climax. Instead, disintegration is the re-curring theme; being absorbed into the universal ephemerality of things has a force that is deeply affecting to Japanese sensibilities, as the expository twist at the end of a thriller is to us. Internal truth, characterisation, and reality don't figure large in Japanese literature, not in the way atmosphere does. Harry Guest touches upon this theme repeatedly in *Traveller's Literary Companion to Japan*. Under the influence of Buddhist thought, reality can only be apprehended once a state of enlightenment, *satori*, has been achieved, and who would be haughty enough to claim that? Better to confine oneself to introspection and fleeting sensations.

Pico Iyer comments that the large issues of state are rarely dealt with in Japanese literature, whereas ordinary domestic situations are its stock in trade. For me, the story that encapsulates everything I feel about Japanese literature is *The Lady Who Loved Insects*. It is an an-onymous little tale, which in a couple of pages touches on the follow-ing: the idea of the 'answer' always being somewhere else (the writer refers the reader to chapter two though there isn't one); self-reference; reverence for what is natural; and this 'The world in which we live has no reality, it is a mirage, a dream.' I wonder if Emi has read it.

For its perfect suggestion, and evident appreciation, of mood, I also love the short exchange between Sei Shonagon and her beloved Emp-ress in *Pillow Book*:

'Why so silent?' said Her Majesty. 'Say something. It is sad when you do not speak.'

'I am gazing into the autumn moon,' I replied.

'Ah yes,' she remarked. 'That is just what you should have said.'

Emi once showed me her favourite *haiku* by Basho Matsuo:

Natsu-kusa ya

Tsuwa-mono-domo ga

Yume no ato

In English, it might go as follows:

In summer grasses

Are now buried

Glorious dreams of ancient warriors

She told me that 'summer grasses' referred to the Sekigahara battle-grounds, not far from where she lives. The bones of many soldiers lie just below the surface of the ground, she said. For four hundred years they have lain there undisturbed, lonely, forgotten, mutely mocking all 'glorious dreams.' It is a poignant image, inextricably linked with loss. As Emi told me about the poem she looked and sounded completely possessed by it. Her eyes were wide and held mine in a steady gaze. Her voice was touched with a childlike wonder. I felt the back of my neck tingle and tears prick at my eyes. I held her face in my hands and kissed her many times. It was an unconscious response to what she made me feel.

Hard facts

A few days later I was still so moved by Emi's feelings for Basho's poem that I went to the library in Himeji and did some research on it. I wish I hadn't. The *haiku* is not about Sekigahara, but about Hirai-zumi, where the Fujiwara clan were overthrown by the Minamoto clan in 1189. Hiraizumi is a place that means nothing to me. I found seventeen English translations of Basho's original, and pointlessly combed through them all, eventually deciding that the one Emi showed me was my favourite. I also stumbled upon the following poem by Fujimoto Junya:

Natsu kusa ya

Tsuwa mono domo mo
Doudemo yoi
Donna jidai mo
Shikabane no yama

This is translated as:

The summer grasses –
Brave soldiers' dreams.
I'm not interested in them.
All through the times,
There have been mountains of bones.

Somehow, I've lost the aching feeling that Emi gave me, and all I've gained is useless knowledge and a dose of someone else's cynicism.

Ways of the hand

The Japanese have a distinctive way of fingering things. The principle area of contact between hands and objects is the inside of the fingers, not the tips. This gives an impression of something precious being cradled in the hands. Westerners often casually hold objects between the fingers, using the sides, or between fingers and thumb; aborigines use the grouped tips of their fingers. As a child in South Africa I was fascinated by the way Zulu and Swazi people used the backs of their fingers, cuffing objects into place. We must learn these ways by watching our parents.

Pretending not to know

While the goal of Buddhism is to reach nirvana and know that there is nothing to know, along the way we may find people pretending not to know what they do know. In most places this is certainly rarer than its opposite, pretending to know what one does not know, but not in Japan.

Ladies of the court, like Sei Shonagon and Lady Sarashina, were great pretenders of ignorance – particularly of agricultural, unpoetic things. Emi allows herself to be uninformed about anything I explain to her, sometimes even when she knows I am wrong. For her, it would have been impossible to say 'I know.' Instead, rapturous feigned interest, which if discovered, would upset me much more than her.

Untruths were fine for Emi, if committed for the right reasons. But it wasn't just that the end justified the means; for her there was some-thing unimportant about truth. For her, believing was a matter of choice.

Japan and the official virtual reality

The computing and media fraternity is in consensus that Japan was late to the Virtual Reality (VR) party, and has only latterly been help-ing to lead the way. This is the semi-official view, and it concerns only the technological VR defined by highly interactive computer inter-faces with advanced visual, aural, and haptic feedback.

Whether Japan is ahead or behind in conjuring up and dealing with alternatives to ordinary space and its ordinary objects is another, and altogether larger, question. I am less interested in questions of who got to specific platforms of VR technology first, and more interested in what we think is real and what we think isn't.

All other things being equal, people take the real more seriously than they do the unreal. When two people differ in their tacit beliefs about what is real and what isn't, strange misunderstandings occur; behaviour appears inexplicable, logic-defying, irrational, inscrutable even.

It's not cricket

I am watching a sports program and, in particular, a press conference that has been called by the Australian cricketer, Mark Waugh. He re-veals that when he and his brother Steve were young boys, they in-vented a kind of semaphore using cricket strokes. Mark says that he secretly developed this a great deal further. He invented encodings of letters and musical notes, and has performed works such as T. S. Eliot's *The Wasteland*, and Erik Satie's *Trois Gymnopedies* in his in-nings. He reveals that particular innings in Sydney, Cape Town, and Mumbai were actually interpretations of major works of art. A spell of short innings for which Waugh was unfairly criticised appear to have coincided with his discovery of Japanese poetry. The reason for the press conference, says Waugh, is that he is on the verge of retiring from test cricket, and is about to perform his magnum opus. For this he considered both Joyce's *Ulysses* and Trotsky's *War and Peace*, but has finally decided upon Wagner's *Ring of the Nibelungs*, which will be performed during the next Ashes series. It is at this point that I realise I must be dreaming, but then I wonder whether the realisation is a dream or a thought. This question spins out of control and I must have either stopped dreaming, or fallen asleep.

Later, Harumi runs up to me with a message in her hand. I unfold the paper. It reads 'I am outside your house but you are not home. We arranged to meet today.' I draw back the curtain and see her car moving away down the road. I call her back and apologise for not answering the door. I see the car slowly turn around on the waste ground halfway to the main road, and draw back up the hill. It parks outside and Harumi waves to me as she walks around to the door. We meet at the *genkan*.

'Maaku-san, I rang the bell many times!' she says reproachfully. 'Were you sleeping?'

'Not asleep, no. On the computer. The doorbell is too musical. I must subconsciously assume it is music playing in another house.'

It is true. That doorbell has tricked me quite a few times, but Harumi is having none of it, I can tell by her expression. I haven't shaved, but we have to leave the house immediately, as we are late for her English class. Harumi assures me that she can make some brunch while I am working with the children, ignoring my protestations that I ate only an hour ago. So I arrive ruffled, dishevelled and unprepared for a class of serious little children.

During the lesson there is something I am bursting to discuss, but I know I cannot. It is Mark Waugh's amazing revelations. In my mind, the reason for not being able to discuss this is that the children know nothing about cricket and it would be meaningless to them, rather than that it was just a dream. I try, instead, to improve their pronunciation of 'very.'

Extremely interesting language

Avoiding the absolute – that is how I see much of Japanese language and thought. Might this be part of the desire to remain childlike and subjective, and avoid objective reality?

Emi once told me that when she learnt the meaning of the English word 'absolutely' she though she would never want or need to use such a word. Similarly, when a Japanese character in *A Circle Round the Sun* by Peregrine Hodson starts to use words like 'tremendous' and 'absolutely' he is described as becoming English.

Once, when Emi and I went to a stylish bar, she said 'I can see nice polished floors, I can see lovely brown walls...' then caught herself and observed it was strange that rather than saying 'the polished floors are very nice, those brown walls are really lovely,' as we would in English, in Japanese one makes the observation subjective, a statement of personal sensory impressions, in preference to anything that might be taken for an absolute, and therefore contestable, statement.

I was at first pleased when I learnt *taihen* and *totemo*, the words in Japanese that are used to translate 'very,' because so many of the observations I wanted to make seemed to depend on intensifiers. In common English usage, we are not content to say simply that today was hot, it has to be '*so* hot.' We conventionally describe people as 'very smart,' 'extremely cute,' 'totally mad,' rather than just smart, cute or mad, which is probably all they are. This is a form of verbal inflation, strictly speaking often untrue, and like other forms of inflation, ultimately undermining. There is something unpoetic about hyperbole, and as might be expected, it does not occur often in Japanese. So now I have been using *taihen* and *totemo* less often, like native Japanese speakers who use these words sparingly, and therefore to better effect.

What is a god to do in Japan?

The history of Christianity in Japan is a peculiar and inauspicious one. Compared to the bizarre cults that number many thousands of adherents, Christianity is a fringe-dweller in Japan. The religion suffers, in Japanese eyes, from absolutism and isolationism but, given the choice of polite acquiescence or rebutting the ardent and impassioned entreaties of western missionaries, the outcome was inevitable.

The question of religion in Japan is akin to that of Australia before the coming of the Europeans; it is either everywhere or nowhere. The Japanese are as passionately uninterested in religion as they are in politics, but they are religious about almost everything they do, and their god is aesthetics. The promised land is beauty, but there are no commandments except one: do what pleases others.

Gods have little to do in Japan other than hear pleas and bestow good fortune. Few critical judgements, such as who is naughty and who is nice, for example, need to be made. Gods are essentially receivers of messages. It has even been suggested that the first use of the written language of China and Japan was to communicate to ancestors and gods (the two groups blur together). Obviously this is different from the more common uses of *spoken* language: communicating thoughts to one's allies and confusion to everyone else.

Language reform – a little or a lot

The Japanese language is as multi-branched and evolving as any major language. It varies so markedly that many Japanese speakers appear to be mutually unintelligible. On almost any night in Japan it is possible to see Japanese subtitles applied to native Japanese spoken on television, for a Japanese audience. Regional differences in the lexicon and prosody of Japanese are much celebrated. The language of the Kansai region, *kansai-ben*, also called *kinki* Japanese, is mellifluous and expressive where the Kanto Japanese of Tokyo is a monotone. Japanese slang is fantastically inventive, particularly in regard to terms for sexual organs, of which there are hundreds. These are all signs of a healthy and vigorous language and, though the Japanese counterpart to 'BBC' English – that of NHK, the public broadcaster – implies that there is a proper way of speaking, ordinary people just get on with the job of reinventing Japanese every day.

Like English, Japanese has a history of absorbency. Approximately half its words are of Chinese origin, smuggled into the language along with the *kanji* writing system. About a quarter of modern Japanese is English, brought in to describe new things or to add new meanings to old things. This leaves only a quarter of the language for 'native' Japanese. For historical reasons, these simple original Japanese terms have a strong naturalistic flavour, concentrating on flora and fauna, animist beliefs, agriculture, hand tools, the bare necessities of life.

Logogrammatically, Japanese is both profligate and parsimonious. The Nelson dictionary identifies nearly two-hundred *kanji* with the sound *ko* (with a long *o*), yet there is only one *hiragana* representation of this sound. The same is true for most other sounds: many *kanji* forms (and meanings) for only one meaningless phonetic *hiragana* form. Regular reforms and a love of systemisation have expunged countless deviations found in early written Japanese.

English has had a more *laissez faire* history. Many years ago at a voice recognition conference in New York, Isaac Asimov cited an impressively long list of letter forms for the long *o* sound. I can think of aprop*os*, b*eaux*, ch*au*ffeur, dep*ot*, *eau*, f*aux*, G*o*gh, h*oe*, J*oh*, l*oa*n, m*ow*, n*o*, *owe*, phar*aoh*, q*uo*, r*ho*, s*ew*, th*ough*, and w*hoa*. From this it is clear that it is far simpler to do sound-to-text conversion with *hiragana* Japanese than it is for English. Indeed, my Australian GSM phone must be trained specifically with my voice to understand a vocabulary limited to just ten names, whereas my Japanese phone can understand *all* Japanese names spoken in *any* voice, with *no* training.

To have so ordered the language that it can easily be understood by machines has not been without its problems. The details of the modifications are often glossed over in linguistic histories and, now I know a little about them, I am not surprised. There was chaos for hundreds of years. At times, competing writing and sound systems overlapped. Systems were arbitrary, short lived, and incomplete, each trying in its own way to marry the Japanese spoken language to derivatives of the incompatible Chinese writing system. Christopher Seeley's *A History of Writing in Japan* gives a good account of the twists and turns of written Japanese from the 1st or 2nd century to the 1980s.

I can just imagine the uproar if written English had undergone such overhaul. I decide to do an experiment.

For a start, no one will really miss *q*. It is kuickly dismissed.

And *x* and *c* can be easily replaced. They are eksised.

Nekst, drop *y*. Easi.

The voised konsonants *v* and *z* are on borrowed time. Thei are fankuished and their homes rased.

Let's see if we kan dispense with *d*. Tone!

Similarli, *b* ant *p* are too klose. Pegone!

Ant now that I think of it, all foiset konsonants kan go, so out with *g* too. Kone, nefer to return.

Japanese kan ket alonk usink *r* for *l*. Ret's to the same.

Now we are town to just fife fowers ant erefen konsonants:

a e i o u

f h j k m n p r s t w

So insteat of 'The kuik prown foks jumps ofer the rasi tok' we kan now sai 'When Mark tops Fuji.'

Hmmm.

Selfless selfishness

I wake up one morning uneasily remembering something that was said to me in a dream the night before.

'If you don't believe in the self, how can you contemplate writing a book about yourself?'

At the time the question had felt devastating, like a sudden realisation that I had been fatally wounded, or permanently crippled. It still has a disturbing power. Agitation stirs somewhere under my rib-cage. I imagine various disaster scenarios: author loses way, wastes years, book gets forgotten; publisher sees straight to the heart of the problem, reiterates the words of the dream, book gets rejected; publisher fooled, critics aren't, book gets panned; critics fooled, public isn't, book gets remaindered.

I get panicky, as if trapped in darkness with an evil presence nearby, but then my cell door moves a fraction and a thin light streams in through the crack. I force myself to think in straight lines again.

First: I assert that there *are* references.

Second: references can refer to other references.

Third: if reference A can refer to reference B, and B can refer back to A, then A can refer indirectly to A.

Fourth: B can be removed with a grammatical flick and then A refers to A directly. When this happens we say A refers to itself.

Its *self*. Hah! So it is the reference that calls the self into existence, not the other way around. I punch the air in goal-scoring, serve-breaking, line-taking celebration.

So, if we use the explanatory expediency of the self only to facilitate talking about references, not because it is an axiomatic concept, then the dream was wrong. I am free to write the book, publishers will clamour, critics will swoon, the public will flock, I will prevail.

Later in the morning I notice another interesting aspect to this. The power of language or references to reify selves can be weakened through overuse. Too many references, too many branches and roots, too many banyan-like transformations from branch to root and back again, and the result is that individual selves get lost in the tangle, they fade out. The trunk, if we are to continue the tree analogy, loses its identity. Something much bigger and undefinable swallows it whole. What should we call this thing? The grapevine, society, universal consciousness, the media, the Internet, nirvana, nothing?

Is this what has happened in Japan? Has the referential overload tipped the balance and given the network a greater identity than the individual? Has the volume of information begun to ebb and flow like a tide, washing away all the individual little contributory rivulets and streams? Then isn't this going to happen everywhere, not just in Japan?

Water world

Several times during the day I try to refine the idea. I incline towards a water analogy, rather than that of the tree. The water cycle has no point of self, the water is always anonymous, but at times it is rain or river or sea. Each of these has a kind of identity, but each is really just a phase in a process. Similarly, individuals subsist on a flow of thoughts from other sources, we stir them for a while, in eddies or tempests, pass them on in a leak or a deluge, and eventually dry up like an ox-bow lake, forgotten by the mainstream.

If our minds and all our impressions and experiences are as water, then the whole notion of cores begins to collapse too. Imagine trying to get to the core of water. We pack our boat and sail out into the middle of the biggest ocean, we dive halfway to the seabed and open our hermetically sealed canister. Later, when the core water has been brought, under armed guard, to the laboratories of the Institute of Advanced Hydrosciences, significant scientific figures of the century gather, the media cluster in the second row, billions of people are telepresent, and then... it's just a can of water.

Any can of water would do. Any can of water does do.

The Truman Show

I never found a sympathetic ear for my theory of what should have happened at the end of Peter Weir's *The Truman Show*. The conventional view is that Truman Burbank, the poor victim of a huge, fascinating, inhuman fraud, would escape to the real world and... well, no one could tell me quite what kind of fulfilling normality or desirable life they had in mind for Truman, but it didn't matter; they all wanted Truman out of that fish bowl and into *reality*.

I don't think it could be so simple. If the only life you have known is a fraud then reality is not going to fit you like an old shoe. As Christof says in the movie, 'We accept the reality of the world with which we are presented.' Anything else is a nightmare. Just think... human cloning, organ smuggling, twice-reversed sex-changes, napalm and Prozac, Michael Jackson's face, Foot and Mouth pyres, testicular elephantiasis, snuff movies, necrophilia, cluster bombs, Martin Bryant, the visible human project, soccer assassinations, Aids, Rushdie's exile, Panama, Thalidomide, body modification, Smoky Mountain, merkins, Stelarc, Ricki Lake, Ok Tedi, Georgetown, the Spice Girls, flesh-eating bacteria, Derek and Clive, stapled stomachs and ears on mice – The Untruman Show, the whole of human life is there. In such a world the only future I saw for the pathetically ill-equipped Truman was fifteen minutes of fame as a has-been TV celebrity with nothing new to say. It would be utterly confusing and terrifying for Truman to undergo total immersion in reality. In the real world he would know *absolutely nobody*.

Better, I thought, to stay in the game, live in Seahaven, but play on at a meta-level. This has the appeal of those moments when we suddenly realise we are dreaming and know that we can do anything. Slide our hands inside the dress of the attractive woman, slap the bully around, treat everything as if it is ours, indulge, take control, act with impunity! So my advice to Truman was... spin it out, let the organisers *deal* with it, spin them out! Face reality on your own terms and your own schedule. Get real when you want to, but only for as long as you want to. Don't, whatever you do, fall into the trap of thinking that, having looked outside, you have finally discovered what is really going on.

And I think Truman knows all this. It is the unbreakable umbilical cord tethering us to *our* reality that makes such a choice hard for us to accept.

And one more thing, the world that held Truman captive is in any case a real town in a real place: Seaside, in Florida. It is one of many such developments, and is even now being copied in Australia, at places like (the creatively named) Seaside, and Casuarina Beach in Queensland. Truman's putative nightmare actually turns out to be real people's dreams.

Non-tyger

The time arrives for me to set off once more to meet tyger at Kansai airport, this time without mishap, I hope. I catch the bus into Himeji, then the train to Kobe, another bus-ride, then I take the hydrofoil across Osaka Bay to the airport terminal itself. The water crossing is enjoyable. Midway between Kobe and the airport I am almost lost in a world of grey: waves, clouds, the silhouettes of ships on the horizon.

In the terminal building everything is exactly the same as it always is, but the expected sense of reliving the moment does not arise, despite my attempts to force a bit of resonance by calling Satomi and Miho again while I'm waiting.

Satomi is pleased to chat, and tells me that she has dumped the number-two boyfriend because of his stinginess. I ask her if she is now worried that she won't be getting enough sex, but she tells me she has already organised his replacement, who is quite capable of 'keeping his end up' – using an arresting phrase I think I taught her.

Miho appears to be overseas at the moment, if I correctly understand her voice message.

Just like last time, the wait for tyger is a long one. The sudden flood of English accents in the concourse tells me the passengers on her plane have debouched, but there is still no sign of her. I get a hard feeling of disappointment in my throat.

A lad of louche middle-eastern looks, carrying a Casino du Liban bag, swaggers through the doorway and gives me a hard stare, as if I resemble the person he's looking for. I look past him at the other new faces coming out. Suddenly he brushes past my shoulder quite unnecessarily and walks out towards the taxi rank and bus stands.

Half an hour later, I realise that tyger has done it again, and this I cannot forgive so easily, because I feel I am being messed about. It takes hours to get back to the village from here, and I castigate myself for being so, so... what? naïve? soft?

The next day I send her an email.

Dear tyger,

    What happened? I hope nothing is wrong.

    I can't really believe that I've just repeated the experience of waiting to meet you at Kansai airport, only to discover that you're not on the plane.

    Just tell me why. I am sitting here trying to describe how I feel, but I just can't. Very very disappointed, I guess.

    love

    Leo

There is no news from her this time – which might indicate that affairs had been out of her control. I wish I knew.

Science fiction dreaming

It is a punk poet. It is not John Cooper Clarke.

Metal is the only element left. Air and wind have been replaced by AC effluent, earth by concrete, water by designer *eau*, fire by a TV in the hearth, wood by plastic. Hear the Banshees: 'Metal is tough, metal will sheen, metal won't rust when oiled and cleaned. Metal.'

Who would have thought that metal would be our last surviving scion? We all thought for a while that applied biology was poised for a century of ascendance, didn't we? Almost was, but the poison was too deep. Our clones and gene-splices, our species and superspecies, our mutant digitising and genetic algorithmics exercised our imaginations but didn't exorcise the virus vectors, the ozone depletion, the carcinogens, mutagens, fatal phages and preying prions, the microwaves, the x-rays, the solar particles and spermicides, insecticides, pesticides, infanticides, suicides and genocides. There was no one on our side. And metal didn't even feel an itch.

Roboticus robustus just kept designing its own mind-children, each brain-child a selfless devotee of its new gold dream, each dream a fabrication bristling with invention, intentionality, and fecundity. Assemblers makers builders fabricators instantiators instantiated fabricated built made assembled multiplied. The grammar of strict exponentiation, poetic redundancy.

A simple deadly function. Arguments: nanotech, curious hacker, self-replication, abundant energy; result: metal. Only metal. Nothing more to dream.

I really suspect that the change of diet is to blame for these strange dreams. It is either the vegetables, or a cold. I often have surreal nights just before starting to cough.

Not all the surrealism is mine, though. Net-surfing off the Serendib coast this morning, I hit an article exploring the structural homologies of the Star Wars series and the *Ring of the Nibelungs*. I cannot believe what I am reading. It reminds me of the multiplex coincidence of the Kennedy and Lincoln assassinations. Each story, says the article, has, for example, incestuous hero twins, training and initiation by dwarfs, magic swords, and many other curious links. The article goes on and on, enumerating connections between the musical scores, the artists, the public receptions, even between the films' cinematography and engravings illustrating the operas. Given all of this, how can there not be a connection between Mark Waugh's batting and Wagner's Ring? I am sure the headline 'Star Waughs' has been used more than once in the last few years, as have 'May the fours be with you' and 'The umpire strikes back.' And if Mark Waugh is so closely connected to Star Wars, then he is also closely connected to the Ring. What is going on here? How much of this have I dreamt, and how much have I imagined or remembered, or simply foreseen?

I am driving. Japan has small cars and small streets, so the Mini (British racing green, of course) is a good choice. But it was not such a good idea to be driving a Silver Cloud at the same time. What is worse, the Mini is swimming around inside the Rolls-Royce as if it is on ice. I have to start steering well in advance of any intended turn, the Mini responds to me and then after a short delay the Rolls-Royce responds to the Mini. I brush a polished bumper against a bamboo screen. People gather to watch me manoeuvre the two cars round the corners of the alleys. They are all commenting on how strange it is to see one car inside another, and a driver inside both of them. They all encourage me, saying it must be difficult. I point out that they are all driving two cars at the same time too, and they, for the very first time, notice that this is indeed true. Events stop suddenly. I thought it was a dream, but it turns out to be a VRML site. No, that can't be true because the onlookers were not on screen – I imagined them. It was both.

I kick back from the Internet, the tool that promised to make us all producers but turned us into round-the-clock hypnotised consumers, where once a search would uncover all sorts of amateur sites with excursive links to other points of departure, but now drops us into corporate sites with recursive links designed to keep us captive by force, not choice.

I am obviously feeling a touch dystopic today, but I don't know what to take for it. A run, probably. So I run though my options: play the MagA game on the net (don't want to use the net any more), email friends (same), netsurf (same), telephone friends (too much hard work), eat (not hungry), *shodo* (not in a good mood for it), walk to Harumi's house (may have to help teach the kids).

A kind of tyger

dearest dearest leo,

It begins,

    obviously something has gone terribly wrong,
    and i don't understand what it is. i don't know
    what gave you the idea i was coming to japan
    after the one debacle for which i remain
    extraordinarily apologetic. i have never been
    able to work up the nerve to make such a trip and
    feel that, in the first place, it must only have
    been my deepest sincere fondness for you that
    ever let me contemplate travelling alone to a
    very foreign country and putting myself in the
    hands of someone i've never actually met, or even
    spoken to on the 'phone.

> i'm awfully sorry for how you must be feeling,
> but please, please believe me that i'm certain
> that i've done nothing, since my one pitifully
> aborted trip, to suggest that i'd make the
> journey to japan. oh, dear leo, what gave you the
> idea?
>
> i'm terribly worried about what you must be
> thinking of me. my hands are shaking again now,
> and i think i've got to stop. please write and
> explain everything to me as soon as you can, and
> i will do the same.
>
> love, oysters and lard
> your truest, but terribly undeserving furry
> friend,
> tyger the maintainer of the holy staple

At first I don't know how to react. Then I write a response, saying I believe her, for why would she intentionally lie, and asking her not to worry. I recount as clearly as I can, using cut-and-paste on some of her later emails, the relevant conversations and plans I thought we made. Either she has somehow lost track of what she is doing – this is possible – or it was not her that set me up to expect her the second time. It could have been Tiger, or anyone else able to hijack her identity online. And yet our conversations about her coming to Japan were so interwoven with what appeared to be classic idiosyncratic tyger-isms that I begin to wonder just how much of tyger the phenomenon has been real. How many times could I have been talking to Tiger, but thinking it was tyger? Could the whole thing have been a horrible joke? My trust in, and enthusiasm for, tyger have taken a severe blow. I sit and try to examine my feelings. Is there any pleasant expectation of receiving another email from her? No, there is not. It is a surprising realisation, but I don't know what to believe or who I am talking to any more.

Emi returns

Emi is at the door and is keen to eat at the tavern. We walk in single file down the road to the junction, and I follow her in. The room is hot and noisy, full of the smells of cooking and fish. She turns and embraces me, then we are on one of the tables.

Next we are beside the river. Then swimming – against the flow. Emi moves easily but I seem to be going backwards. A *tanuki* watches me from the bank. Slowly Emi moves out of sight.

Playing truant

Harumi calls and tells me that she was disappointed when I didn't come to tea earlier today. This is something of a surprise to me, as I cannot remember being invited. I check my diary, though, and see that she is right. And the children were also disappointed when she told them that I wasn't there to help with their lessons, she says. I apologise. She goes on to tell me how much the parents appreciate my help with the lessons, how important it is for the children to hear a native English speaker. I think that by the time I hang up I have said 'sorry' fifteen times.

Harumi carries around with her an unearthly feeling of sadness and unrealised dreams – reminding me always, in a tenuous way, of Lady Sarashina. To add to her disappointments is therefore something I regret deeply.

What puzzles me is that Harumi seemed to think I have failed to turn up more than once. She sounded truly offended, in her terribly well-mannered way.

I make amends by building an elaborate extension to her tree house.

English in Japanese

I get little notes from the children, at the lessons and in my (real) mailbox. They are usually addressed to 'Mr Mark.' They are decorated with coloured flowers, smiling faces, and little animals. They invariably thank me for whatever it is I do in the English lessons, and often include a Japanese translation in wobbly *kana*, just to be sure. They are deeply endearing. I make sure to thank the children, and praise their written English, next time I see them. This makes them even more shy than usual.

Interesting things happen when languages meet. The meeting of English and Japanese, languages so different in structure and use, is no exception. Imaginative, surreal, and idiosyncratic uses of English in Japan are often cited quite derisively, but little of illumination is ever actually said about the phenomenon. I am ashamed that I too occasionally succumb to poking fun at Japanese English. The temptation is strong of course; I saw a restaurant in Kyushu offering 'last food.' *Arsenic and strychnine sauces a speciality, tables for thirteen*, I immediately thought. At the Itsukushima-jinja on Miyajima, I read a sign over a gateway:

> This is only for the exit. An enter from this is refused.
>
> An entrance is an opposition side. An admission fee is
>
> necessary for this shrine.

And there actually appears to be something of a cottage industry gathering and distributing funny bits of English for smug *gaijin* amusement. *Kansai Time Out* runs a regular column on the subject. Its own eschewal of any imaginative use of language is evident in its flatly prosaic title: *Funny English*.

The fun to be had from Japanese English derives from two origins: actual mistakes caused by unfamiliarity with English ('last' instead of 'fast'), and more deliberate attempts to create a vague dreamlike impression, rather than a specific message. These mood-setting phrases are interesting because they show language being used in a loose, almost poetic way that gives a distorted reflection of the Japanese language itself. For example, on the wall of a Matsumoto hairdresser I found:

> We stare at an age to be new always and improve our
>
> sensitivity, and we are the artist groups which express it.
>
> Then, we support "you who has pride to itself who
>
> doesn't flatter a person"

I have no idea what it really says, but I sense the *avant garde*, openness, pride and purity, and I can see that something inspiring is struggling for expression in these strangely assembled words.

Game on

It is days since I began, but I estimate I am still only half finished. I've figured out quite a bit. The procedures that people are working on are actually segments of the game's code – the whole game is still a work

in progress. This constant enhancement explains the unexpected rich-
ness and variety of everything here, and probably also accounts for
the occasional changes in causality I've been experiencing. I've been
learning how to make procedures of my own, and what I've focused
on, even though it was initially just a whim, is textures and non-solid
substances, such as bundles of thatch. I've stripped the old thatch off
my roof and replaced it with my new stuff. This is *real* thatch; it can
be interpenetrated, magnified endlessly, and has a non-periodic surface texture. It is based on close-up photographs of the *susuki* reed.
I've set the house up so that it automatically updates as I make imp-
rovements to the basic material.

The more I dig into the code the more I can do. I put in some
routines for calling lists of functions that create images. These are abstract images, but full of multi-level structures that suggest objects,
space, and movement. I intend to offer them up as works of art to
other game players. I'll be able to open a gallery. I am just about to
compile and test a few modifications when suddenly the screen goes
blue. *System crash* I think. I get that dreadful jolt of cold water in the
veins, sigh loudly and wonder how much work I've just lost. But
something is not quite right. There is a small green blob on the blue of
the screen, and the cursor is a hand, not an arrow. I hold down the
mouse button and drag – the blob moves. Another irregular green
blob comes into view, and another - a ring of five of them. I pan left
and find a large green area that fills the screen. An old memory suggests I hit the minus key a few times and, sure enough, I am zooming
out on a map of some kind. Up, up, up and then I see the Malaysian
peninsula come into view. A few more steps up and now I see all of
eastern Asia, including Japan. Odd that, because if I am still in the
game, this is the first time I've seen real places. I pan over until Japan
is centre-screen and zoom in on Honshu. Down, down towards the Inland Sea, down towards the Honshu coast. There's Awaji Island, the
bridge. Left a bit, left, up, I find Himeji. In a bit more, there's the Sugo
River, and Araki. Keep going, there's the cluster of houses and right...
there is my house. In some more, and now down a bit and I see the
path to Engyo-ji, down, down, and I'm almost at tree level now. Down
again and it is exactly as if I am on the path, and with a small shift of

the mouse I can raise my direction of gaze and look up the hill towards the...

Fern glade

So there I am hiking up towards Engyo-ji, hoping for fresh spring air, some quiet, and an opportunity to clear my head. I plan to find a spot on the hilltops where I can sit and look out over the valley, eat my lunch and work out why I feel so out of sorts these days. Whenever I feel like this, I usually make a list of everything that bothers me, without any concern for how big or small each problem is; so a list can often include items such as 'result of election' and 'broken shoelace' side by side. I then go about fixing as many items as I can. Just lately, the problem has been that I can't think of any items.

I stumble into the fern glade I passed through a few times on previous walks. It is cool and silent. The peacefulness provokes me to shrug off my backpack and settle down. I sit cross-legged on the pack and open my Thermos for a drink of tea.

The phone rings.

'*Moshi moshi.*'

'*Konnichiwa*, Maaku-san,' says Emi, using the cadence of *Konnichiwa Aka-Chan*, the Japanese nursery rhyme.

'Hi baby, how are you?' I say, pleased it is her.

'*Genki desu.* And you?'

'I'm fine. What are you doing, having a lunch break?'

'Maaku, you sound tired. Not fine.' She's pretty hard to fool, is Emi.

'Yeah, you're right. I'm feeling odd. I've just climbed a hill to find some peace, to feel that I'm above my problems.'

'You need a holiday, *ne?*'

'This *is* a holiday,' I point out.

'So maybe it is time to stop?' she says.

'I don't know. I've got this feeling of being pressured coming from somewhere, and I can't figure out what's causing it. I've been spending far too much time in that game, too.'

I'm also still troubled, I suppose, by the whole tyger debacle, but I don't mention it. I know tyger is a touchy subject with Emi.

'The game,' says Emi. 'Are we in it now?'

'That's too hard to think about, Emi.' I laugh. 'But anyway, did you have any particular reason to call today?'

'Just talk,' she says, softly.

'Thanks. I wish you were here. Are you at work now?'

'*Hai*. At work… but I have to go soon, *ne*?'

'Now?'

'*Hai. Gomen, ne*?'

'OK. Well, thanks for calling. I needed it,' I say.

'*Do itashimashite. Jaa, mata…*'

'Bye bye.'

We, Mark Peters

Somehow my great survey of Japan seems to have spun down to a un-healthy kind of self-absorption. The irony of this is not amusing.

I know better than to seek myself. I once had the odd experience of meeting someone called Mark Peters. It was in Notting Hill, some time in the late 1980s. He was of average height and build, brown-eyed with curly dark hair. Not a bit like me, which struck me as deeply wrong.

Odd then, that I keep typing "mark peters" into Internet search en-gines. So now I know that it is a name by which hundreds of men are known, and most of them are ordinary in a very humbling way. Such a great name – the sign fades, money dwindles, rotation of Peter Smark; transposition of Peter Marks; spoonerism of Park Meters; ana-gram of tramps reek and perk master; familiar throughout Europe; easily pronounced by all races – but such ordinary nominees. One of them enjoys writing about himself in the third person:

> What Mark Peters has done for writing and new talent in writ-ing is unbelievable! I can't tell you how much he means to all of us. He's one of a kind! There will never be another!

That can't be right. But this sure is:

> Sometimes, Mark Peters and reality collide.

Someone doing something somewhere

It is warm enough today to go walking without a jacket. A quiet path meanders alongside the river for several miles. I realised a few weeks back that this must have once been the old road that linked all the little hamlets of the valley. It is the long way to wherever I want to go, but in the days before the bridges were built, it would have been the only way.

I stop to sit on the embankment and peel a hard-boiled egg. A small black car pulls up in front of a house maybe a hundred metres away on the other bank. The woman driver gets out and stands there, watching me, wondering who I am and what I am doing here. If she asked me I couldn't tell her. What could I say? I'm on holiday, I'm doing research, I'm just staying away from home?

I gather the pieces of egg-shell into a tissue and ball it in my hand. I'm a house-sitter, a social observer, a *shodo* apprentice. I'm an AI researcher working as an unpaid teacher's assistant. I'm in a relationship of indeterminate type with a Japanese girl whom I never see any more.

I transfer some tea from my flask into the cup that also serves as its lid. How can I explain what I do? I'm writing everything down because I've got nobody to talk to about it. I'm spending half my time in a computer game because someone asked me to. I'm looking for questions that have no answers because they fit my thesis.

I repack the flask and shoulder the pack. When I stand up a small animal down at the water's edge takes fright and plops into the water. All I see are a few ripples expanding and fading into the eddies.

Repeat offender

I am not sure why, but now when I meet people in the village they are all asking me if I am feeling any better, and wishing me that special 'take care of yourself' greeting that is reserved for the sick: *o-daijini.*

Nakamura-san ushers her children to the far side of the lane and scuttles by with a confused series of nods, smiles, cutting motions, and indecipherable whispering.

The teenagers who hang out in front of the convenience store fall silent as I approach. They all look away.

I tried explaining my dream to another one of the parents, who laughingly suggested I see a doctor. This is, I feel, very unfair. It all smacks of conspiracy. Either that, or I really have done something I shouldn't have. Perhaps tupping Emi in the tavern was the last straw. But how would they know about that?

Self-translation

The first Japanese approximation of 'Mark' is the nearest *romaji* rendering: *maaku*. The sound can also be approximated in *kana*, or even using a set of *kanji* precursors. But should it be the sound or the meaning that has priority? And should either of these characteristics be given such priority that the overall length, look and consonance of the name be overlooked?

Only two *kanji* actually have the pronunciation *maaku*, and neither is well-known. One actually means 'mark' too, in the sense of trade mark, symbol, sign, etc. *Kanji* being symbols, and this particular symbol symbolising 'symbol' symbolises the kind of symbolism that I like. Forget that 'Mark' doesn't mean 'mark.' The fact that this *kanji* symbolises symbolism is enough. And its right hand element is itself the *kanji* for ink, an appealing calligraphic connotation, so perhaps I should chose this one as my *shodo haimei* or *gou*. The other *kanji* that is read as *maaku* has negative connotations; it means 'betrayal,' which I take as a kind of betrayal in itself. In the end I choose neither of these *kanji*.

For my *gou* I eventually select the character *ma*, meaning 'space,' with connotations of interval, opening, distance, time. This *kanji* captures many appealing ideas: the emptiness between walls, between characters in a work of calligraphy, Zen enlightenment, the essential Japanese corelessness. *Ma* is used to describe the long comfortable pauses that take place in conversations between people who know each other well or, more correctly, the harmony that enables such conversation. The synergy that results from a few stones placed in an open garden can be described as *ma*. It is also used to describe the pared-down minimalism of *noh* drama, where a mere tilt of a head is used to indicate an emotion. The *kanji* character for *ma* combines elements for gate and sun (or the moon), clearly suggesting space or light seen through an opening. It's an empty space – a good symbol for what I feel I am becoming.

Openings and closings

It's funny, but long gaps now seem to be appearing in my diary. I know I should capitalise on this and get more work done – make hay while the sun shines. Never look a gift horse in the mouth. Strike while the iron's hot, and so on. But instead, I get up late each day, sit beside the computer with my toast and coffee, and try not to succumb to the desire to go back to bed.

Shodo is a graphic index of one's mental composure. My latest efforts are lined up against the wall, and I can clearly see that every one of them is dreadful. I cannot show them to Segawa-sensei.

It's lonely. I do wish Emi could be here.

If I were really sick, I wouldn't have to worry about anything. I could just stay in bed and be looked after. I hastily push away this thought; it is too rash a temptation of fate.

Fade out

Japanese endings are not abrupt things. They are often unheralded, and only noticed retrospectively. Stories unravel, just like experiences. Without dying, they simply fail to go on. Death and failure are not closely connected in Japanese thought; when nobly achieved, failure is not thought of as death. It is the manner of the performance, not its outcome, that is important. Indeed, dying well, boldly and unflinchingly, is something that many Japanese aspire to even today, and suicide can still be seen as an appropriate *solution*. Old people once took themselves off into the mountains when they felt they had become a burden (or they were dumped there by a helpful younger relative, after an uphill piggyback ride). In Japanese culture, death is more often poignant than tragic. We are all impermanent, transient – fading away into the evening like the sound of a temple bell. It is a remarkably mature view that such a fate is a matter for embracement rather than futile denial. Awareness that each day may be our last, and that one will, might earn us a greater sensitivity to its sad fleeting details. Sadness can be such a fulfilment of the soul, and lends a gentleness to our actions that elation does not.

Niki Jumpie, the anonymous male character of *The Woman in the Dunes* by Abe Kobo, allows himself to be absorbed and buried in an existence without meaning and without a future, comforted by the thought that everything is illusory and unimportant. Twenty-five hundred years ago, Buddha already knew this. If, as much eastern thinking holds, to exist is meaningless, then is ceasing to exist meaningful

– or is it equally meaningless? There is a Japanese word, *umu*, which means both existence and non-existence – as if the inexorable sliding from one to another is just part of an indivisible process. And so, with the end so near at hand, it is easy to avoid the need for a climax, a resonant last word, a full stop…

Wrong dream

Everything we learn about our sensory systems suggests that we construct all we experience, from the most improbable dreams to the blue of the sky. And all we learn about the world out there on the other side of our senses suggests that it is nothing like anything we hold familiar. In the *terra nova* of quantum physics and cognitive science, what do our common notions of real and unreal mean? Are our common beliefs and customs any less foreign than those of another country? Can we any more explain our way of thinking than we can that of another culture's – even though we are prepared to die trying to enforce it?

A feeling of not knowing Japan has contaminated my every certainty. I've lost objectivity, I've lost direction, and I've lost my thread.

After feeling like this for several days it occurs to me that if I lose touch with reality, I have really lost touch with nothing at all. Unfortunately, this does not improve my sense of well-being – it worsens it. If I have created a space for myself here, it echoes with a maddening cacophony. Is it all just words? Instead of feeling loosened, I feel I am fraying at the edges. If I must live in a dream, then why not a familiar reassuring one? It is perverse and self-destructive to insist on another.

My joy in the hills and solitude seems to have left me. And worse still, I cannot think of anything else I want to do now. I sense that many things are coming to an end. It is sad but inescapable – like waking from an impossible dream.

The solution is as clear as it is unexpected. I need a different dream. I must rewrite my own dream one character at a time. There is a limit to how much one can say with a single brush-stroke. If I press on here I will soon over-write myself or run dry. At times, the brush must be lifted from the paper, refreshed and reformed if necessary, and placed down on a new sheet. Without doubt I must leave Japan.

I call everyone to say goodbye.

Akiko is stiffly formal, but cheerful. She wishes me *bon voyage.*

Miho laughs that in all the time I've been in Japan we have only ever managed to talk on the phone, and hopes to see me again in Sydney, or maybe in the air.

Satomi jokes and teases, and says she looks forward to my next visit.

I even call Kayo (though she doesn't answer and I resort to a left message).

I leave my call to Emi to last, knowing that it will be difficult. She is rendered almost speechless by my news. Her voice is tiny, quavering. I feel guilty, as if I am hurting her for purely selfish reasons. I wish I could be there to somehow soften the hurt with a touch, but perhaps that might just make it worse. I simply don't know what to do with Emi. Valiantly, she reminds me that it will soon be St Valentine's Day. A lump grows in my throat; I have to fight to keep control. We talk emptily about what we might do in the future, promise to speak again soon, and that is it.

That is it.

After all, what more can I do in Japan? The only plausible answer to that question is: submerge, get work and become an inhabitant, not a traveller; the object, not the subject.

But it is more than that. Despite all my efforts, the understated aesthetic of Zen, *shibui,* has eluded me, and instead I have created a palimpsest, written over and over so many times until everything seems to have been blurred by cross-hatching. Instead of an empty space, a noisy scribbling reigns; too much information. Where I have sought simplicity, things have become awfully complicated. Everything, everyone, I most wanted seems most unattainable.

I call the airline as I walk along the road, my eyes unconsciously following the hawks as they wheel high over the hills. I force my voice to sound neutral and business-like.

Such a beautiful day to be thinking of leaving. I imagine sympathetic signs of spring everywhere. Shoots are pushing up all over the fields and buds are appearing on the trees. The days are noticeably warmer.

It takes only a few minutes to pack. I'll be gone in the morning.

Real 'Japan'

We, the non-Japanese, the *gaijin*, the hypnotised and the cauterised, the Japan-crazy and the Japan-sick, flock to a fictitious land.

No view of life can encompass itself. That way lies the inconsistency of infinite regression: $V_L > V_L$. We'll never know our own lives, but perhaps we can believe something about them. And if we never really see ourselves in the picture, at least we can look at the rest of it.

If I were to now confess that I have just, let's say, been woken by my daughters on a cold morning in suburban Montreal, that I have never been to Japan, that there has been no seeking, no journey, no discovery, that everything so far reported was part of some long-running and lucid dream, redolent of a soap-opera that had written itself into a dead-end, that nothing I refer to means anything – then what of it? Or instead of a dream, what if all these words were nothing more than fatally flawed memories, unintended inaccuracies, or even lies? Would this mean disappointment for the reader, to discover that one has been reading barely credible fiction and not the truth? Or that artifice made obvious is somehow fake? Does it make any difference now, as you read this?

And finally, the thought to start with:
There is Japan and then there is Japan...

Epilogue

THINGS AND PEOPLE CHANGE, and hence time passes. It wasn't long before I was back in Japan. It wasn't long before I left again. It is always there, always there.

Satomi still lives in her tiny Tokyo apartment. Practically nothing about her has changed except her boyfriends. These days her English is deteriorating through lack of practice. This annoys her, but not enough to dull her spirits or dampen her appetites.

Akiko sent me a letter, decorated with little stars and glitter, saying that she was moving to Dublin, and after that I heard no more of her.

I did meet Miho again. She has left the airline and is pursuing a career in what they call the hospitality industry. She is working long hours, and misses the opportunity to fly overseas.

Maya, the priest's daughter, is completing a PhD, and looks destined for a career in academia. Now that her father has retired, her parents spend every day at the temple.

I sometimes imagine Kayo, striding through the streets of Kobe, but of course I'll never see her again.

Friends remember Kyoko from time to time. I don't know what she is doing these days.

Harumi and Naomi still live in the house in Sugo Valley.

tyger disappeared for ever soon after the second no-show at Kansai airport. Occasional Internet searches on her real name have failed to turn up any links.

Emi's friends all left the Kyoto area. Katsuya went north without telling the others about it. Yoko took a job as a teacher in a small town some distance away at the north end of Lake Biwa. Kasumi became a tour guide and now lives in New Zealand, often travelling overseas with Japanese parties. Yoko has visited her in Queenstown.

And Emi herself? She's married now, Kasumi tells me, and has moved away from our playgrounds around Kyoto. She and her husband live in Gifu prefecture. I wonder – in her evenings alone, waiting for her husband to come home – does she ever recall the night of the *torii* beside the waters of Lake Biwa?

The three great *sumo yokozuna* of the day have all now retired; Akebono after winning eleven championships, Musashimaru after twelve, and Takanohana after an astonishing twenty-two. Thus a *sumo* generation passes into history. Kotomitsuki, the charismatic newcomer, went on to win a championship of his own in September of 2001. Within a year, however, a new *yokozuna*, Asashoryu, rose up, and has since dominated the sport as thoroughly as the old triumvirate.

I fixed up the old letterbox and each month I find there a large envelope from Segawa-sensei, containing *shodo tehon*, calligraphy exercises. I do several copies and post the better ones back to her. She forwards the best to her association, *Kansai shodo kyukai*, for monthly grading. My *kyu* grades have steadily improved, and I am now within striking distance of first *dan*.

And I've worked on robots, and methods that enable them to construct their own models of reality. There seem to be good reasons to do this.